Log Buildings
of Southern Indiana

Log Buildings
of Southern Indiana

Warren E. Roberts

Trickster Press

BLOOMINGTON

Dedicated to Wallace Sullivan, companion on many a house-hunting expedition, who has held one end of a tape measure more times than either of us cares to remember.

Contents

Acknowledgements to the First Edition

MUCH OF the fieldwork for this study was done while I was a Fellow of the John Simon Guggenheim Memorial Foundation. Some fieldwork, too, was made possible by grants from the Indiana University Foundation.

I have received help and encouragement from many individuals, far too many to list by name. The owners of countless log buildings have permitted me to visit, photograph, measure, and generally climb around in their structures. Many have shared with me information of various kinds about the buildings, the builders, and the way they built. Many conversations with long-time residents of southern Indiana have provided me valuable information. I have always found the people with whom I have come into contact while hunting log buildings to be friendly and willing to help, indeed, ready to postpone important tasks to answer the questions of a stranger.

Many individuals have told me of log buildings to look at and a number have gone with me to guide me over back roads and across fields. Students in both my graduate and undergraduate classes have given me photographs, have accompanied me on trips, and have helped me in a number of other ways. Discussions both inside and outside the classroom have helped shape my thoughts on log architecture.

The chapter on the tools used in building log houses was originally printed, in slightly different form, in *Pioneer America* in 1977. The excellent drawings appearing both in the article and in the chapter in this book were made by Ada L. K. Newton.

The map showing the distribution of log construction in Europe is taken, with minor changes, from Terry Jordan's *Texas Log Buildings* (Austin: University of Texas Press, 1978), p. 22.

The editors of the Trickster Press, especially Tom Walker, have devoted many hours to changing a manuscript into a book.

My family has constantly encouraged me over the years I have worked on this book and has tolerated inconveniences of many kinds for my sake. My daughter, Sarah L. Roberts, devoted many hours to producing finished drawings from the roughest of sketches I provided her. I owe her special thanks.

Preface to the Second Edition

IN THINKING back over the years since this study of the log buildings of southern Indiana was published, there is little information that has come to light to supplement the study. Certainly, nothing has come to light to change or invalidate any data or conclusions.

However, I would like to comment on the general method of research embodied in this study. For a long time it has been a general assumption that in order to understand the past it is necessary to locate and probe written documents. When one is trying to learn about the common people—about 95 percent of the population—the attempted reliance on written records usually proves futile. Folk architecture is a good case in point. There are very few written records that deal with the houses of the average person in the preindustrial era, but there are a great number of such houses that have survived. When written sources do not agree with evidence derived from examining old buildings, does one accept the word of the written source or the evidence provided by one's own eyes?

In working with old buildings, almost everyone, it seems to me, accepts the word of the authors of books on old houses. If a specific old house has narrow floor boards, for example, the restorer is likely to say: "The books agree that old houses had wide floor boards. These narrow boards must be later." So the original narrow boards are taken up and wide boards installed in their place, or they are covered with wide boards. And so, in a few years visitors to the house are provided with further "evidence" that all old houses had wide floor boards.

My experiences with log buildings convinced me that I should examine the buildings first and draw whatever conclusions I could. Only then would I look at the written sources to learn what they had to say on the subject. Consequently, over the years I have come to realize that written records fail the folklife researcher in three important ways.

First, written records are often inadequate as sources of data for the folklife researcher. A simple case in point is census records and their treatment of crafts. The federal census takers, beginning with the 1840 census, were instructed to record the trade or profession of adults. In the countryside almost all adult males were listed as "farmer" or "farm laborer." (An adult son living at home was normally listed as "farm laborer.") To use a simple example, one would assume that in most counties in Indiana there was not a single basketmaker! Actually, the typical basketmaker was also a farmer, and so he came to be listed in the censuses as a farmer. If one has done fieldwork and has found that many farmers made baskets when they did not need to work in the fields or otherwise farm, the census figures present no problem. By placing too much reliance on the censuses, people writing on crafts far too often ignore these rural craftsmen because the censuses largely ignored them. Likewise, if the folklife researcher is trying to accumulate data on the number of basketmakers working in the past or the number of baskets produced or their size and shape, he or she will find few or no written records to help.

Second, written records can be misleading or can be misunderstood without the insights provided by fieldwork. A good illustration of this point may be found in a book devoted to Indiana cabinetmakers. In an early document, the book's author found an entry in which a cabinetmaker stated that he owned "Dogs for turning." The author includes a print of a canine running inside a big wheel-shaped cage and states, "In this period dogs would have been used as demonstrated in Plate II."[1] Fieldwork shows, however, that in this context the craftsman was saying that he had the metal parts ("dogs") for a lathe. The wooden parts of the lathe would have been made by the craftsman himself.

A third problem with written records is that they can be inaccurate. Every historian knows that this generalization is true, but the historian normally does not depend on fieldwork to correct inaccurate written sources. While I do not want to devote much attention to this point, I once again cite census records. In a trade journal entitled *Stone*, published in Chicago in 1891, is an angry editorial critical of census figures. Under the heading, "Indiana Sandstone and the Census," it is stated that the 1890 census shows that 334,000 cubic feet of sandstone was produced in Indiana at a profit of $711 while actually there was at least 9,000,000 cubic feet of sandstone produced with a profit of at least $75,000. The editor asks who would invest in Indiana sandstone quarries if they accepted the census figures?[2] In this case the editor of the journal himself did the necessary fieldwork by travelling around Indiana and talking to quarry owners before compiling his statistics.

There is an even greater problem with the work of most of those who write about the way in which people used to live: Because many writers ignored the vast majority of the population, the nontypical five percent of the population is presented as typical. In most parts of the United States, more than ninety percent of the population lived on small, largely self-sufficient farms. The federal census of 1790 showed that ninety-five percent of the population lived on farms, and Benujamin Franklin rightly observed in 1787, "The great business of the continent is agriculture. For one artizan [sic] or merchant, I suppose we have at least a hundred farmers."[3] As time went on, of course, towns and cities flourished and grew, but throughout the nineteenth century, great areas of the country, especially the Upland South, remained predominantly rural. Yet it is these rural people, the bulk of the population, who are almost completely overlooked in the written records.

Writers on the past and the few museums devoted to showing what life was like in the past constantly make the grievous mistake of assuming that all people in the past lived in mansions or in large towns. As I demonstrate later in this Preface, up until roughly 1900, at least eighty percent of the population lived in one-room houses. Yet museums such as Colonial Williamsburg and Old Sturbridge Village have scores of mansions and multi-room houses but not a single example of the one-room house. Anyone can easily find examples of writers who use such phrases as, "The typical hostess in colonial America set her table with ...," then proceed to list table ware that the typical hostess, in actuality a farm wife living on a small farm, could not possibly have owned.[4] But because the writer has been able to find some written inventories of wealthy people and has been unable to find or has not even looked for household inventories of the small farmhouses, that writer has fallen into the trap of assuming that the wealthy family is representative of everyone. Or how many museums have invited visitors "... to learn what life was like in colonial America" when the museum shows only the homes and the material possessions of the atypical elite? Surely, a major service that folklife researchers can perform is to constantly point out these and similar mistakes as well as to make available research showing who was typical of the whole population and how they lived.

One point that I have continually had to defend over the years since the publication of this study revolves around my conviction that hewn-log houses were usually covered with siding at the time they were originally built. This conviction of mine runs directly counter to what many people—and many who have has extensive experience working with log buildings—firmly believe. I cannot repeat here the evidence that has led to my conviction since it is laid out in considerable detail in the body of this work. I will, however, report on an important piece of evidence that has come to light more recently.

People have shown me photographs taken years ago which show log houses without siding. In some instances the photograph in question was taken at a family reunion. The family members are posed before the "old home place" which is a log house—and the house has no siding. Actually, when a house was abandoned, it seems to have been a common practice to remove the siding. Why? Because siding was valuable, it could be easily removed, and it could be re-used on some other building.

A piece of evidence to support this assertion comes from a newspaper report dated May 3, 1884. It seems that a fire had started in a flue of a house a mile north of the town of Ellettsville, Indiana, and a brisk wind was blowing the fire towards the smokehouse. Neighbors had saved as much from the house as they could, so they turned their efforts towards the endangered smokehouse. The first thing they tried to salvage was the siding, here called weatherboarding. They were removing the siding—obviously considering it the most valuable contribution they could make—when blasting caps stored inside the building exploded, sending scraps of metal flying through the air like shrapnel. Three men were killed and ten injured, which explains why this was considered a truly newsworthy event.[5] For our purposes, however, it is only necessary to emphasize that in 1884 the siding was considered to be so valuable as to be worth saving from destruction. The value of wood siding helps explain why early photographs of abandoned log houses often show the houses without siding. I might add that photographers wishing to emphasize the "old-timey" character of certain regions of southern Indiana, such as Brown County, would persuade people to pose outside an abandoned log house to make it appear that the house was still being lived in. In this way they wanted to perpetuate the idea that pioneer living conditions lingered on in the backwoods of southern Indiana.

My final point in this essay concerns the size and shape of log houses. Again, I will not repeat all the data in the body of this work but will merely reiterate that 65 percent of the hewn-log houses found in southern Indiana were one-room houses with a sleeping loft overhead. I am convinced that in earlier times the proportion of one-room houses compared to multi-room houses would have been rather higher. I say this because multi-room houses have survived better than one-room houses. One-room houses in more recent times have not been considered adequate as family houses and many have been destroyed.

It is important to note that in earlier times, especially when as much as 95 percent of the population consisted of self-sufficient farm families, most houses in Great Britain and the United States were of one room. It is unfortunate from the standpoint of trying to understand what life was like in earlier times that historic preservation groups and museums have clouded the issue. Historic houses restored and opened to the public by organizations such as the National Trust for Historic Preservation are usually the multi-roomed mansions of wealthy people. Moreover, the houses in "outdoor" museums such as Colonial Williamsburg and Old Sturbridge Village are mostly multi-room houses. These large houses are aesthetically pleasing and important for the history of the architecture of five percent or so of the population, the upper classes. But one who is trying to learn how most people lived in earlier times will be led astray if he or she thinks that the multi-room houses are in any way typical or characteristic of the houses of most people. In short, these early multi-room houses are long on charm and aesthetics, but they can be used only with great caution for history.

Over the years data have accumulated showing how common the one-room house was in Great Britain and the United States. For example:

England: For the year 1631-32 in Wiltshire, there are records on 355 houses, and "many of these had only a single ground floor room."[6]

Ireland: In 1779 an English traveller, Arthur Young, wrote, "The cottages of the Irish, which are called cabbins. . .generally consist of only one room."[7]

Wales: In many hilly regions of Wales there are great numbers of "cottages" about 28 feet by 18 feet built in the eighteenth and nineteenth centuries by small farmers who also worked in the mines or at other jobs.[8]

New England: Out of 144 houses built before 1725 that were documented in 1979 for the Massachusetts Bay area, 82 were of one room. "Documented" means actually observed and recorded, and many of the one-room houses have disappeared without a trace, leaving a higher proportion of larger buildings that tended to survive. Also, it is worth noting that every house that was investigated had been enlarged since 1725.[9]

Maryland: "Numerically, the most significant plan form was the one-room house. Usually flimsily built and frequently extremely small—as little as eight or ten feet square—these houses form the background against which everything else must be set. As late as the eighteenth century, the one-room house characterized the accommodations of eighty to ninety percent of the white population of much of the Chesapeake, and, of course, of all the black population."[10]

Delaware: "In the mid-eighteenth century, in Delaware, three out of four land-owning families lived in houses measuring twenty-six by twenty feet or smaller." Note the term "land-owning."[11]

This rather lengthy listing of data is important to our understanding of the houses built by and lived in by most early settlers in southern Indiana. In short, Indiana houses were neither better nor worse, neither bigger nor smaller, than those that most people lived in "back east." It is a mistaken notion that life for most people in the early 1800s in southern Indiana was mostly different from—and much harsher and cruder than—life in the regions from which the settlers originated. The mistake is to compare the restored multi-room houses of the museums and the historic preservation groups with the simple one-room log houses of southern Indiana. The only valid comparison would be between the one-room houses of most families "back east" and their Indiana counterparts.

Such a comparison would shed valuable light on the pioneer era in southern Indiana. It would help us realize that life in the pioneer era was not too different from life in the periods directly before and after it. It was vastly different, of course, from life at the end of the last century and throughout this century, but that generalization holds true for almost all parts of the country, not just southern Indiana.

Chapter One

Introduction

THE LOG buildings found in southern Indiana are interesting and important in a number of ways. They are picturesque in themselves and hence have attracted much attention, but also they represent a local adaptation of an immensely old building tradition. Moreover, they can tell us much of a way of life, itself very ancient, that flourished in this country until relatively recent times but which now has almost disappeared. This way of life, the main feature of which was the self-sufficient farm, was markedly different from modern, urban life in almost every respect, yet traces of it are apparent everywhere around us. Not only is it as worthy of study as any which is remote geographically, but also it is important as being the basis upon which modern life in the United States is built. Many of the values, ideals, and customs of this earlier era still influence modern life. In understanding it, we can better understand ourselves. The architecture created by people living in southern Indiana before the Industrial Revolution wrought its many changes is a useful guide to understanding the ways in which those people lived. If we can understand how they built and why they built, we have come a long ways toward understanding their ways of life.

This study is based upon an examination of log buildings rather than written records. In doing my fieldwork I visited 470 log buildings in all. Of these, 296 are houses while the rest are barns, smokehouses, churches, and other buildings. I have also helped dismantle about ten log buildings and helped reassemble a few so that I have been able to examine every feature of log buildings in considerable detail.

LITERATURE ON LOG BUILDINGS

Log buildings have aroused a great deal of interest in the past probably because they have become firmly associated in the minds of most people with the pioneers. While I will not review here the entire literature on log buildings in the United States, I will cite several works that represent different approaches to the subject.

Articles such as Howard W. Marshall's "The 'Thousand Acre' Log House, Monroe County, Indiana," and John Vlach's "The 'Canada Homestead': A Saddlebag Log House in Monroe County, Indiana," are detailed studies of individual log buildings.[1] While the authors of these articles give as much of the history of the buildings as they have been able to assemble, their primary object is to describe the buildings they are studying as thoroughly as possible. Hence it is fair to say that their articles are primarily descriptive in nature. As such, they give a valuable record which can be used by others for comparative and other purposes.

Another approach may be characterized as historical. C. A. Weslager in *The Log Cabin in America* covers a number of topics, but his main concern is not detailed description of existing log buildings.[2] Indeed, while a number of photographs of log buildings illustrate his book, he hardly mentions them in his text. Instead, he concentrates on historical records about log buildings and brings to light a mass of new material useful to anyone concerned about the early dates at which log buildings were constructed and in what areas. If he is unable to solve the vexing problem of what ethnic group first introduced log buildings to the New World, he has nonetheless put on record a mass of data to help in its solution. Donald and Jean Hutslar's "The Log Architecture of Ohio" likewise covers a number of topics.[3] It is more detailed than Weslager's book in that it does describe a number of extant buildings. Nonetheless, this work also lays primary emphasis upon early written records and hence may also be considered an example of the historical approach.

A third approach to the study of log buildings is concerned with diffusion. An attempt is made to discover the source of a building type or feature and to trace its geographical spread. Needless to say, this approach is deeply concerned with migration patterns especially within the United States. Examples of this approach are the sections devoted to log buildings in Henry Glassie's *Pattern in the Material*

Folk Culture of the Eastern United States and Fred B. Kniffen's article, "Folk Housing: Key to Diffusion."[4] For this type of study it is of course necessary to describe log buildings in more or less detail and to establish types of buildings. Nonetheless, the main purpose of each author is to show that there are certain regions in the United States that share common building traditions and to demonstrate how people from these regions, as they moved, took these traditions with them.

A recent book by Terry Jordan, *Texas Log Buildings: A Folk Architecture,* consists largely of a detailed description of log buildings in the state.[5] Although the log tradition in Texas is markedly heterogeneous in comparison to that of Indiana, I consider this present volume a companion work to Jordan's in many ways.

GOALS OF THIS WORK

The main goals of the present work are three in number. I have first attempted to describe, as others have, existing log buildings in southern Indiana. Because of the large number of log buildings included in this study, a total of 470, this descriptive process has been schematic for the most part. It has been possible to generalize to a large degree for there is a great deal of homogeneity in the log buildings of southern Indiana. Insofar as possible, I have established a simple typology and relied upon statistical averages. If my descriptions have any merit in comparison to those of other writers, it is that I have based them on a greater number of examples than have been used in most studies.

The second objective of this work is to try to describe why log buildings were built as they were, or to deal with what may broadly be termed "functional" considerations. For the most part, other writers have not used this approach. If I have been successful in this approach to any extent, it is because I have devoted considerable time over the last twelve years to observing log buildings and because I have been able to be present when a number of log buildings were disassembled and when a few, at least, were reassembled. This experience has led me to conclude that there was always some good, practical, functional reason why the builders of log houses built as they did, and it is these reasons that I have tried to pinpoint. I firmly believe that the functional reasons should be clearly understood before other speculation is undertaken. I must quickly admit that I realize that I have been unable to treat all the functional considerations that influenced the builders of log structures. Nonetheless, it is this topic that I have emphasized.

A third goal has been to discuss the European and American sources of the log buildings in southern Indiana. While I have previously dealt with the European sources of log constructions,[6] new information has come to light. Hence I feel it valuable to take up that question once more. My discussion of the diffusion of log construction from the east coast to southern Indiana has necessarily been sketchy. I have myself been unable to do much significant fieldwork in the states from which came most of the settlers in southern Indiana. Published information on log buildings in those states is rather scanty. I have tried, however, to assemble data showing that log construction was common in those states before about 1800, the date at which the early migrants left those states for Indiana. Wherever possible, I have given information in more detail concerning the way in which log houses in those states were built.

In this work, one approach has been largely neglected. I have not attempted to examine large numbers of historical records in search of information about log buildings. I have felt it more rewarding to examine buildings themselves than to look for records about them. As I will show later in this work, the early written records tend to deal with a type of log building that no longer exists, so that the examination of the early records is, to some extent, a separate and distinct task. It would be valuable to have this task done for southern Indiana, it is true, but the results of such research would not be of major importance for this work.

LOG CONSTRUCTION AND FRAME CONSTRUCTION

Buildings that are constructed mostly of wood may, generally speaking, be of log construction or of frame construction. When the main part of a building is composed of a number of horizontal timbers that interlock with one another at the corners it is customarily called a log building. The timbers may be the trunks of trees that have been cut to length and left round in cross-section, or they may be shaped until they are rectangular in cross-section. Either way, a building so constructed is termed a log building.

Up until the twentieth century most frame buildings also had some large timbers in them but these were far fewer than in log buildings. In a frame building of the simplest kind, a wall will consist of a horizontal timber at the bottom, another at the top, and a vertical timber at each end. Smaller timbers running vertically are fitted between the large bottom and top timbers. Between these smaller vertical timbers the doors and windows, if any, are placed, but otherwise the wall is generally covered on the outside with boards of some sort while the inner side of the wall is also covered with plaster or wooden paneling. It is clear, then, that the presence of large timbers in a building does not tell whether it is a log or a frame building. The number of timbers and the way they are fitted together are the decisive elements.

THE RELIANCE UPON ORIGINAL STRUCTURES IN THIS STUDY

There are many hundreds of log buildings of various kinds still standing in southern Indiana today. Some of these have been built of small round logs or poles in the twentieth century. While these buildings are certainly interesting, they represent a special subject that will not be treated in this work. Most of the extant buildings, however, use hewn logs. Some may be called, for the purposes of simplicity, original structures in that they have been in continued use in substantially the same form in the same location since they were originally built. Of course, each building has been subject to changes over time. The original roof covering of wooden shingles has worn out and been replaced, for instance. Usually, at some time the original fireplace has been closed off and a stove installed. In recent years, electric wiring and water pipes have often been installed. Nonetheless, a careful examination of a building can yield a great deal of information about the way it was originally constructed. Many of these buildings have been abandoned in recent years and are falling into decay, so that it is possible to examine almost every detail of them. It is these original buildings that are the objects of my study.

For many years in southern Indiana it has been a common practice to salvage log buildings, usually by disassembling them, moving them, and re-erecting them on a new site. Often this has been done to provide a vacation home or similar sort of recreational structure. Since this has often resulted in saving—we might even say recycling—a number of original parts of a log building that was threatened either by immediate destruction or slow destruction by decay, this practice has, in the main, been beneficial.

The amount of care devoted to salvaging and reusing the original material in a structure has varied from example to example. On one extreme we have the very careful reconstruction wherein every original element that was in usable condition has been saved and reused, while elements that were so far decayed as to be unusable have been carefully duplicated in old materials from other sources. This careful reconstruction, I am sorry to say, seems to have occurred very infrequently, even at the museums I have visited that included reconstructed log buildings. At the other extreme is the all-too-frequent case in which only the logs from an old building have been reused or logs from a number of buildings have been worked into a single structure. It is impossible in most instances to tell how much of a log building is original when it has been reconstructed in the twentieth century or whether it is made up of materials from several buildings. For these reasons I have tried to exclude reconstructed buildings from this study. Needless to say, I may have been mistaken in specific instances. I may have included some reconstructed examples and excluded some original examples, but I am convinced that virtually all of the buildings included in my study fall into the category of original buildings.

My attempt to focus on original structures has been prompted by more than narrow antiquarian interests. The question that has intrigued me is: how did people build before the Industrial Revolution? Because of a lack of transportation, they were restricted to using locally available materials almost exclusively. They were also restricted to using hand tools almost entirely, water-powered and animal-powered machinery being the only exceptions. Moreover, they relied upon tradition as their main guide in choosing the design of their buildings, the construction materials, and the techniques with which to work the materials. While it may be true that the Industrial Revolution was well under way elsewhere in the land and that its effects were certainly being felt in a number of areas of life in Indiana, those people who were building log structures in the nineteenth century were largely following old traditional patterns, and it is on these patterns that I have tried to concentrate.

GEOGRAPHICAL COVERAGE OF THIS STUDY

It is unfortunately true that my survey of log buildings has been carried out over a decade and that I have not made anything approaching a scientific survey from the geographical standpoint. Using Bloomington, Indiana, as a starting point, I have tried to cover as much of the southern part of the state as I could. If I have not worked in northern Indiana, it is because it has not been practical for me to do so. Many days I have driven out and tried to cover as many of the roads in a county as I could. Whenever I have been told about a log house I have tried to visit it, even though it may have been some distance from Bloomington.

On the map shown in the appendix I have indicated the number of log buildings that I found in each county I visited. The appendix also gives the names of counties I have worked in and the number of buildings found. In the case of counties close to Bloomington in which I have located a substantial number of log buildings, the number of buildings is also given for townships, though I must acknowledge these figures have little relationship to the number of log buildings actually existing in each county. For the counties close to Bloomington, I have made a number of trips and have probably found a large percentage of the extant log buildings. Farther from Bloomington, however, my visits have been fewer so that the number of buildings found has little or no corelation to the number actually extant.

I am saddened by the fact that many of the log buildings included in this study have been destroyed in the years since the study first began. In the summer of 1976, for instance, I revisited the site of a fine log barn in Dubois County. I was in time to see the still smoking remains of the barn, which had caught fire the night before and had burned to the ground. Due to limitations on travel, I have been unable to make an accurate count of the number of buildings no longer standing. I would estimate, however, that more than 25 percent of the buildings investigated are no longer standing. Some have been taken down, moved, and re-erected. Some have been torn or bull-dozed down because they were in the path of a new highway or in an area to be flooded by a reservoir. Some have been torn down by their owners because they were dilapidated and the owners wanted to be rid of them. Some have simply decayed to the point where they have tumbled down. In the last few years there seems to have developed an awareness that log buildings can be sold. Since this awareness has caused some owners to save buildings that they otherwise might have destroyed, this development is all to the good. It is my hope that the reckless destruction of these buildings will end while there are still a substantial number left. They are far too valuable to be destroyed, for they are tangible indicators of how people used to live.

THE DATING OF OLD BUILDINGS

Determining the date at which an old house was built is a very difficult and time-consuming task, one that usually is informed by four general types of available information. First, there may be a date on the house itself that was put there by the original builder. In some parts of the United States, it was a common practice to thus date a house. In the vicinity of Lancaster, Pennsylvania, for instance, there are a number of masonry houses with date stones set in a prominent place. These stones often have the names or initials of the original owners as well as the dates of construction. This was not a common practice in southern Indiana, and I cannot remember ever seeing a log house with the date of construction prominently displayed. Only on extremely rare occasions will one discover a date left by a builder in a casual manner somewhat akin to doodling. Several years ago I was helping to disassemble a large log house east of Columbus, Indiana. The logs in the walls had been covered with siding on the outside and plaster on the inside ever since the house was built. On one of the logs, the date 1848 had been carved in large numerals. The log was fitted into the wall in such a way that the date was upside down. It would seem likely that one of the builders carved the date into the log while it was lying on the ground before being placed into the wall. Had the date been carved after the log was in the wall, it would have been right side up. By contrast, the date 1864 was seen on a log granary in Owen County. It had been daubed onto an overhead beam with black paint. The owner of the granary said it had been done by his great-grandfather when he came home from the Civil War and that the granary had been built some years before 1864. On a number of log barns one finds dates carved into the log near the doors. Usually there are a number of dates and initials. It seems possible that farmers who were kept from working in the fields by inclement weather may have carved their initials and dates while waiting in hopes that the skies would clear. While dates of this sort do not provide the exact years of construction, at least they give helpful indications. (See Plate 1.)

Written records are a second type of information. The records maintained at county courthouses in southern Indiana deal, for the

Plate 1. *Inscription carved into one of the logs of a barn. The date is not necessarily the date of construction but may have been carved at some later time.*

most part, with land and not with the buildings on the land. It is only rarely that such records are helpful. They can tell us who first bought the land from the land office and when. However, it is never safe to assume that the buildings now standing on the land were built at or shortly after the time the land was originally purchased. Other buildings may have been built first and then destroyed. A large piece of land may have been bought at first and then divided into smaller pieces at a later date before any buildings were constructed. Nineteenth-century records do give the price of the transaction, and sometimes it is possible to see that a person bought a piece of land for a certain sum and sold it a few years later for a much higher amount reflecting the addition of buildings that had been erected on the land. At any rate, seaching through official records in hopes of finding the date at which a house was built is a time-consuming and often unrewarding pursuit. Because of the large number of log buildings included in this study, it has been impossible to investigate the official records for most of them.

The third type of information that may be used is oral tradition. Sometimes the owner of a building or his neighbors will know a great deal about the history of the structure. The fieldworker soon learns to treat the statement , "Oh, it's over a hundred years old," with caution. It is a statement that people use to indicate that they are impressed with the great age of a building rather than an exact indication. More specific answers may range all the way from "We bought the place twenty years ago and the building was standing then" to "My grandmother was born in 18 and 52 and she always said that her father built the house when she was six years old." Perfectly reliable statements such as the latter one are, unfortunately, all too uncommon. Moreover, it was often impossible to find the owner of a building while doing the fieldwork for this study, and it was often necessary to talk to tenants or neighbors who could give little information.

An investigation of the house itself may yield the fourth type of information. There are a number of features in a building that may be general indications of age and some that are rather precise indicators. Most of these features, insofar as they pertain to log buildings, are discussed in their proper place later in this work. They need not, therefore, be listed here, but they include such things as the type of saw used in sawing boards from a log as indicated by marks left by saw teeth and the type of hardware used. There are a number of problems in trying to discover evidence of this sort. Original hardware, for example, often has been replaced with more modern hardware. In a house that people are living in it is usually impossible to go into attics, bedrooms, and closets where useful evidence may be found. Often, too, valuable information is hidden so that it is only possible to find it when a house is being torn down. Bearing these circumstances in mind, one can realize that it was often impossible to gather information from the buildings I visited that would have helped to date them.

All in all, therefore, the *exact* dates of construction for most of the buildings included in this study are unknown. Construction methods and other details were little changed for log buildings throughout the nineteenth century. Because of this fact, it has been possible to describe building practices with reasonable accuracy even though the date of construction of the individual buildings is not precisely known.

There is, however, one general indicator of the age of a house, and that is the fireplace. Research with log houses and with houses of other types whose dates of construction can be discovered with reasonable accuracy always bears out one conclusion: in Anglo-American areas in southern Indiana, fireplaces were almost universal before about 1875. It was only after that date that stoves came into wide use. In houses that had been built with fireplaces originally, the fireplaces often were closed up and stoves installed after 1875. Transportation was undoubtedly an important factor in determining the use of stoves. In the nineteenth century, stoves usually were made of cast iron and were very heavy. Hence it was costly to ship a stove any distance, and it was not until the network of railroads was established that stoves could be obtained at a reasonable cost by most people. It is quite likely that people who lived close to the Ohio River had stoves at an early date because of relatively inexpensive river transportation. It is also likely that people who lived in larger towns had stoves before most rural dwellers. In trying to understand how quickly people would accept an innovation such as a stove, one must remember that more is involved than heating. In most one-room log houses, the fireplace or the stove was also used for cooking the year around. Changing from a fireplace to a stove involved buying new pots and pans as well as learning new cooking techniques. Moreover, the fireplace was an important source of light especially in the winter, and when a stove replaced the fireplace, dependable sources of light such as coal oil (kerosene) lamps had to be used regularly. All in all, then, it is easy to see why stoves were not instantly accepted as soon as they became available.

It is possible, then, to judge in a general way how old a house is by determining whether or not it had a fireplace when originally built. In many houses, when a stove was installed the fireplace was closed off and a hole was made into the chimney above the fireplace so that a stovepipe could be run into the chimney. In some houses the fireplace and chimney were torn down when a stove was installed and a new chimney was built. In cases of that sort, a window was often built into the hole in the wall left by the destroyed fireplace. A careful examination of the wall will usually show whether or not a fireplace was ever present. In working with log houses, therefore, I was able to tell whether or not a house was built before about 1875 by using the one important key. It was possible—then—to get some information as to general building trends and to make some generalizations concerning the age of buildings. Seventy-three percent of the nearly three hundred houses located for this study had fireplaces when originally built.

The Sites of Log Buildings

While it is always possible that log houses have been moved from their original locations, most of the buildings included in this study are presumed to be placed where they were originally built. In a number of instances the present owner of a log house has confirmed that tradition within his family has held that the house is on its original site. In other cases the owner has been able to locate the orginal site on the basis of family tradition.

In the majority of instances, the precise location of an early house was due to the availability of water. In the parts of Indiana where I have done my fieldwork, most log houses seem to have been built near springs. It is most unusual to find an early log house built near a stream of any kind unless, of course, we have a spring with a stream running from it. This means that most early log houses are not located on ridge tops or at the bottoms of valleys, but in the land in between, where springs occur. Usually a level spot close to the spring but above it on slightly higher land is chosen for the site for the house.

It is very rare to find a log house in a context with other farm buildings of comparable age. Either the log house stands virtually alone and other buildings that once stood on the farm are no longer standing, or a log house stands on a farm surrounded by more modern buildings. Consequently, it is impossible to discuss the relationship of log house sites to other farm building sites.

I have also been unable to find any consistent attempt to orient houses in relationship to specific compass directions. As far as I have been able to discover, the house is usually constructed in such a way that it faces the nearest road, and this means that a house may face any point on the compass. Rural roads frequently follow property lines and township lines in southern Indiana, and since springs and other sources of water are often far removed from the roads, the log houses often are, too.

It seems to have been a common practice in southern Indiana, as elsewhere in the midwest, to plant two large evergreen trees in front of houses. When this practice was common, it is impossible to say, but in most cases when trees have survived until today, they have attained a huge size. Most of the trees that I have noticed seem to be white pines *(Pinus Strobus)*. It would be interesting to know how the seedlings of this tree, which does not occur naturally in southern Indiana, were brought to the area in earlier times.

A NOTE ON LOG HOUSES BUILT BY GERMAN IMMIGRANTS

Most of the log buildings in southern Indiana resemble one another in a number of ways, especially in the ways the logs are shaped and fitted together. There are a number of log buildings that were built by people who moved to the area from Germany. These German-American log buildings resemble those built by British-Americans in many respects, but they have some special features. These features are described in a separate section. In most sections where log buildings are being described, the descriptions apply to both BritishAmerican and German-American buildings. Any exceptions for the German-American buildings can be understood by referring to Chapter 5.

Chapter Two

On the Origin and Diffusion
of Log Construction

To TRACE in great detail the origin and diffusion of log construction is an impossible task. While much has been written on log buildings both in Europe and the United States, available information is both spotty and uneven. If one considers only the log buildings that are still standing, there are large areas for which there is no published information. For earlier centuries information is practically nonexistent. The buildings themselves have mostly disappeared, leaving only a few traces that can be uncovered by painstaking archaeological research, and written records are not only scarce but also are often hidden away in obscure manuscript sources.

Writing on the origin and diffusion of log construction must, therefore, be at best speculative. Much has already been written on the subject, but since new evidence continually comes to light, older theories must be reassessed.

THE THREE DIFFERENT TYPES OF LOG CONSTRUCTION

I. ROUND-LOG CONSTRUCTION

One general point needs to be made at the very outset. There are three different types of log construction. I will call them round-log, shaped-log, and hewn-and-chinked-log construction. The fact that there are these three types of log construction has never previously been pointed out. Nonetheless, in order to understand the history of log construction, we must distinguish between the three types and keep them separate.

In round-log construction, the horizontal timbers are simply tree trunks cut to appropriate lengths. In cross section, they are, of course, round. Large logs are generally not used. Instead, small straight logs less than eighteen inches in diameter are usually selected.

There are three construction features that almost invariably appear in round-log buildings. The first is that there are lengthwise gaps or interstices between the logs because the logs are never perfectly straight and because every tree trunk tapers to some extent from the butt end towards the top. These gaps may be left open if the building is a barn or an outbuilding, but in dwelling houses the gaps are filled in or chinked with odd pieces of wood or stone and clay.

The second feature is that the corners of the buildings are made so that the ends of the logs are not flush with the corners but protrude some distance past the corners. Although several different notches may be used to hold the logs in place at the corners, most have this feature (Fig. 2.1, following page).

The third feature is that the walls in these buildings normally are not covered with exterior siding. The different sizes of the logs and the way the logs protrude past the corners make it very difficult to apply siding of any sort.

Only very scanty evidence is available for round-log construction in Europe. Some outbuildings using round logs are found in Scandinavia and in Germany, for example, but it would seem that round logs were used only in temporary or crude structures.[1]

In the eastern United States round logs have also been used for temporary or utility buildings. Typical examples are the log cabins of pioneers used only until some better and more permanent house could be erected, barns and other outbuildings, and the shelters of hunters, loggers, and the like. Round-log houses have also been built as vacation homes in the twentieth century as well as in areas where coniferous trees are common. I will discuss the use of logs from coniferous trees in round-log construction below.

II. SHAPED-LOG CONSTRUCTION

The second type of log construction uses shaped logs. The logs often are shaped so that they are gently rounded on the inside and outside surfaces, but the most important consideration is that they are shaped on the tops and bottoms so that they fit together without lengthwise gaps or interstices. There is, therefore, no need for chink-

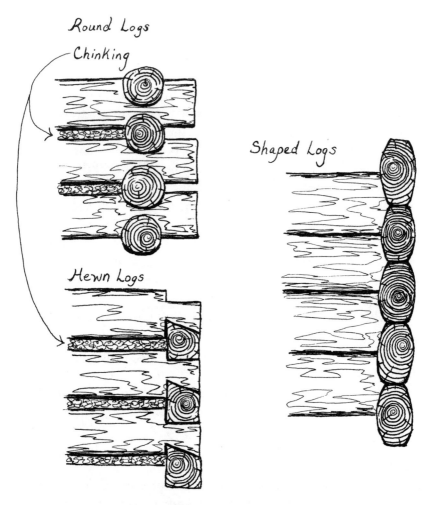

Fig. 2.1 *Round, hewn, and shaped logs.*

ing. There is much variety in the actual shape of the logs, in the ways they are joined at the corners and in the lengthwise joints, but the absence of interstices and chinking marks the principal distinction between this type of log construction and the other two types.

However the logs may be joined at the corners, often a short length of log protrudes past the corner. As with the round logs, shaped logs usually are not covered with exterior siding.

Shaped-log construction is the predominant form in Europe. Round-log construction, as I have already said, is very rare there, and hewn-and-chinked-log construction, which I will describe below, seems to be unknown.

Shaped-Log Construction in Europe

The areas in Europe where log construction is found today can best be shown by means of a map (Fig. 2.2). If one compares this map with a map showing the areas in Europe where coniferous forests predominate (Fig. 2.3), one fact is immediately obvious: log construction is found in Europe where coniferous forests predominate. Log buildings in Europe, therefore, are usually made of logs from coniferous trees. Since coniferous trees tend to grow in the north and at high altitudes elsewhere, log buildings in Europe are found in the north and in mountainous regions.

To emphasize the degree to which the distribution of log buildings and coniferous forests correspond, let us look more closely at

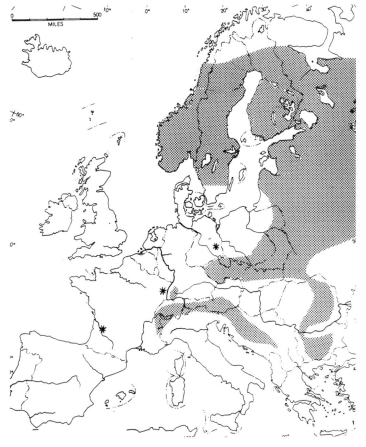

Fig. 2.2 *Distribution of notched-log construction in modern Europe.*
Star indicates a minor occurrence.

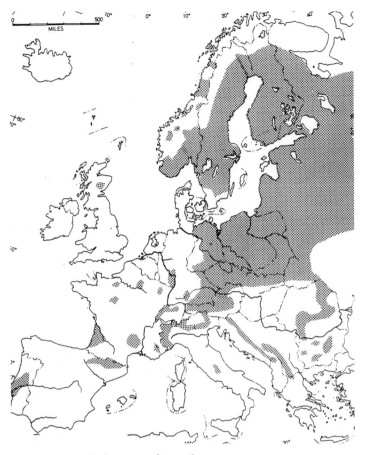

Fig. 2.3 Coniferous forests in Europe.

certain areas. Notice, for example, that log buildings are found virtually all over Sweden except in the southern tip where deciduous forests predominate. Although Sweden and Norway have great numbers of log buildings, Denmark has none. Pine forests predominate in Norway and Sweden while Denmark has forests of oak and beech.

Log buildings and coniferous trees are found in the Alps. A small finger wherein log buildings are found protrudes into southwestern Germany. This corresponds to the Black Forest which is made up largely of coniferous trees. Most of the rest of Germany has no log buildings nor has it coniferous forests. Konrad Bedal, in describing log construction in southern Germany and neighboring areas, provides confirmation on this point. He states that, with the exception of some timbers that need to be exceptionally strong, log buildings consistently use wood from coniferous trees.[2]

Notice, too, that the areas of "minor occurrence" are areas where coniferous forests are found. Especially noteworthy are the two areas of minor occurence in France, for these are within areas of coniferous forests, even though most of France has deciduous forests.

It should be pointed out that there are areas such as northern Poland where there are coniferous forest but there are no reported log buildings. We may, therefore, make the following generalizations. In Europe, log buildings are found in areas where there are coniferous forests. Where there are coniferous forests in Europe, log buildings are usually found.

One can only speculate as to why buildings in Europe are built of logs from coniferous trees. Probably one important reason is that evergreen trees such as pine tend to grow tall and straight so that suitable house logs can be easily obtained. Moreover, the wood is relatively soft so that logs can be carefully shaped and closely fitted to one another in the building.

Shaped-Log Construction in Northern Asia and the United States

While it is true as I have stated that shaped-log construction predominates in Europe, it is also found elsewhere. A few pictures that have been published show that it is found in at least some parts of Asiatic Russia. Henry Mercer, for example, reproduces a photo taken in Siberia in 1918 showing a family standing by the wall of a log house.[3] The logs appear to be nearly round, and they protrude some distance past the corners. It is clear from the photo, though, that each log has been carefully shaped, for the bottom side of each log has a curved groove running the entire length of the log so that it can fit closely down over the top of the log below it so that no chinking is needed. Making such a groove must have required much time and special tools, for such a groove could not have been chopped out with an axe.

Some European immigrants brought shaped-log construction with them to the United States in the nineteenth century. I have elsewhere cited examples of Norwegian-American shaped-log houses and also the fact that while a few Norwegian immigrants built shaped-log buildings, most got their British-American neighbors to help them build hewn-and-chinked-log buildings.[4] A number of pictures of Finnish American shaped-log buildings in Wisconsin have also been published.[5] These nineteenth-century examples of shaped-log construction have had no influence on most log buildings in the eastern United States.

The origin and diffusion of both round-log and shaped-log construction cannot be adequately treated in this work. Since round-log structures have often been considered temporary, there are very few surviving examples that are old. While many round-log houses have been built in the twentieth century as vacation homes, information on how to build them has been spread by books, magazines, and newspapers. Hence these modern houses can tell us little about the history of this form of construction. Further, while round logs were used in barns and other outbuildings in the past, very little has been written on such buildings in Europe especially. It is true as I have noted that round logs were used in temporary shelters and in roughly built utility buildings in Sweden and Germany. It is also possible that round logs were used in a similar way in other parts of Europe. Hence this form of construction could have been introduced to the New World by the Swedes in Delaware, by the Pennsylvania Germans, or by other immigrant groups. Because of the paucity of relevant information, I doubt that we will ever know who introduced it to the New World.

The history of shaped-log construction must be left to European scholars, for there is too little published information available to an American to deal with it, and this type of construction is found in the United States only in areas where Fenno-Scandinavian immigrants settled in the nineteenth century.

III. HEWN-AND-CHINKED-LOG CONSTRUCTION

The third type of log construction uses hewn logs or, as they are sometimes called, planked logs. The logs are worked so that they are flat on both sides to an average thickness of six or seven inches. Their other dimension, their height as placed in the wall, varies depending on the size of the original log. Only rarely does this size exceed two feet, for the giant trees of the virgin forest were not used by most log house builders, probably because there would have been far too much waste wood to remove from each side.

The logs, then, are much different in shape from those of the other two types. Moreover, they are joined at the corners in such a way that the corners are flush and no part of the log protrudes past the corner. Because the outside surface of the logs is flat and because the corners are flush, these log walls are normally covered with siding, usually overlapping, horizontal clapboards. Because of this siding, which protects logs from the weather, lengthwise gaps are left between the logs to be filled with chinking consisting of chips or pieces of wood or stone covered with clay.

While the term "hewn-and-chinked-log construction" is a very awkward one, I have decided to use it in this chapter to avoid any possible confusion. In shaped-log construction it is likely that the preliminary shaping of the logs is done by hewing with an axe even though the final shaping is done with other tools such as drawknives. Hence the simpler term "hewn-log construction" might be misinterpreted in this chapter. I will use the simpler term, however, elsewhere in this work.

To summarize, then, I may say that the three types of log construction are distinct from one another. The shape of the logs is usually different in each case; the corner notches are usually different in each case; the hewn-and-chinked logs are covered with siding; and the shaped logs use no chinking. The round logs and most of the shaped logs have corners that are not flush while the round logs and the hewn-and-chinked logs both use chinking.

Hewn-and-chinked logs are found only in the United States and Canada. In this area they are normally made of logs from hardwood or deciduous trees. Round-log and shaped-log construction, on the other hand, normally use logs from evergreen trees. This and other generalizations that I have made thus far have never been made before, even though the origin and diffusion of log construction have been discussed for at least fifty years, and because the generalizations I have made have a direct bearing on this much-discussed subject, I feel that I must elaborate on certain points.

Resemblances to Hewn-and-Chinked-Log Construction in Central Europe

The first point is that several recent writers have stated that hewn-and-chinked-log construction is found in an area in Central Europe, the "Czech hills." Glassie states, for example, that "it is in Bohemia, western Moravia, and Silesia . . . that log construction of exactly the American type can be found."[6] Jordan makes a similar point in his book *Texas Log Buildings*.[7]

Log construction techniques in the Czech hills do superficially resemble American hewn-and-chinked techniques even though there

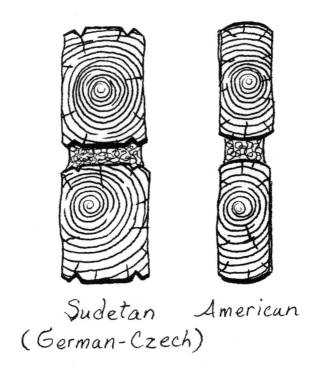

Sudetan   American
(German-Czech)

Fig. 2.4

were very few early immigrants to America from this area. Closer inspection, however, reveals that beneath the superficial resemblances lie some marked differences. In his *Ostgermanische Holzbaukultur,* Heinrich Franke gives drawings showing cross-sections of logs used in walls.[8] I have reproduced one such drawing (Fig. 2.4) that Franke says is from the Sudetenland. This illustration shows that interstices are indeed left between the logs and filled with mortar. The construction of the logs at the top and bottom, though, is very different from that in hewn-and-chinked construction. In hewn-and-chinked construction the logs are simply not shaped on the top and bottom surfaces at all. Hence the top and bottom surfaces retain the natural curvature of the tree trunk from which the timber was hewn, and the width of the interstices varies from mere cracks to large gaps, for the trunks taper from one end to the other and are never perfectly straight. In the Sudetenland logs shown by Franke, the bottom and top surfaces of each log have been shaped so that the log is straight from one end to the other and so that the top and bottom surfaces are flat. Moreover, big grooves have been cut in the corners of the logs so that the mortar packed into the gap will be better retained. The shaping of the Sudetenland logs, therefore, required much more careful workmanship and different tools from the hewn-and-chinked system, for the long grooves could not have been cut with an axe or a broadaxe. For these reasons I believe that the log construction method found in the Czech hills should be considered a special type of shaped-log construction and that my generalization concerning the distinctiveness of American hewn-and-chinked-log construction is a valid one.

The fact that the American hewn-and-chinked-log technique is indeed different from that found in Central Europe is emphasized by a statement from a leading German scholar who has studied log construction extensively. Joachim Hahnel has informed me that, as far as he knows, the hewn-and-chinked method of building log houses is unknown in Germany and Central Europe.[9] The methods that he describes as used in southern Germany are all variations on the shaped-log technique that I have described above.

Moreover, Terry Jordan has recently done extensive fieldwork in those areas in southern Germany, Switzerland, and Austria from which came many of the German-speaking immigrants who settled in colonial America. After examining large numbers of extant log buildings in those areas, he concludes, "Log shaping, corner timbering, spacing in walls . . . all differ in fundamental ways from American types and methods."[10]

TYPES OF WOOD USED IN LOG CONSTRUCTION

The second point that I want to discuss concerns the types of wood used for the different log construction methods. There can be no doubt that softwoods, as woods from coniferous trees are usually called, are used in shaped-log construction in Europe. Bedal's statement cited above concerning the use of softwoods in German log buildings helps confirm this assertion. Moreover, the coincidence between the distribution of softwood forests and of shaped-log construction in Europe is too exact to permit any other interpretation.

I am also convinced that logs from coniferous trees are usually not strong enough to make the kind of corner joints used in hewn-and-chinked log construction that produce flush corners. In hewn-and-chinked logs, the part of the log that holds the log in place is actually quite small. I once watched a demonstration of how to make the two types of corner joints most commonly used in the United States for hewn-and-chinked logs. Unfortunately, the man giving the demonstration was using pine logs rather than hardwood logs. As the work proceeded, for each type of joint he actually broke off the important part of the joint in the process of trying to cut out the joint with an axe.

In the kind of joint customarily used with round softwood logs in the United States, a portion of the log several inches in length protrudes past the notch giving enough strength so that the locking part of the joint cannot break off. In Figure 2.5, I have shown the important parts of the joints, the parts that actually lock the logs in place, by means of arrows.

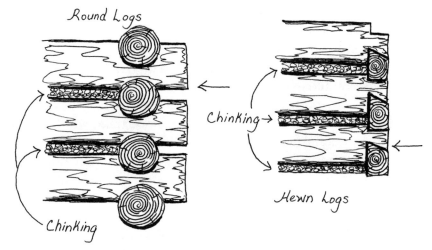

Fig. 2.5

Round-log and hewn-and-chinked-log construction are found in the United States and Canada. It must at once be said that information on the distribution of log buildings in these countries is very incomplete, and information on the kind of wood used in these buildings is even less complete. There does, however, appear to be a clear tendency in the United States for round logs to be made of softwoods and for hewn-and-chinked logs to be made of hardwoods. The only other writer who has addressed this question is Terry Jordan. After I had discussed this matter with him, he examined the large amount of data he had assembled on log buildings in Texas. He found that the data for Texas supported this conclusion, for Texas has areas both of softwood and hardwood forests.[11]

There are, however, several exceptions to the generalization that round-log construction uses softwoods in the United States while hewn-and-chinked-log uses hardwoods. The first is that hastily built temporary houses may use logs of hardwood and so may barns and outbuildings. The fact that round-log construction takes far less time and skill than hewn-and-chinked-log construction explains why this is so. In most areas in the United States people were familiar with both types of construction. Where hardwoods were available before the twentieth century, if one wanted a permanent structure and if one had the time and skill, one built hewn-and-chinked-log buildings. In an area such as southern Indiana, therefore, people built large numbers of carefully crafted houses, barns, churchhouses, sheds, and smokehouses of hewn-and-chinked hardwood logs. When they were in a hurry and did not need a permanent structure, they sometimes used round logs of hardwood. In the twentieth century when the old skills had become rare and when people wanted rustic looking vacation homes, they used round logs also.

The second exception to the softwood-hardwood generalization concerns people who moved from an area where hewn-and-chinked-log construction was common into a new area where only softwoods could be found. Such people sometimes built hewn-and-chinked-log buildings with softwood logs. As a case in point, I saw a fine log house near Aurora, Oregon, built of fir logs that had been shaped so they were flat on both sides and chinked. The builders of the house had come from Missouri where most log houses used hewn logs of hardwood. Terry Jordan also reports that early houses in softwood areas of Texas often used hewn logs, although later in the same areas round logs became common.[12]

At any rate, it seems clear that round-log and shaped-log construction are used mostly where logs from coniferous trees are used. Because of the use of softwoods in shaped-log construction, the builders can shape the logs in special ways and fit them so closely to one another that no chinking is needed. In shaping and fitting the logs, drawknives and similar tools are used to cut away the wood. Hewn-and-chinked-log construction, on the other hand, uses mostly hardwood logs. In hewing the logs, broadaxes are used and large chunks of wood are split away from the logs. These points underscore the fact that hewn-and-chinked-log construction is markedly different from the other two construction methods.

THE USE OF SIDING ON HEWN-AND-CHINKED-LOG HOUSES

A third point to be made concerns the use of siding on hewn-and-chinked-log houses. In discussing below how southern Indiana houses are built I will elaborate on this subject. At this time let me say only that much evidence has led me to conclude that the use of siding on hewn-and-chinked-log houses was the normal practice in the eastern United States.

THE EUROPEAN SOURCES OF AMERICAN LOG CONSTRUCTION

The discussion on the preceding pages has shown that the predominant form of log construction in the eastern United States and adjacent areas in Canada is markedly different from log construction in Europe. It has shown that there are three important differences. The logs are shaped and fitted together in different ways. The exterior of log walls in the United States and Canada is usually covered with siding. Finally, in America logs from hardwood trees are normally used for houses built before the twentieth century.

As we turn to the history of log construction in the United States and a discussion of its European sources, we may hope to find why log buildings in the United States were built in ways that were so markedly different from European ways.

SEVENTEENTH-CENTURY BRITISH-AMERICAN LOG BUILDINGS

Much has been written on the European origins of log construction in America, for all evidence points to the fact that Native Americans did not build houses of horizontal logs notched together at the corners before the coming of Europeans to these shores. For many years scholars believed that it was Swedes who introduced log construction to this country while more recently the belief that it was Germans who were responsible has gained some adherents. Because new evidence has recently come to light, I want to review the extensive material on seventeenth century British-American log buildings in order to demonstrate that no single European source can be considered to be the origin of log buildings in the United States. After this review I will describe the Swedish and German origins theses and point out why I consider them inadequate.

LOG HOUSES IN EARLY NEW ENGLAND

Although there are at the present great gaps in our knowledge of early log buildings in British-American areas, enough information is available to show that there were log buildings in these areas at a very early date. Richard Candee has described a number of very early New England log buildings.[13] Those that he describes in greatest detail are found near the Piscataqua River, which divides the states of Maine and New Hampshire. These buildings date between 1650 and 1750. He has also described other early log buildings in Maine, New Hampshire, Massachusetts, and Connecticut. A number of log buildings in these states must have been destroyed long ago without leaving any trace or record. John Rempel, for example, cites an account, not found in Candee, that is dated 1724 from Londonderry, New Hampshire, ordering a schoolhouse to be built "sixtine foot long and twelve foot brenth . . . to be a log house seven foot side wall."[14] Probably there are surviving examples elsewhere in these states that have not yet been discovered, for Candee concentrated his fieldwork in the Piscataqua region. Candee, for instance, does not mention three early log houses that Henry Mercer illustrates, one of which Mercer found in Gloucester, Massachusetts, supposedly dating from 1638. The other two, from Rockport, Massachusetts, and Kittery, Maine, were built well before 1700. All three of these log houses were standing and in use in 1920.[15]

Some of the buildings Candee describes were used as garrison houses, that is, houses that could be used as forts in case of attack, but most were simply dwelling houses. Some are relatively large, two-story houses, while some are small, with one room. Whatever the purpose or size of the building, most used in the walls logs that were worked in a special way.

These logs were cut so that they were flat on the inside and outside surfaces, and they were joined at the corners with dovetail joints so that the corners were flush. Most of them were probably covered with siding right from the time they were built. Candee does not deal with the question of siding in any detail, and it is quite likely that it was impossible to determine for many of the houses whether they were originally sided. Early documents he cites show that some of the houses were sided at the time they were built, and, certainly, all of them have been covered with siding for a long, long time.[16]

The logs in these early New England houses, therefore, conform in three important respects with the hewn-and-chinked-log model I have given above. To show the inadequacy of terminology, though, these logs were sawn, not hewn. Candee explains that the logs were sawn because there were a large number of early sawmills in the area. Whether hewn with a broadaxe or sawn at a mill, the shape of the logs is the important consideration, for it is their shape that makes it possible to join the logs at the corners so they do not protrude past the corners and to cover them with siding.

The log construction method Candee describes deviates from my hewn-and-chinked-log model in one important respect. In all the early buildings he was able to inspect, the logs fit closely upon one another so that there are no lengthwise gaps between them. In this respect, therefore, they resemble shaped logs rather than hewn-and-chinked logs. Actually, the absence of gaps can best be explained by the fact that the logs were sawn at sawmills. While the logs were at the mill being sawn so that the sides were straight and flat, it would have been a simple matter to saw them so that the tops and bottoms were also straight. The absence of gaps made for better insulated and warmer houses in the cold New England winters.

Candee believes that the method of building with logs that he describes is unique in the United States, that it first appeared along the Piscataqua River and spread to a few other New England areas but that it is unconnected with any other form of log construction and had no influence on log building methods elsewhere. While it is true that the method he found does differ in one important respect from methods used in most areas, I feel that he has not used evidence about early log buildings elsewhere. Also, Candee has to some extent confused round-log construction with hewn-and-chinked-log construction when he says the method he describes is unconnected with any other form of log construction. Certainly, the form he describes differs markedly from round-log construction. As I have shown, however, it is very close to hewn-and-chinked-log construction elsewhere in the United States.

To turn to other early examples of British-American log buildings outside New England that use the same method that Candee describes, it should at once be mentioned that Donald and Jean Hutslar found one such log building constructed in Ohio shortly before 1800.[17] The builders of this Ohio structure came from New England. The logs were sawn on all four surfaces so they fit closely on one another without chinking, and they were covered with siding. This technique of working the logs must, therefore, have been well known in New England and still flourishing around 1800.

Henry Glassie has also found two houses in Middle Virginia that are built of logs shaped exactly like those found in early New England buildings. The logs are "planked," that is, they are only about five inches thick; they are joined at the corners with dovetail joints; they are fitted so there are no interstices between them; and they are covered on the outside with clapboards.[18] As happens so often with log houses, Glassie was able to find no precise date of construction for them but was forced to rely on the general phrase "built in the eighteenth century."

There are at least two other areas where early log buildings built in this way are found, North Carolina and New Jersey. The Horton House at Horton Grove in Durham County, North Carolina, is thought to have been built around 1770. It uses the same techniques as those buildings found by Glassie.[19] The same may be said for a number of houses in southwestern New Jersey whose exact dates of construction are unknown, but which are believed to date from the early 1700s.[20]

How are we to explain the fact that these Virginia, North Carolina, and New Jersey houses are built in the same way as the New England ones? There are at least three possible explanations. First, it could be just an accident, and four different groups of people invented the same way to build independently. Second, some New Englanders from the Piscataqua River may have moved to these other states taking this form of construction with them. Third, the British immigrants who settled in New England, North Carolina, and New Jersey knew about log construction before they came to the New World. Because other British-Americans in other parts of the country were building log houses at a very early date, I believe that this third possibility is the best explanation for the resemblances. Information on early log buildings outside New England will be given below.

NEW ENGLAND AS A SOURCE OF LOG CONSTRUCTION

To further demonstrate that log construction flourished in New England at an early date, it is possible to show that some New Englanders who emigrated to other areas took a knowledge of how to build log buildings with them. Moreover, it was the hewn-and-chinked-log technique that they took. This method probably developed in New England out of the earlier method used there that featured sawn logs joined without lengthwise gaps.

Emigrants from the other New England states who moved into parts of Vermont that were being settled in the late eighteenth century built some hewn-and-chinked-log houses shortly after the Revolutionary War.[21] Much of New York state was settled by people from New England, and many of these early settlers built houses of hewn logs that were chinked.[22] Some of the New Englanders who moved to Ohio before 1800 built houses there of this type.[23] Some New England people who moved to Canada also built hewn-and-chinked-log houses. Indeed, when a group of Loyalists from New England and New York state moved to Nova Scotia, Benjamin Marston, a government surveyor, wrote of an area known as Roseway:

> The first location upon house lots was on the 23rd of May 1783, and on the 1st of February 1784, there were 1127 houses built. 80 of which were indeed only temporary ones put up for the winter by some latecomers who could not be immediately provided for. 231 of these were framed houses, the rest (816) what are called Log-Houses, built of pieces of timber framed together at the ends—and these are sometimes clapboarded over; that they may be made permanent buildings to endure many years.[24]

Houses using clapboards over the logs are almost always built from hewn-and-chinked logs.

The evidence that the New Englanders took the knowledge and skills of log construction with them as they moved to other areas is important for two reasons. As has been noted, this evidence shows that log building techniques were widely known in New England and not confined to only a few areas. Moreover, this evidence can serve as a supplement to the generalization made by Fred Kniffen and Henry Glassie that log construction spread from the Pennsylvania German areas to virtually all other parts of the United States. They write:

> The horizontal log construction with true corner timbering that came to characterize the American frontier was, then, not a New World adaptation to environment, nor was it a Scandinavian introduction; rather it was introduced by the Pennsylvania Ger-

mans and carried by them and by the Scotch-Irish in all directions from southeastern Pennsylvania.[25]

While it is doubtlessly true that the diffusion of log construction from Pennsylvania was of great importance, it is impossible that it is responsible for the early log buildings in New England, some of which date from 1650. Moreover, it is clear that log construction spread from New England as well as from Pennsylvania.

EARLY LOG BUILDINGS IN OTHER COLONIES

We have seen that New Englanders built log houses when they moved to other areas. People in other colonies, however, were also using at an early date log construction, and this log construction cannot be explained as coming from New England. In dealing with early British-American log buildings in other colonies we will have to rely upon evidence that comes only from written records. Unlike the reliable fieldwork evidence from Candee, the Hutslars, Glassie, and others mentioned, the early records are often tantalizingly unclear and incomplete. Following are references to log buildings dating before 1700 arranged by state or province.

A pamphlet published in England in 1650 was designed to attract settlers to land owned by Sir Edmund Plowden in New Jersey. Entitled *A Description of the Province of New Albion,* it lists the types of houses new settlers could build. One is "A log house of young trees 30 foot square notched in at the corners."[26] How the author of the pamphlet learned about log houses we cannot know, but it is likely that reports from the New World were his source, for the first two editions of the pamphlet do not mention the log house, the reference to which was added in the third edition.

A visitor to Port Royal, Nova Scotia in 1687 reported that, "All the houses were low, made of rough pieces of wood, one on top of another, and roofed with thatch."[27] It sounds as if the visitor is trying to describe log construction that he is seeing for the first time.

In Maryland, British-Americans were building log houses at a very early date. C. A. Weslager has compiled an impressive listing of early references to log structures in the state.[23] The earliest is dated 1658 and there are many others before 1700.

There are likewise early references to log buildings in the Carolinas. A letter writer in 1690 mentioned log structures in South Carolina, including one built by a Nathaniel Johnson, and a log jail was built in North Carolina in 1680.[29]

Weslager also has found documents referring to two log houses that had been built in Philadelphia by 1685, one by a Patrick Robinson and one by a George Bartholomew.[30]

Finally, another writer refers to "a solid and substantial log house built by William Thompson in 1699" in Falls Church, Virginia.[31]

SEVENTEENTH-CENTURY BRITISH-AMERICAN LOG BUILDINGS—CONCLUSIONS

To sum up, then, the evidence, some of which has only recently come to light and hence could not have been used by other writers on log construction, supports three important points. First, a special type of log construction flourished in New England as early as 1650. This special type resembles hewn-and-chinked-log construction also was known in New England well before 1800. It seems reasonable to assume that hewn-and-chinked-log construction developed from the special type of log construction. When logs were sawed at a sawmill to use in log houses it was possible to saw all four surfaces so that the logs fit closely upon one another without lengthwise gaps that would have needed chinking. When the builders were some distance from a sawmill, it was easier to hew the logs with a broadaxe than to haul the logs long distances to a mill. When they hewed the logs. they did so only on two surfaces and left the top and bottom surfaces unshaped. The gaps left between the logs could then be filled with chinking. Since the houses were covered with siding on the exterior, the presence of the gaps filled with chinking was not objectionable. The third point is that log construction was used in many other British-American areas well before 1700.

The early dates at which log construction was used by British-Americans and the wide geographical extent of its use—from Nova Scotia to the Carolinas—lead to one conclusion. British-American immigrants must have known about log construction before they came to this country. The problem is that there are no clearly documented examples of log buildings in Great Britain.

Candee agrees with Mercer that it may have been Scottish immigrants who brought a knowledge of log forts and fortified houses to New England and who used that knowledge to construct log houses there.[32] It was certainly Scottish settlers who were building log houses in Nova Scotia before 1687. It may also be Scottish immigrants to other colonies such as Virginia and Maryland who introduced log construction there. Unless more information should come to light from England and Scotland, it may never be possible to be more precise about the British origins of log construction.

RESEMBLANCES BETWEEN LOG AND FRAME CONSTRUCTION

In support of the thesis that the most common form of log construction in the eastern United States, namely, the hewn-and-chinked method, may be of British origin, the following further points may be made:

1) The primary technique in shaping the logs is hewing with a broadaxe, even though in a few cases we have seen that the logs were sawn to shape. Hewing hardwood logs with a broadaxe in order to shape them into usable timbers is an ancient technique for buildings of frame construction both in Great Britain and in the United States. This technique was also widely used in ship building and many other crafts using wood. The earliest settlers from Great Britain brought broadaxes with them to the New World.[33] Hence they had the tools and the skills for hewing house logs.

2) The use of clay and chips of wood to chink the interstices between the logs bears some resemblance to a widely practiced technique used in the construction of half-timbered frame houses in Great Britain. This technique involves filling large spaces between timbers with sticks, over which a mixture of clay and straw is plastered.

3) The dovetail notch used at the corners of many buildings to join the logs together was a joint well known to craftsmen of many kinds who worked with wood. Many of the early New England houses of log used this joint at the corners.

4) Many of the British-American hewn-and-chinked-log houses had the exterior of the walls covered with siding of clapboards, as I have noted. Covering the exterior of the walls with clapboards is an old building practice in England, especially in the areas in the southeast from which many immigrants to America came.[34] Frame houses built in New England and the other colonies throughout the seventeenth and eighteenth centuries were, of course, regularly sheathed with clapboards.

5) Log houses built by British-Americans have always been similar in almost every respect to smaller frame houses built by the same

people. They are similar in size and shape, in the location of fireplaces and chimneys, in the location and construction of doors and windows, and in many other ways.[36] The main exception is, of course, the actual construction of the walls, and, in finished log houses intended to be permanent, the wall construction is hidden anyway. It is true in New England, and it is true in Indiana, that a finished log house covered with clapboards looks almost exactly like a frame house covered with siding.

OTHER THEORIES OF EUROPEAN ORIGINS
OF AMERICAN LOG CONSTRUCTION

THE SWEDISH THESIS

Now that the evidence concerning early British-American log construction has been presented, we can examine the other suggestions that have been made as to the European origins of American log construction. As we look at these other suggestions, we must bear in mind that the important evidence on early log buildings provided by Candee did not come to light until after those who put forward these other suggestions had published their findings, and thus they could not have used Candee's material.

It was not until 1924 that the European origins of American log construction attracted the attention of scholars. In that year Henry C. Mercer read his paper on "The Origin of Log Houses in the United States" at a meeting of the Bucks County Historical Society at Doylestown, Pennsylvania.[36] After discussing what evidence was available to him, he decided to agree with Fiske Kimball who had casually remarked in 1922 that log houses in the United States should be traced to the Swedes who settled in the Delaware Valley in 1638 and the years following.[37] Later, in 1939, Harold R. Shurtleff elaborated on the topic,[38] and since that time many writers have repeated the thesis of Swedish origins.[39]

Simply stated, the Swedish thesis assumes that since log construction is known in Sweden and since Swedes were in this country at an early date, they must have introduced log construction here. There are two major objections to this suggestion.

The first objection is that the thesis ignores the point that the dominant Swedish way of building with logs is markedly different from the dominant American way. In Sweden there are a few utility buildings built of round logs, but most log buildings use the shaped-log method described above. In the eastern United States, as I have shown, the hewn-and-chinked-log technique predominates. The logs themselves in Sweden are not hewn flat on both sides with a broadaxe. They are joined at the corners with a variety of complicated joints, but not with the single dovetail or V-notch joints commonly used in America. The logs in Swedish walls fit closely upon one another so that chinking between the logs is never used, and the logs are normally not covered with siding.

I have dealt in much more detail with the differences between Swedish and American log construction in my article, "Some Comments on Log Construction in Scandinavia and the United States."[40] These differences are so many and so fundamental that I cannot believe that the typical American method of building with logs owes anything to Sweden.

The second objection is that British-Americans were building with horizontal logs at a date far too early to be explained by influences from the small Swedish settlement on the Delaware. It is hard to believe that New Englanders, as described above, who were building log houses as early as 1650 could have learned this building method from the Swedish settlers who had arrived in the Delaware Valley only a few years earlier.

All in all, it seems to me that, in the light of present-day information, the Swedish origins thesis as the explanation for the source of all American log construction should be abandoned.

THE GERMAN ORIGINS THESIS

Another hypothesis that has been advanced is that German immigrants to Pennsylvania brought log construction to the United States and that British-Americans learned to build with logs through contact with them. The first detailed presentation of this thesis was made by Fred Kniffen and Henry Glassie.[41] It has also been repeated by Terry Jordan.[42]

There are three major objections to this thesis. The first concerns the dates at which the German immigrants reached Pennsylvania. By 1702 only two hundred families had come, and until 1727 the numbers were still very small. In that year, the number of immigrants increased substantially and large numbers continued to come up through 1764.[43] It is clearly impossible, therefore, that the Pennsylvania Germans could have been the source of the British-American log buildings dating before 1700 discussed above, and it is very unlikely that the German people could have exerted much influence before at least 1727.

The second objection is that there are only a few areas in Germany in which log construction is found, in the extreme south. The map giving the distribution of log construction in Europe (Fig.2.2) shows this very clearly. Moreover, very few of the immigrants came from these areas in Gerrnany where log construction occurs.[44]

The third objection to the thesis of German origins is that there are marked differences between the methods of log construction in Germany and in America. As I have shown above, in Germany and nearby areas shaped-log construction predominates. In the northeastern United States, on the other hand, it is hewn-and-chinked-log construction that is most common in early houses.

If one examines Pennsylvania-German log houses, one finds that in many other ways they resemble British-American log houses and differ from German log houses.[45] The floor plan and general size and shape of Pennsylvania-German log houses are much more similar to British-American houses than to German log houses. The fireplaces and chimneys in many Pennsylvania-German log houses resemble those in British-American houses in shape and in placement.[46] In most German and Central European log houses, the apex at the gable end walls is built of logs. That is, the upper part of the gable end walls is built of logs that get progressively shorter to fill in this triangular area. In British-American and Pennsylvania-German log houses this way of building the gable end walls is virtually unknown. Logs are used only up to the level of the eaves. This upper, triangular-shaped part of the wall is framed in with small vertical timbers and covered over with siding.[47] Moreover, most Pennsylvania Germans preferred houses of masonry or frame construction. Log construction never became the dominant form among them. Terry Jordan has also pointed out how different log buildings in Germany are from those in the United States. He was able to carry out extensive fieldwork in those areas in southern Germany, Switzerland, and Austria from which the German-speaking immigrants settling in colonial America came. Because he was able to examine closely large numbers of extant log buildings in those areas he concludes:

The evidence presented so far would lead any objective scholar to reject the likelihood of significant Alpine-Alemannic influence in Midland American log architecture. By the time I had completed field work in the Black Forest and Canton Bern, the districts which seemed to offer the greatest possibility of linkage to America, I had found little to suggest such a cultural tie. Log shaping, corner timbering, spacing in walls, roof construction, and dwelling floor-plans all differ in fundamental ways from American types and methods.[48]

As these points demonstrate, it is unlikely that the German immigrants to Pennsylvania are responsible for introducing log construction to America. It is much more likely that they learned this type of construction from British-Americans with whom they came in contact. It is undoubtedly true, however, that Pennsylvania is an area from which log construction spread westwards and southwards as Kniffen and Glassie have shown.[49]

THE WESTWARD MIGRATION OF LOG CONSTRUCTION

The foregoing discussion has amply shown that log construction was known and used by British-Americans on the East Coast both in the north and the south. The Pennsylvania Germans also built log buildings. With the exception, perhaps, of some small areas, log construction never was the predominant form. Buildings of frame construction undoubtedly were far more common. Studies such as Herbert Wheaton Congden's *Early American Houses for Today,* a description of early Vermont houses, document large numbers of early wooden frame houses and some of masonry, but mention few log houses.[50]

As settlers moved westward, though, they took with them a knowledge of log construction. Indeed, they built so frequently with logs that the "log cabin" has become the symbol for later generations of this westward movement. I have already shown that people migrating westward and northward out of New England built log houses in New York state, Ohio, Nova Scotia, and Ontario. Kniffen and Glassie have shown how the Germans and Scotch-Irish moving westwards and southwards from Pennsylvania took log construction with them.[51] I do not wish to duplicate this information here. Rather, I will cite some evidence to show that the hewn-and-chinked-log house was built by people moving westward from the East Coast. This evidence will help to establish the fact that not all pioneers built round-log cabins. It will also show that the hewn-and-chinked-log construction method must have been known in many areas on the East Coast.

Hewn-and-chinked-log houses were common in western Pennsylvania at an early date, for example. David Thompson passed through the north-western corner of the state in 1816 and mentioned the 150 dwelling houses in the town of Meadville, most of which were of hewn-and-chinked logs.[52]

Hewn-and-chinked-log buildings were also built in great numbers in Ohio. Donald and Jean Hutslar have carried out extensive research both in early documents and in the field, and they have shown that hewn-and-chinked-log houses were built in the state from the very earliest period of settlement. Moreover, settlers from both the northern states and the mid-south built hewn-and-chinked-log houses. I have cited the instance of Major John Burnham from Essex, Massachusetts, who built a number of such houses in 1790. As in Indiana, while some round-log cabins were undoubtedly built as temporary shelter by early settlers, none of these has survived to the present day. Instead, large numbers of carefully built hewn-and-chinked-log houses, as well as barns and other outbuildings, are still standing in the state today.[53]

In Michigan in 1851 a writer reported, "The house Mr. Campan built is still standing; it is what is called a blockhouse, i.e., a house built of logs that have been hewed square before being laid Up."[54]

THE SOURCES OF LOG CONSTRUCTION IN INDIANA

The settlers who moved into southern Indiana were thoroughly familiar with hewn-and-chinked-log construction for they built large numbers of hewn-and-chinked-log houses, barns, churches, and other buildings. Most of the early settlers came from Virginia, Pennsylvania, the Carolinas, Kentucky, and Tennessee.[55] The records of an Old Settlers meeting held in Monroe County in 1858 supply typical data. To be considered an Old Settler at that time one had to be over fifty years of age and to have lived in Indiana at least thirty years. The places of birth of these Old Settlers were as follows: Kentucky, 30; Virginia, 24; North Carolina, 10; Tennessee, 8; Maryland, 6; Pennsylvania, 4; Indiana, 3; and Ohio, Vermont, and Delaware, 1 each.[56]

I have already listed very early references to log buildings in some of these states. Wherever it is possible to do so, I will at this point cite examples of hewn-and-chinked-log houses that were built in these states in the eighteenth century, for it is with houses of that period that the people who moved to Indiana would have been familiar.

In Maryland, for example, one writer noted that in 1795 there were about two hundred dwellings in the town of Hagerstown, and that "the greater part of the Houses are built with Logs neatly squared."[57]

From South Carolina we have detailed information about a large log house built about 1765, Walnut Grove Plantation near Spartanburg. Published photographs of the house before, during, and after restoration show it to be a large, two-story house with chimneys at each end that are outside the walls, just as in southern Indiana. The building stands on stone pillars located at each corner, again as in southern Indiana. The logs are hewn with interstices between them. It is obvious from the photographs that the house had been covered with siding right from the time it was built. In this case, the siding was replaced during the restoration.[58] This house is remarkably like southern Indiana log houses. We can assume that the people who moved from South Carolina to southern Indiana had known houses of this type before their move.

Both in Tennessee and in Kentucky there are many log houses, even though published information about them is not plentiful. Moreover, the picture is clouded by some examples of faulty restoration. Log houses such as the birthplace of Abraham Lincoln have received considerable attention, but it is impossible to tell what the buildings were really like originally. Certainly, the Lincoln "cabin" is an imaginative creation that has no claim to authenticity.[59] If we disregard such examples, the published information for these two states shows, as we would expect, that log buildings there are very similar to those in southern Indiana. Indeed, on one point, the use of siding on early log buildings, there is information that published sources usually neglect. The Pioneer Farmstead at Great Smoky Mountains National Park includes a large two-story log house with an exterior end fireplace and chimney of stone. It is built of hewn logs joined at the corners with half-dovetail notches. A pamphlet describing the house states that, "Instead of being chinked with clay and mud as was common practice, handsplit clapboards were used."[60] If no chinking was used between the logs, the siding must have been installed as soon as the house was built. I suspect that careful field-work in the area would show that many log houses were originally covered with siding.

I will show that the log houses built in southern Indiana in the nineteenth century that are still standing are all remarkably similar to one another. This similarity can be explained by the fact that the early settlers were thoroughly familiar with hewn-and-chinked-log con-struction, for they came from areas where buildings of this type had been used for a long time. Moreover, they came from areas with a markedly homogeneous log building tradition. It is because these people knew how to build such fine buildings that so many of them are still standing today.

Chapter Three

Early Round-Log Cabins

THERE ARE or were three general types of horizontal timber or log construction in southern Indiana. One was a kind of temporary construction characterized by round logs. It was common only in the early decades of the nineteenth century. Another is a kind of finished, permanent construction characterized by hewn logs. It flourished from the earliest period of settlement until well into the twentieth century. The third is a type of temporary or utility construction using small, round poles. It has been common mainly in the twentieth century. It is the hewn-log, permanent type of building with which this work is primarily concerned since most extant horizontal timber buildings use this type. The twentieth-century pole construction will be mentioned only in passing. The early round-log construction is known only from historical accounts, since no extant examples have been located. It cannot, therefore, be treated in much detail.

There are several historical accounts of the building of early, temporary, round-log "cabins." These accounts must, however, be suspect to some degree. If they were written by contemporary travelers, it must be understood that their descriptions were written after they had returned from their travels. How good were their memories of what they had seen? How complete were the notes they had taken while actually in southern Indiana? How much were their perceptions influenced by what they expected to see? If the accounts were written by "oldtimers" in the nineteenth century, drawing partly on their own experiences, partly on what they had been told by their parents and others, how much were their recollections clouded by a romantic haze, how much influenced by a desire to emphasize the hardships of earlier times? Because there is no known extant building of the early, temporary type in southern Indiana, it is impossible to say how accurate the historical accounts may be.

When one examines early accounts, he finds that both the round-log, temporary structures and the hewn-log, permanent structures were built in roughly the same time period. There seems to have been a tendency in the early nineteenth century to call small, usually one-room round-log structures "cabins" but to call the larger, hewn-log structures "houses." Thaddeus M. Harris's carefully made distinction based upon his experiences in the early years of the nineteenth century on the western Pennsylvania frontier has often been cited:

> The temporary buildings of the first settlers in the wilds are often called Cabins. They are built with unhewn logs, the interstices between which are stopped with rails, caulked with moss or straw, and daubed with mud. The roof is covered with a sort of thin staves split out of oak or ash, about four feet long and five inches wide, fastened on by heavy poles being laid upon them. "If the logs be hewed; if the interstices be stopped with stone, and neatly plastered; and the roof composed of shingles nicely laid on, it is called a log-house." A log-house has glass windows and a chimney; a cabin has commonly no window at all, and only a hole at the top for the smoke to escape.[1]

It would be unsafe to generalize from Harris's statement that such a distinction between cabin and house held true everywhere in the United States and at all periods. Nonetheless, it also must have been a distinction common in southern Indiana in the early nineteenth century. Baynard Rush Hall, who lived in Bloomington and the vicinity between about 1822 and 1830, was very consistent when he wrote about his experiences in The New Purchase: a small, round-log structure he calls a "veritable cabin," but a two-story dwelling of "hewn and squared timbers" he calls "a house."[2] Since there are no extant early structures that fit the contemporary description of a "cabin," we should use the term "log house" if we are to be consistent with early usage when we are talking about an extant horizontal timber dwelling.

The bottom logs in the long walls of such a cabin rested directly on the ground and the floor was either of dirt or of puncheons resting on joists which rested on the ground. In these sources, a puncheon seems to be a thick slab hewn or split from a log rather than sawn from a log. It may be flat on only one side with the natural curvature of the log on the other side. The logs themselves were cut from fairly small trees and were usually not much more than a foot in diameter. Certainly, the huge trees of the virgin forest so often described in early accounts were not used for house logs. Usually the logs were simply left in the round with the bark on, though sometimes the inner face of the log was flattened. The logs were notched together at the corners in such a way that several inches of each log protruded past the corner. If the logs were eighteen or twenty feet long, the lengths most frequently mentioned, the inside dimensions of the cabin would be considerably smaller.

Holes for doors, windows, and a fireplace were cut out after the log walls were completed. Puncheons of appropriate size were set against the cut ends of the logs at the openings and pinned in place. After the walls had reached a height of about eight feet, the gable ends were built up of progressively shorter logs with poles running back and forth between the gables to secure them in place. Over these poles were laid clapboards some four feet in length which had been split from straight-grained oak, and heavy poles were placed on the clapboards to keep them on the roof. The doors were made of puncheons pinned together and swung on leather or wooden hinges while the windows were covered with greased paper. Into the cracks between the logs pieces of wood and moss were crammed and covered with clay. A fireplace was made of sticks covered with clay on the inner surface and a chimney was built up of sticks laid atop one another like the logs and plastered with clay on the inside.

If structures of this sort were as common in southern Indiana as early sources and later writers would have us believe, why is it that none have survived to the present time while many other early nineteenth century buildings have survived? It is, of course, impossible to tell how many of these cabins were ever built in Indiana. While early writers stress the fact that this is the type of structure that the settlers first built on their land, it is likely that this was not always the case. Moreover, these cabins seem to have always been considered as temporary expedients, to be abandoned as soon as something better, be it a larger hewn-log house, a frame house, or a masonry house, could be built. When they were abandoned, they probably were used for miscellaneous storage for a time, but, since they were built directly on the ground, decay and termites probably destroyed them fairly quickly.

Unfortunately, it is true that most people in Indiana in the twentieth century have tended to confuse the round-log, temporary cabin with the hewn-log, permanent house. They have tended to associate all log buildings with the very earliest pioneer conditions. When attempts have been made to "restore" a log building to its "original" condition, in every case which I have ever investigated, the restorers have taken a hewn-log structure and tried to make it look like a "pioneer cabin." While there are, of course, a number of similarities between the two, there are likewise a number of differences. The difference which strikes the eye most forcefully is in the use of exterior siding or clapboards on the walls. It would have been extremely difficult to put clapboards over the exterior walls of a round-log cabin. The fact that no two logs could be of the same diameter, for instance, means that the exterior wall would be extremely uneven. Since none of these temporary structures are extant, it is impossible to say that they were never covered with siding, but it is unlikely that they ever were and all early accounts agree that they never were. On the other hand, one of the reasons why the permanent type of house was built of hewn logs was so that it would be possible to put siding on the exterior walls as well as plaster or some similar covering on the interior walls.

I will discuss later the evidence which has led me to such conclusions, but at this point I need only say that most houses made of hewn logs were covered with siding when they were originally built or very shortly thereafter. Yet in every case that I know of in southern Indiana, including museums, restorers have stripped the siding from hewn-log buildings under the impression that they were restoring the building to its original condition. Unfortunately, they have created in the process the condition which made the round-log cabins temporary structures. That is, they have exposed the logs to the elements thus causing them to decay. In their eagerness to restore the buildings, they have contributed to their destruction rather than their preservation. A correct understanding of the differences between round-log and hewn-log buildings, therefore, will contribute to the preservation of the structures.

Chapter Four

The Construction of Hewn-Log Houses

A COMPLETE description of a building or a group of buildings will include a number of details. A discussion of the size and shape of the buildings is important, but so also is a description of how they were put together. In describing the extant hewn-log houses of southern Indiana, I will begin by discussing the details of the construction. Most of what is said about how houses were built will hold true also for other buildings. Later in this work when these other buildings are described, any differences will be noted.

THE FOUNDATION

In considering the way in which hewn-log houses were built, it is probably logical to begin with the foundation. In the vast majority of cases we find what can best be called a corner foundation as opposed to a perimeter foundation. Either a single large stone or a pile of smaller stones is placed at each corner and on these stones the bottom timbers rest. If the house is unusually large, there may be pillars under the timbers towards the center of the house to provide additional support, but most houses have only the four pillars, one at each corner. In at least two cases I have been present when a log house was moved, and I have moved the pillars of stone and dug underneath them to see whether additional stone was put under the pillars to keep them from sinking into the ground. In both cases the pillars seem to have simply been placed directly on the ground with no additional stone under them.

As is true with most early building features, there is usually some sound, functional reason for any consistent practice. Older craftsmen may be able to tell us what these reasons are either from their own experience or from the craft tradition passed on to them by an earlier generation of craftsmen. Sometimes, however, it is immediately apparent what the reasons are. The houses are set up on pillars so that the air can circulate under the houses, keeping the bottom timbers dry so that they will not rot. Whenever significant changes have been made in this pattern in old log buildings, decay has usually developed in the lower timbers.

In the Ketcham log house south of Bloomington, the builders put a full foundation wall of dressed stone under the front wall of the house facing the road but used only a corner foundation for the other three walls, perhaps feeling that the facade that faced the road should present a more finished appearance. After roughly one hundred and fifty years, the bottom log at the front of the house was badly rotted and thoroughly termite ridden, while the bottom logs on the other three walls were in remarkably good condition.

In some instances, an owner in relatively recent times has built a concrete floor up against a bottom log for a porch or some other addition to a house. Usually, the bottom log has rotted as a result. In far too many cases, an abandoned house has settled down onto the ground as the corner pillars have sunk or as dirt has washed up against the house and accumulated, causing the bottom logs to rot.

Whenever I have found a log house where the corner pillars are still keeping the bottom timbers well up from the ground and where the air can still circulate freely under the house, I have found the bottom timbers still in good condition. It seems obvious, therefore, why the early builders followed this practice.

While it has been impossible to investigate large numbers of log buildings in other states, I have found that the use of corner foundations is a common practice in the southern United States, while a perimeter foundation is common in the northern states. More research is necessary before a dividing line between these two traditions can be located. I can only say at present that I have observed the corner foundations used in log buildings in Virginia and the perimeter foundation used in Pennsylvania. Therefore, builders in southern Indiana were following traditional southern practices, just as they did in many other ways, when they put their log houses up on corner pillars.

The corner foundation, then, had the distinct advantage that the lower timbers in the house were protected from decay. However, it had the distinct disadvantage that the cold air blowing under the house in winter time made the floor cold. It seems to have been a common practice in the nineteenth century and well into the twentieth century to cover the floor completely with woven rag rugs or some other kind of carpet which extended from wall to wall. Under the rug a layer of straw was put down and the rug was taken up once or twice a year so that it could be cleaned and so that fresh straw could be put down. The rug plus the straw, of course, helped keep the floor warm. A number of older people with whom I have talked have mentioned this use of rugs and straw. There are a large number of devices for stretching the carpet tightly against the walls before tacking it down. The frequency with which they appear at farm auction sales testifies to the widespread use of wall-to-wall carpets. It is also indicative that the weaving of rag rugs is a craft still flourishing in southern Indiana. The craft has probably been passed down from earlier times.

It is also true that houses with corner foundations rarely have cellars or basements under them. Prior to the widespread use of coal-fired furnaces and other forms of central heating, very few houses had basements. The main use for a cellar in earlier times was for storage of fruits and vegetables. It was, of course, important to have such a cellar dry at all times. Before the introduction of poured concrete, it was very difficult to build an underground masonry wall that was watertight and an underground wooden wall would have decayed rapidly. To have a dry cellar, a builder had to choose the site carefully, and most fruit cellars were built into a bank rather than on the level site under a house. Moreover, rain guttering was not common on early log buildings because sheet metal was scarce and expensive. The water that poured off the roof during a rainfall fell directly to the ground and would have seeped into a cellar under a house. When metal guttering was first used on most buildings in southern Indiana, it was to gather rain water and carry it to a cistern where it was stored for later use. Modern houses need guttering to keep rain water from the roof from soaking into the ground around the house and seeping into the basement, but such was not the case in earlier times.

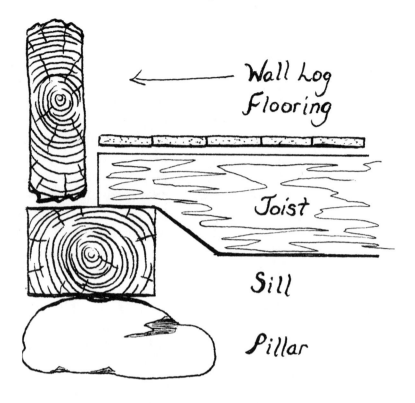

Fig. 4.1 Typical southern Indiana foundation system.

Directly on the corner pillars two sills are placed which will be the lowest members in the longest front and rear walls. These sills are rectangular in cross section and lie flat, that is, with their greatest width in the horizontal plane, so that they will extend inside the wall for several inches while being flush with the outside surface of the wall (Fig. 4.1). These sills are normally hewn on all four surfaces, unlike the remainder of the logs which form the walls which are hewn only on two surfaces. Often the sills are as large as 10-by-14 inches. There are at least two reasons why the sills are so large. They must support the weight of the entire floor and everything on it while themselves being supported only at their extreme ends. Moreover, the sills must extend some distance inside the walls to give a bearing to the floor joists, the ends of which rest on the sills.

It is impossible to tell the exact sequence that builders of log houses followed, and it is quite likely that the sequence was not always the same for every building. It is possible that the walls were built up

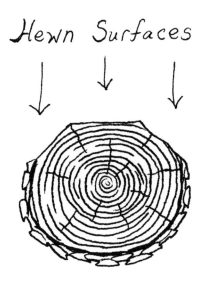

Hewn Surfaces

Fig. 4.2 Cross-section of floor joist.

first and the floor joists were laid down later, but since having the floor joists in place would provide a platform which the builders could stand on as the work progressed, it is likely that the joists were put down early in the construction process. Hence, it will not be out of place to describe the joists at this point. They are always placed in such a way that they run parallel to the gable-end walls.

There are two kinds of joists for the first floor which have been observed. One type consists of relatively small, straight logs which have been hewn with a broadax, or perhaps adzed, to give a straight top surface. (See Plate 2.) While it is not always possible to discover the fact when the joists and the flooring of a house are in good condition, in almost every case where I have observed joists of this type when the floor boards were removed, the tops of the joists have been shaped so that there is one flat surface about four inches wide with two more narrowly hewn surfaces at about a forty-five degree angle to the flat surface. Usually the rest of the log is untouched with the bark still on it. Figure 4.2 shows a cross-section of a typical floor joist of this type and depicts the three hewn surfaces.

The ends of the joists are cut partially away so that they can rest solidly on the sills and so that they will have their top surfaces in a level plane in order to make the floor level, even though the joists

Plate 2. *Floor joists made from round logs. Each has three hewn surfaces on the top, which are not visible in the photo.*

themselves are not all of the same diameter (Fig. 4.1). The ends of the joists are pinned or nailed to the sill partly so they will not shift about and partly to help overcome any tendency of the sill to bow out or in. In most instances these floor joists are small in comparison to most of the other timbers in the building, eight inches to a foot being a common diameter, but sometimes they are much larger. I will deal later with the question of why timbers were sometimes used that to us appear to be wastefully large.

The other type of floor joist used for the ground or first floor consists of sawed timbers. These are usually of substantial size, at least by modern standards, a full 3-by-8 inches being common. They may be notched on the ends to rest on the sills like the other type of joist or they may be morticed into the sills. It would seem logical to assume that the log joists are earlier historically than the sawed joists, but the inability to date most log houses with accuracy precludes a definitive statement to that effect.

The Walls and the Logs

Once the sills are in place, the first of the logs for the wall may be set in place, for they rest on the ends of the sills, forming the bottom logs in the gable end walls. Usually they simply rest on the sills with a flat surface, no specially shaped joint being formed. The weight of the logs, plus, of course, the weight of the entire structure above them, is enough to keep them in place. It should be borne in mind that the logs in the structure touch one another only at the corners so that the entire weight is placed only on the corners. This point will be discussed later in connection with the roof construction. Occasionally, however, a more complicated joint is made between the two bottom logs in the end walls and the sills.

From this point on until the walls are completed on all four sides, the walls are constructed by alternately placing two logs one way and two logs the other. That is, after the two logs for the gable end walls are placed on the ends of the sills, two logs for the front and back walls are placed on the gable end logs, then two logs for the gable-end walls are put in place and so on.

Exactly how the logs were moved from where they were cut to the site of the house, where they were hewed and how they were raised into place is hardly possible to tell from examining the buildings themselves. Even when we can find early accounts of how log houses were built, we cannot assume that these are truly typical because they mostly describe the construction of the hastily built, temporary round-log structures rather than the more carefully built, hewn-log ones. From an examination of the buildings themselves only a few hints on a few points can be gained.

First, it is clear that no attempt was made to secure huge logs from the forest giants that certainly were standing in Indiana throughout much of the nineteenth century. It is quite rare to find a log house with a log in it over two feet in diameter. A huge log would have required a huge amount of hewing to reduce it to the thickness of seven inches, which most house logs conform to, and a huge log in a suitable length would have required great effort to move to the site of the house and to lift into place. A poplar log twenty-six feet long, seven inches thick, and averaging twenty inches in width (over twenty inches on one end, but under twenty on the other because of the tapering of the tree trunk) would have weighed, when freshly cut, about nine hundred pounds. Surely, this is enough weight to move without looking for even larger logs. In those few houses that do have in them a log of two feet or slightly more in width, these logs are usually near the bottom of the wall, as one might expect. My impression is that the builders tried to find reasonably straight trees free of branches for the required length (for where there is a branch, there will be a knot in the log), to find logs of a manageable size, and to find them as close to the site of the house as possible.

While it might seem that hewing the log where the tree was cut down before moving it would make the log more easily moved, the evidence does not seem to indicate that this was done. In dragging a hewn log any substantial distance, it surely would have been dragged over rocks which would have put long gouges in the surface. I do not recall ever having seen a log in a house showing such marks. I have been able to examine the inner faces of logs in a number of houses where the logs are in excellent condition, showing no signs of decay, and also the outer surfaces of logs which have been protected by siding and are likewise in excellent condition. Since they never show signs of having been dragged for any distance, it seems safe to conclude that the hewing was done mostly at the site of the house. Oxen probably did the dragging, and they are capable of moving heavy loads. It is unlikely that the logs were loaded onto sleds before moving them unless they were to be moved a long distance.

The lower logs in a house were probably partly lifted, partly shifted into position with levers of some sort. It is generally believed that the higher logs were raised into place by leaning poles against the house and sliding the logs up the poles. Considerable manpower was necessary for this task, but both written and oral accounts testify to the fact that neighbors turned out to help at the time a house was being built. Many men now living have taken part in barn raisings and they speak of scores of men helping to raise the heavy timbers of a barn. Far fewer men would have been needed to raise the house logs into their places.

Many writers have repeated the story that four men stood at the corners of the house to notch the logs.[1] It is possible that this was frequently done, but an examination of the corners of log houses leads me to conclude that the corners of a particular house were all done by one man. First of all, there are differences from house to house in the angles at which the corner joints are cut. In one house, the slopes of the corner notch may be rather flat, while in another house the slopes may be much steeper. For any one house, however, the corner joints will usually be remarkably uniform all around the house. It is possible that a pattern was made for the corners and all four men used exactly the same pattern to mark out their joints. However, a second consideration is that the corner joints in almost every house are made with great skill, seemingly with an ax only, so that the two logs fit together so smoothly that it would be impossible to push a piece of paper between them at that point. It is possible that in any group of men there would be four who were equally skilled at making these joints, but it seems more likely that there was one highly skilled craftsman in the group to whom this demanding task was consigned and who made all the joints for all four corners of the house.

It has already been mentioned that the logs for the walls were usually dragged to the site of the house and hewed there. The process of hewing was by no means complicated, though it required great skill. (See Plates 3, 4, 5.) The log was rolled up onto two blocks of wood of some sort, probably short lengths of log, so that its bottom surface would be a foot or two off the ground. At first the weight of the log would keep it in place without any need to fasten it down, but as hewing progressed, it probably was necessary to block it up so that it could not tip over.

Straight lines would be laid out on the log as a guide for the hewing by using a string rubbed over some substance that would leave a mark. Usually the string was rubbed over a piece of chalk, pulled taut at each end of the log, and snapped or twanged so that the chalk dust left its mark. At least two proverbial phrases, "as straight as a string" and "to hew to the line," are probably derived from this process. On a few early nineteenth-century buildings, I have seen traces of a mark seemingly made by a string and some substance other than chalk. These marks seem to have been made by soaking the string in some reddish or purplish fluid, perhaps pokeberry juice. Perhaps chalk was unavailable or perhaps a mark more permanent than chalk, which is easily wiped off in handling a timber, was wanted. The use of a fluid with a string is well known in other countries, but has not been commonly mentioned from the United States.[2]

Once the necessary two lines had been established, the craftsman cut V-notches at intervals of two to three feet down almost to the lines using a chopping or felling ax. Then with a broadax he went along splitting away big slabs of wood between the notches. Some general observations should be made here about the broadax and its use because evidence gathered in southern Indiana from men who have actually used broadaxes sometimes conflicts with statements made by

Plate 3. *This and the following two photos show steps in the process of hewing a timber such as would be used for a sill or plate in a large log house. Here Wallace Sullivan surveys the felled tree.*

Plate 4. *Mr. Sullivan and Lonnie Hamm true one side of the timber. (Mr. Sullivan is using a broad ax, but Mr. Hamm did not own one and is using a felling ax.)*

Plate 5. *The completed timber, which is fifty feet long.*

writers who seem not to have gathered their data from such sources. It is frequently assumed that the broadax went out of use long ago, but such is not the case in southern Indiana and probably not in many other parts of the country. While it is true that house logs have not been hewn in large numbers in the twentieth century, railroad ties certainly have been and the basic hewing process is almost the same in each case. Well into the twentieth century, farmers could supplement their incomes by cutting trees from their woods, hewing them into ties, and selling them. I have been told by a number of people that hand-hewn ties brought a higher price than ties sawed at a sawmill because the hewn ties did not decay as rapidly as the sawed ones.

The process of hewing is primarily a process of splitting rather than cutting. As such, it seems to have been especially adapted to hardwood timbers rather than to softwood. Hence it flourished especially in those areas of Europe and the United States where hardwood forests flourished. It is an immensely old technique whereby usable timbers could be produced from tree trunks without the very laborious process in earlier times of hauling a log to a sawmill, which could only be located at a suitable site on a stream or river, and then hauling the sawed timber back to the site of the house. Moreover, most sawmills could not handle logs of the length required in most buildings.

It is true that timbers could also be made from tree trunks by hand-operated saws, the so-called pit saw or whip saw, but sawing a log lengthwise by hand was slow in comparison to hewing. Moreover, it was necessary to raise a log on trestles or dig a pit and roll the log over it, for the pit saw required two men, one above and one below the log. The log also had to be shifted several times in the process of sawing it. Pit saws may have been used to produce boards from logs in southern Indiana in the nineteenth century, but I have never found any evidence in houses that they were.

Logging and the sawing of timbers and boards have changed markedly in the last century as new machinery has replaced the ancient techniques. At some time in the second half of the nineteenth century, probably about 1875, steam powered portable sawmills were introduced which could be moved about from one stand of trees to another. In the twentieth century trucks and a network of roads have made it possible to haul logs for long distances from the forests to permanently located sawmills.

Some writers have maintained that there are many ways of handling a broadax and many positions the hewer could take. Donald and Jean Hutslar, for instance, write, "Various techniques were used in handling the broadax; one man might work the ax horizontally, another vertically."[3] However, very man I have talked to who has ever used a broadax has always demonstrated or described the same technique: standing with his left leg against the log, the craftsman (if right-handed) swings the broadax downward, normally at a slight diagonal, across the vertical face of the log. While it is undoubtedly true that special circumstances might require variations from this practice, it is hard to believe that a craftsman would customarily swing a heavy broadax horizontally or that he would want to raise a log high enough off the ground so that he could swing the ax horizontally.

It should also be emphasized that the broadax is a specialized tool especially adapted to hewing and that, except in cases of emergency, it would not have been used to chop down a tree or to split up firewood. At the same time, a chopping or felling ax would not normally have been used for hewing. I have heard older craftsmen tell with amused contempt about beginners who have tried to hew a log with a chopping ax. To them, this is a sign of utter ignorance, roughly equivalent to trying to eat soup with a fork.

Most broadaxes are easily distinguished from other axes by several features. They are larger, for one thing, with a cutting edge ranging from eight to fourteen inches. There are smaller hewing hatchets used with one hand that resemble broadaxes in most respects except for their size, but these would not be of much use in hewing a log. Broadaxes are made in such a way that one face of the ax is perfectly flat so that it can slide along the flattened face of the log like a huge chisel. Chopping axes, on the other hand, are basically wedge-shaped, neither face being flat. Moreover, the handle of a broadax is bent in such a way that the flattened face of the ax can lie flat on a plane surface and the handle curves away from the plane surface. The handle is bent in this way so that the hewer's knuckles will not get skinned as the ax slides along the face of the timber. About two out of three of the broadaxes which I have seen sold at farm auctions in southern Indiana are what turn-of-the-century catalogs call the Western pattern, but the origin and significance of this term is unclear. (See Chapter Six.)

Once one face of the log is roughly shaped by the process of splitting off big slabs, the hewer went along log chopping into the face a short distance with his chopping ax. Next he went along the log with the broadax, shaving off small quantities of wood until he reached the line. The finished log almost always shows the marks left by the chopping ax in this final step. Had it been desirable to produce a smoother surface, it could have been done with an adze, usually called a "foot adze" in southern Indiana. Since the outside of the wall was normally covered with siding, and the inside covered with plaster or paneling, the final smoothing step was usually not taken. Then the log was probably turned over so that the other face could be hewn. Hewers preferred to start at the top end of the log and work towards the butt because the direction of the grain of the wood was more favorable for splitting in this way. Only two faces of the log were hewn so that the finished log was very nearly seven inches in thickness. The bottom and top surfaces of the log as placed in the wall were not hewn in ninety-nine out of a hundred cases. As a matter of fact, the bark usually was not removed from the top and bottom surfaces.

A question naturally arises as to how much time it would take to hew enough logs to build a house. The question cannot be answered with any great degree of certainty, because the size of the logs, the skill of the hewer, and other factors would vary from case to case. Some rough indication can be gained, however, from evidence concerning the number of railroad ties that skilled craftsmen could hew in a day. One man whom I shall call "Shorty," who lives in the countryside in eastern Greene County and who was born in 1890, told me an anecdote that threw some light on this matter. In the 1930s, Shorty worked out an arrangement with an older man named Uncle Billy whereby Uncle Billy and Shorty would together cut down trees and cut them to length for railroad ties. Uncle Billy would hew them on all four sides to make the ties, and Shorty would haul them to town with his team and sell them at the tie plant. For his share of the work, Uncle Billy was to receive ten cents for each tie he hewed. The arrangement worked out very well except for one habit of Uncle Billy's that annoyed Shorty somewhat. Uncle Billy would only hew twenty railroad ties in a day and insisted on going home at about two o'clock in the afternoon. Two dollars a day was as much as he wanted to earn, and when he reached that sum he just stopped working.

Other men with whom I have talked have given almost exactly the same information: if a man had help in cutting down the trees and cutting them to length, he could hew about twenty ties a day. If he were working alone and had to cut down the trees and cut them to length himself, fourteen to fifteen ties a day was a normal day's work. A railroad tie is much shorter than a house log, and ties were often made from logs much smaller in diameter than the typical house log, so smaller amounts of wood needed to be hewn away. Ties, however, had to be hewn on all four surfaces whereas house logs were hewn on only two.

When I have asked the men who gave me information on hewing ties to estimate about how long it would take them to hew enough logs to build a log house, they have replied between three and five days. Although the hewing of the logs would represent a formidable and time-consuming task to a person today who wanted to build a log house from freshly cut trees, to the skilled hewer of the nineteenth century, the actual hewing of the logs would have added relatively little time to the whole process of building a log house.

So far we have dealt only with the shaping of the logs which comprise the walls of the house and have not considered how they are fitted together. As previously noted, they touch one another only at the corners so that gaps, or interstices, of various size are left between the logs for most of their length. Leaving interstices between the logs derives from the practice of hewing the logs on only two sides. If it had been deemed desirable to make the logs rest on one another for their whole length, it would have been necessary to hew the other two surfaces. I feel sure that making the logs fit closely together throughout their length would have presented no major problem to craftsmen who were capable of doing the other work on a log building. They could have done it if they had thought it necessary or desirable. Instead, they left interstices to be filled later with chinking. I have seen only one log building in southern Indiana where the logs have been hewn on all four surfaces and fitted together so that there are no interstices: the log jail in Nashville, where interstices were clearly not desirable.

The corner joints used in southern Indiana are of two main types, the so-called "half dovetail" and the "V-notch." Rather than attempting to describe these joints, I will refer to the illustrations which are far more effective than written descriptions. (See Plates 6, 7, 8.)

In doing the fieldwork for this study, I visited a total of 470 log buildings. Of these, 296 are houses while the rest are barns, smokehouses, churches, and other buildings. Of the 470 log buildings, 338 used the half-dovetail corner joint, 52 used the V-notch, 10 used both, and 14 used other notches, usually a simple square notch. It was impossible to tell what notch was used in fifty-six buildings because the siding was in such good condition. The only place where the V-notch was at all common was in northern Owen County. Since the statistics were compiled for this study, I have been able to visit a number of log buildings in Franklin County, where the V-notch is very common there. Elsewhere the half-dovetail predominates and only an occasional building will have the V-notch.

One might well ask how there can be ten buildings that use both the half-dovetail and the V-notch? In most of the ten cases we have a log house with a log wing attached in some way or another. The house uses one type of corner joint while the wing uses another. The differences in the corner notches would present clear evidence that the two structures were not built at the same time.

Both the half-dovetail and the V-notch share some common features. They do not require that any of the log protrude beyond the corner as with the joints made with round logs. Moreover, the logs are

Plate 6. *Half-dovetail corner notching.*

Plate 7. *The V-notch.*

Plate 8. The square notch.

held firmly in place by their own weight without the need of nails or any other fastening device. Occasionally, someone will assert that a log building using one of these two joints actually has a hidden wooden pin or peg in each joint, but none of the many buildings I have ever seen partly or completely disassembled has ever had such a fastening device in the corner joints. The weight of the logs holds them so firmly in place that there is very little chance of their ever coming apart by accident.

In the summer of 1970, two men and I set about tearing down a log house in southern Owen County near the town of Freedom. The house was in ruinous condition. It had not been lived in for some time, and about 1965 a violent windstorm had torn off much of the roof. A few of the logs were still in reasonably good condition, but there was very little else that could be salvaged. Since it was impossible either to restore the house where it stood or to move it and rebuild it, we determined to salvage what few logs we could. It was actually dangerous to climb around on the upper parts of the house with partly decayed timbers lying about in confusion as a result of the windstorm, so we decided to try to pull one of the lower logs out of the structure, hoping the whole building would collapse and the salvageable logs could be snaked out of the pile. A cable was fastened around one of the lower logs and the winch on a heavy truck began to wind up the cable. When the cable tightened, the log refused to budge. Instead, the truck, with brakes locked, was pulled toward the building. Eventually the truck was anchored by a chain to a large tree and the log was finally pulled out. That corner of the house settled a little but the whole house, despite its ruinous condition, remained solidly upright. It was finally necessary to climb up on the house, remove the decayed timbers, and take the logs down, one by one, in the reverse order of which they had been put together.

As the log walls increase in height, a point is reached where it is necessary to insert the ceiling joists, timbers running parallel to the gable end walls of the house which will form the ceiling of the ground floor room and the floor for the sleeping loft. This is normally done at a point such that there will be between seven and eight feet of head room in the ground floor room. An examination of the way in which the notches for the ends of the joists are cut into the logs in the front and back walls of the house shows that it must have been the common practice to cut the notches and put the joists into place while the walls

Fig. 4.3 Ends of ceiling joists as seen from outside.

were being erected rather than waiting until the walls had been built up to their final height. In almost every case, notches are cut from the top side of a log so that the joists can fit down into them and so that the ends of the joists are clearly visible from the outside of the house before the exterior siding is put on (Fig. 4.3). In this way, there is no chance for the joists to tip over.

Three types of joists have been found. Very rarely, round poles about eight inches in diameter and very straight have been chosen and a flat surface hewn or adzed on their top. More frequently, small, straight logs are chosen and hewn on all four sides into a timber about four by seven inches in cross section. Frequent also are sawed timbers averaging four-by-seven inches.

The choice of joists is largely dictated by whether or not the floor joists will be covered on their bottom sides by plaster or boards forming a finished ceiling for the first floor. It seems to have been a common practice throughout most of the nineteenth century not to have a finished ceiling but to leave the joists, or beams as they are often called, exposed to view from the ground floor. The rectangular joists hewn from logs are usually carefully finished, the ax marks being removed with a hand plane. In many houses these rectangular joists have been covered by boards at some time after the house was built. However, visiting such a house that has fallen into disrepair, one sometimes sees that the joists had been exposed to view for many years before they were covered. In the area above the fireplace where

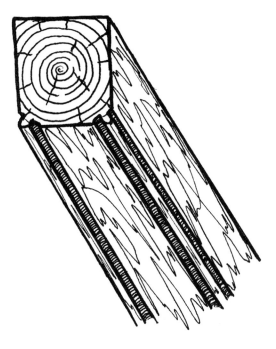

Fig. 4.4 *Bead molding on lower edges of exposed ceiling joists.*

cooking was done or above the kitchen stove, the ceiling joists and the bottom of the loft floor clearly show the black deposits which accumulate from the smoke from the fire and from frying bacon, ham, and similar foods.

In those houses with sawed joists, too, when ceiling material has been removed it is nearly always possible to see that the joists were originally exposed to view. The joists have been carefully planed so that the saw marks on their side and bottom surfaces are removed and smooth surfaces left. Then a decorative and functional bead molding has been worked on each lower corner (Fig. 4.4). Moreover, the boards forming the floor for the sleeping loft also often have a decorative bead molding along their bottom edges. Surely no carpenter would go to the trouble of beading the edges of the joists and floor boards if they were to be hidden from view. In sum, it may be said that the care lavished on the finishing of the joists indicates that they were usually exposed to view.

Nineteenth-century craftsmen went to considerable pains to finish neatly any surfaces exposed to view and which would be handled, cleaned, or dusted. The notion that nineteenth-century log houses were crudely finished is, by and large, erroneous. Especially unfortunate is the prevailing notion that ceiling beams exposed to view were always rough. The prevalence of this notion is clearly indicated by the widespread use of rough beams in the ceilings of modern homes, restaurants, and the like. These beams are either of wood or plastic. Plastic "beams" are currently available at most lumber yards which reproduce convincing facsimiles of knots, bark, ax marks, etc. The vogue for "rough-hewn beams" in modern buildings is probably the result of faulty restoration work in old houses. People have bought old houses and "restored" them by removing original plaster from ceilings, thus exposing beams which the original builder never intended to be exposed. This faulty "restoration" work has given impetus to the use of crude beams salvaged from barns or reproduced in plastic.

At some point after the walls are pretty well raised and before the house is completed, it is necessary to cut through the walls for door, window, and fireplace openings. All available evidence supports the belief that full-length logs were used to build four complete walls and that the openings were cut out after the logs were in place. There seems to be no reason to assume that the logs were cut to allow for openings before they were raised into place. It appears that the openings of appropriate size were marked out on the logs first. Then blocks of wood were wedged between the logs just outside the marks so that when the logs were severed, the cut ends would not sag. A narrow bladed saw must have been used at least to start the cuts, narrow enough so that the blade of the saw could be inserted through the gap between two logs. Occasionally it can be seen that several auger holes were made through a log, one above another, so that the blade of a saw could be inserted to begin the cut, but the use of a saw with a narrow blade that could be started between two logs seems to have been far more common. Once the saw cuts were completed, some of the logs would have been completely severed, but the logs at the top and bottom of a window, for instance, would not have been. It was necessary to split out the wood in these areas.

Against the cut ends of the logs, heavy planks of appropriate size were placed and fastened to the ends of the logs. (See Plates 9, 10.) An approximate historical sequence can be seen as regards these planks and the ways in which they were fastened, always allowing, of course, for considerable overlap in the stages of the sequence. Early planks were split, or rived, from a straight-grained log, usually of oak, for oak

Plate 9. *A plank fitted against the cut ends of logs in a wall at a fireplace opening.*

Plate 10. A plank fitted against the cut ends of logs at a door opening in the wall of a barn.

Plate 11. *The plate overhanging the long wall and supported by a protruding log in the gable-end wall.*

Plate 12. *The log in the gable-end wall that supports the plate.*

splits cleanly and well. Such planks are usually around one-and-a-half inches thick and seven inches wide. Later planks have been sawed at a sawmill. In early work the planks are fastened to the ends of the logs by wooden pegs, pins, or trunnels ("peg" seems to be the term commonly used in southern Indiana) about one inch in diameter and six to eight inches long, driven into auger holes. In later work, large iron spikes, usually of the "square" or cut type, are driven through the plank into the end of the log. It is often possible to discover in an extant log house that one or more doors and windows have been added in later years to the structure by examining these planks fastened to the ends of the logs. The planks for the original doors and windows will be fastened with wooden pegs while the planks for added doors and windows will be held by iron spikes.

The walls have reached their final height for the most common one-and-a-half-story house when the top edges of the two logs on the gable end are about ten feet from the top of the sills. Since these two logs must support the plates, they are longer by about eighteen inches than the other logs in the end walls, for they must extend about nine inches farther out on each end. Usually these protruding ends are shaped to a gentle curve (Fig. 4.5; see Plates 11, 12).

Fig. 4.5

I might mention that in searching for log houses, I soon learned to distinguish log buildings from early frame buildings by looking for these protruding ends. No matter how carefully the exterior of the log house is finished with siding, there seemingly is no way to disguise these protruding ends and no similar protrusions are found on frame buildings. If one can approach close to a house, there are other ways of telling if it is log covered with siding, but from a distance these protruding ends can easily be seen.

On these protruding ends of the logs in the gable ends of the house, the plates are laid. The plates are usually of the same dimensions as the sills, huge timbers hewn on all four sides to a rectangular cross-section averaging ten-by-fourteen inches. Like the sills, they lie flat; their greatest dimension is in the horizontal plane. Unlike the sills, they extend several inches beyond the vertical outside plane of the logs in the walls, overhanging the walls (Fig. 4.5). On the top outside edge of the plates the ends of the rafters rest. Hence the overhang is necessary so that rain water dripping from the eaves will not run down the walls of the house. One of the places in a log house where wooden pegs are of major importance structurally is where the plates rest on the ends of the logs in the gable-end walls. Here a large auger hole is bored through the plate into the log below it and a peg of oak or hickory, often two inches in diameter and eighteen inches long, is driven into the hole. The pegs that I have been able to examine have never been perfectly round as if turned in a lathe. Instead, it is clear that they have been split out of straight-grained wood and shaped into a round cylinder with the aid of a draw knife.

This may be an opportune place to dwell on the reasons for the large size of the plates and what this size tells us about the general structural scheme of the houses. The plate is so large because it bears the entire weight of the roof, the rafters all resting on the plate, and of any load of snow which may accumulate on the roof. It should be borne in mind that a layer of several inches of wet snow covering the entire roof would weigh many hundred pounds, as anyone who has had to shovel a driveway after a typical southern Indiana late spring snowstorm would well know. Since the plate does not touch the logs below it at any point except at the corners, the entire weight of the roof is transferred to the corners of the house. With the exception of the logs which are cut completely through for door, window, and fireplace openings, the logs in the walls likewise touch one another only at the corners. Moreover, as previously mentioned, the entire weight of the first floor rests on the massive sills and hence is transferred to the corner pillars. It is possible to see, therefore, that a number of construction features in log houses evolved to make possible the corner pillar foundation system which in turn seems to have been developed to keep the lower timbers of the log houses up off the ground, dry and free from termite damage. All the wooden members of the house are one structural unit supported by the foundation at four points.

The chimney and fireplace, as we shall see, make up another completely independent structural unit with its own foundation. The house does not depend upon the chimney in any way for support nor does the chimney lean against the house in any way or derive support from it.

Each, we might say, is free to go its own way. If the fireplace and chimney with their tremendous weight of rock and, sometimes, brick sink into the ground faster than the house does, no structural damage can result.

In order to understand more clearly the support system embodied in the southern Indiana log houses, let us compare it with a rather different construction system I have examined in log houses in Pennsylvania. Here a perimeter foundation is used. All around the exterior walls of the Pennsylvania houses is a foundation of stones carefully built up so that their top layer is level all around and so that the stone wall is thicker than the log wall. There is no sill as such. The lowest log in each wall is the same shape and size as the logs above it and the bottom log rests directly on the stone wall for its entire length. The stone wall extends inside the log wall for several inches so that the floor joists for the first floor can rest on the stones (Fig. 4.6; see following page). Should any part of the foundation sink further into the ground than the rest, the joist in that area must sink below the others, making the floor uneven. At the same time, the perimeter foundation keeps the cold winds of winter from blowing underneath the house. Where the doorway openings are cut through the logs, the weight of the logs at this point bears down on the foundation. There is no plate as such at the top of the wall. The ends of the rafters bear on the top log.

In this Pennsylvania system of construction, therefore, it seems that a rather different philosophy of building is present in that the

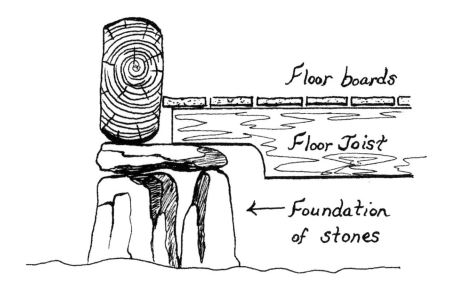

Fig. 4.6 Perimeter foundation found in Pennsylvania log house.

wooden parts of the house are supported all around the outside wall, and if the foundation sinks at any point some structural damage will result. Should one of the corner pillars in a southern Indiana house sink into the ground, of course, structural damage will also result. It would seem, however, as a generalization that we have two fairly distinct ways of building log houses which are closely bound up with environmental factors—the hot, damp southern climate requiring one type of construction and the colder, dryer northern climate requiring, or perhaps permitting, another type of construction. The few previous attempts to study the geographic distribution of construction features of log houses have concentrated on the corner joints, perhaps under the impression that different kinds of corner joints indicate different ethnic origins. It is certainly true that the different types of corner joints as used in hewn-log houses do not appear to be closely connected with factors from the natural environment. Perhaps a study of the corner foundation complex and the perimeter foundation complex would be more significant in terms of environmental factors and their influence.

Although it is probably true that the gaps or interstices between the logs would not have been filled until the house was near completion, while we are dealing with the wall construction, it is logical to

Plate 13. *Chinking: The clay has mostly fallen away, revealing the chips of wood filling the interstices. See also Plate 9.*

discuss all aspects. Besides, there probably was no set sequence of steps which was followed in every case, and it is quite possible that the less experienced workers on the job and children could be put to work filling the gaps while other workmen were completing the roof or building the fireplace.

The filling between the logs is variously called "chinking," "chunking," and "daubing," chinking being the most commonly used term today. Whatever it was called, the actual technique seems to have been quite consistent throughout the nineteenth century. In some places in some houses there are very large interstices between the logs caused by using logs which are not straight or logs that taper considerably from the butt end to the top. Such large gaps may be filled with long chunks of wood of appropriate size, probably by-products of the hewing of the logs. In the vast majority of cases, though, the interstices are seldom more than two or three inches wide. These are filled first with pieces of wood roughly six inches long, four inches wide, and three quarters of an inch thick, laid at about a forty-five degree angle so that they overlap one another. (See Plate 13.) The large degree of uniformity in these pieces of wood suggests that an appropriate sized block of wood was cut out and then pieces were split from it, probably with a froe. A large number of pieces could be made in a relatively short time using this technique. In a few cases, pieces of stone very nearly the same size as the wood pieces just described were used in the same way, but this was made possible by the ready availability of fieldstone or creek stone of appropriate size. Such stone cannot be found in sufficient quantity near the site of the house very often.

Over the pieces of wood or stone, clay is applied both from the inside and the outside. There seems to have been no problem in securing ample supplies of suitable clay. It is nearly always of a yellowish-brown color and probably was put on while damp, using some sort of a trowel. I do not remember ever seeing any clay in well-preserved houses that showed finger marks as if the clay had been put on with the bare hand only. While I have never had samples of the clay examined with a microscope or subjected to chemical testing, it nearly always appears to be just plain clay. In a very few cases, it appears that oat hulls have been mixed with the clay, but I have no record of the use of animal hair or straw in the clay. When a log house was being re-assembled in the town of Ellettsville in 1966 as part of Indiana's sesquicentennial celebration, the coordinator of the project told me that an old man had told her that salt was mixed with the clay to make it adhere better, but I have never heard similar information elsewhere.

THE SIDING

After the chinking of the walls was completed, it was possible to put siding on the walls. Actually, siding was not put on in all probability until the roof was completed. Since we have discussed many aspects of wall construction, it might be valuable to take up the matter of siding while the other aspects of wall construction are fresh in mind, for all aspects of wall construction are closely interrelated and one aspect cannot be discussed apart from the others.

After examining nearly 300 hewn-log houses in southern Indiana, I have become convinced that most hewn-log houses in this area were covered with siding at the time they were built or shortly thereafter and that the technology or tradition of building houses with hewn logs developed with the use of siding as a vital and integral part of the tradition. Since I realize that such an assertion is in direct opposition to both historical writers and current popular opinion, I feel it wise to give at this point a summary of the various kinds of evidence which have lead me to make it.

First of all, every original hewn-log house that I have seen has either been covered with siding in good condition, or partially covered with siding falling off, or showed unmistakable signs that siding was once on the building. The unmistakable signs that siding was once present include many nails and nail holes in the logs and the vertical channels, to be described later, cut into some of the logs to provide for the furring strips to which the siding was nailed. The fact that every extant hewn-log house has siding now or once had siding, of course, cannot be taken as proof that the houses were originally sided, but it certainly demonstrates that the people who lived in log houses realized the need for siding.

I have been able to examine closely a number of hewn-log walls that have been protected by siding. That is, I have sometimes been able to pry away a piece of siding from a house that was covered with siding in good condition so that I could get a glimpse of the logs underneath the siding. This usually can be done only when a house has been abandoned for a few years and the siding is beginning to come loose. In a house that people are living in, it would hardly do to pry up the siding, and in a house that has been long abandoned, the siding has long since fallen off. I have also been able to examine at least a score of houses from which siding in good condition has recently been removed. These include houses which I have disassembled and moved or helped move, houses being disassembled and moved by other individuals and institutions, and houses which stood in and around Fairfield, Indiana which were in the area to be flooded by the Brooksville Reservoir. I have also seen at least a score of houses from which part of the siding had fallen away but part was in good condition so that it was possible to peer up under the siding in good condition. In every case it has been possible to see that the logs were covered with siding at the time the house was built and that the siding has always been on the house. (See Plate 14; see following page.)

It is possible to make such an unqualified assertion for one major reason. Unpainted wood that is protected from direct sun and from rain turns a deep tan or brown color such as one sees in old furniture.

Plate 14. *When original siding is removed, unweathered logs are revealed beneath.*

When unpainted, unfinished wood of most kinds (especially poplar and oak which are most used for house logs) is exposed to rain and sun for a few years, the wood turns a silver grey color. I am not sure how long it would take for wood exposed to the elements to acquire this silvery grey patina. It has certainly happened in one summer in my personal experience, but there are, of course, many factors involved, such as the amount of sun received. Once wood has acquired this silvery-grey patina, the patina cannot be removed save by planing it off or sanding it off. Certainly, if one protects the silvery grey wood from the sunlight and rain by covering it over, the wood is not going to bleach itself and regain the tan or brown color of unexposed wood. The logs that I have seen under siding in good condition have never had the silvery grey patina of exposed wood, proving that the logs were covered with siding when the house was built or very shortly thereafter.

In a log house with the most typical and common fireplace and chimney type, there is a portion of the gable-end wall that is covered by the chimney (Fig 4.7). In the few cases where it was possible to

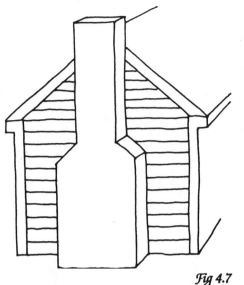

Area where clapboards pass behind chimney. Nails are now covered by the chimney, showing they were installed before the chimney was built.

Fig 4.7

examine this area as a house in good condition was being torn down, it could be seen that nails had been driven into the wall siding in the area covered by the chimney. The only way this could possibly have been done was to have put the siding on with nails driven in before the chimney was built.

As will be explained later, the gable-end walls in the triangular shaped area above the top log are filled in with vertical studs. These studs are almost always covered on the outside with horizontal siding. The siding in this area must obviously be put on at the time the house is built. Otherwise, it would be almost impossible to live in the house because the rain would blow into the loft. In every case where it has been possible to observe a house entirely covered with siding in good condition, it appears that all the siding on the gable-end walls is of the same kind and has been put on at the same time. Certainly, it has never seemed that the siding at the bottom of the triangular shaped area has been pried up and the other siding for the rest of the wall slipped underneath it. Perhaps it should be mentioned that with horizontal siding of the clapboard type most commonly used on log and frame houses in southern Indiana, one has to start at the bottom with the first piece of siding, for the next piece overlaps the top edge of the piece below it (Fig. 4.8; see following page).

There have been a number of cases where log houses have stood for many years with the logs in excellent condition because they were

Fig. 4.8 Clap-
boards on wall
overlapping one
another.

been necessary to replace some. This seems to be what has happened
in the Pioneer Village at Spring Mill State Park near Mitchell. Some of
the houses had stood on their original sites for nearly one hundred
years and were in good condition and covered with siding. I have
talked with two men in and near Leesville where the "Granny White"
log house stood before it was moved to Spring Mill State Park in the
1930s. Both men remembered the house very well as it was before it
was moved and assured me that it was covered with siding and was in
good condition before it was moved. When the house was re-erected
in the Park, the siding was left off the walls. In the three or four
decades the house has stood in the Park, many of the wall logs have
rotted very badly, and several near the bottom of the walls have been
replaced. (See Plate 15.) I feel sure that the house could not have
stood in Leesville for a hundred years with the logs in good condition
unless they had been covered. Yet several people have assured me that
hewn-log houses were never covered with siding when built, citing as
evidence the fact that the log houses in Spring Mill State Park are not
covered with siding.

The truth of the matter is that prior to the development of
chemicals which can be sprayed or painted on house logs, there was
no practical way to keep them from rotting away when they were
exposed to rain water. It is true that wood siding and shingles properly
made of good wood such as poplar or oak will last for a long time
without paint or preservatives, but house logs present some special
problems. As a log that is hewn from a single tree trunk seasons,

Plate 15. Exterior of logs in the "Granny White" house at Spring Mill State Park. Note how the logs have decayed.

cracks of varying size develop in the log. Rain water gets in these cracks and soon causes decay in almost any wood, including oak and poplar. The decay makes the cracks bigger and bigger and deeper and deeper, and eventually the whole log is decayed. Trying to plug the cracks with mortar or putty seems only to aggravate the problem. The mortar or putty loosens due to the expansion and contraction of the wood, and the moisture that does succeed in getting into the crack then is not dried out by the wind and the sun. In such case, ideal conditions for decay—darkness and dampness—are present. More-over, it will be recalled that when the house logs were hewn, the bark was almost invariably left on the top and bottom surfaces of the hewn log. As the log seasons, the bark dries and pulls away from the wood,

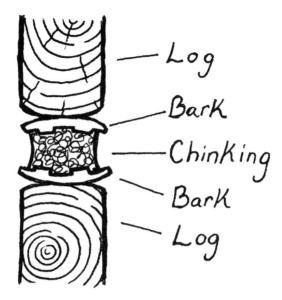

Fig. 4.9 *How pockets develop when bark dries and loosens from log. (The extent to which the bark loosens has been exaggerated in the illustration for purposes of clarity.)*

creating a pocket for the rain water running down the walls to enter and cause decay (Fig. 4.9). Nearly always, when a house has been uncovered for some time, a careful observer can see an inch or two of decay along the bottom of each log where water has stood in this pocket. The people who built the log houses and the people who lived in them in the nineteenth century must have clearly understood the need for siding on a hewn-log house to keep it safe from decay. In this instance, they were wiser than many twentieth-century "preservationists" (Fig. 4.9).

In a few houses it has been possible to see other evidence that proves the houses were sided when they were built. In the Ketcham house south of Bloomington, when the siding was removed as the house was being torn down, it was possible to see that the chinking had only been partly completed. In a number of places in the walls the pieces of wood had been laid in as previously described. The clay had been pushed in over the pieces of wood from the inside of the house, but the clay had never been put on from the outside of the house. The people putting the siding on the exterior of the house must have been in such a hurry that they could not wait for the chinking to be done.

After the exterior was done, there was time to put the clay on from the inside. In a house examined near Helmsburg as it was being torn down, I noticed that the chinking had never been put in many of the walls. Since the chinking would certainly help keep the house warm, one wonders why it was left out.

Now that the physical data have been presented which led me to my conclusions, it may be well to consider further why hewn-log houses were usually sided. The siding protected the logs and preserved them from decay. Moreover, wind-driven rain water hitting the walls unprotected by siding would have washed away the clay from the chinking. Now it is true that the statement has frequently been repeated that the chinking often fell out from between logs and was frequently replaced. This statement is derived from historical accounts and probably applies to unsided round-log cabins. Certainly, the clay could be replaced if it fell off or washed off a hewn-log building without siding. So can a modern homeowner keep his house paint in good condition by occasional touch-up or by caulking cracks, but it is neither possible nor convenient to paint a house in cold weather. It certainly would have been inconvenient to replace a big chunk of clay if it fell out of a log house wall in cold weather. Siding, then, protected the chinking.

It might be worthwhile to raise a general point here as to the interconnections between elements in a traditional craft or technology. It seems to me that stating that siding was used to protect the chinking is oversimplifying the situation. It might be truer to say that chinking was used because it could be protected by siding. The craftsmen who built hewn-log houses had the ability, the tools, and the time to build log houses that would not have needed chinking. They were men who could hew two big sills and two big plates on all four sides so that they were "as straight as a string," and they could make complicated corner joints that fit together very closely. Such men were capable of making log houses that needed no chinking. They must have considered it unnecessary to do so if they planned to use siding. It will not do to say that they used chinking in hewn-log houses because they were accustomed to chinking in round-log cabins and did not feel it necessary to change. Such an explanation ignores the fact that there are innumerable differences between the extant hewn-log houses and the round-log cabins described in historical records. If people were used to dirt floors in round-log cabins, why did they have wooden floors in hewn-log houses? If they were used to a ladder to the sleeping loft in round-log cabins, why did they put in a staircase to the loft in hewn-log houses? The notion that craftsmen blindly follow tradition because they do not know of any better or different way of doing things is a very unfair assumption.

A similar discussion could be given concerning the fact that the bark is usually left on the top and bottom surfaces of the logs. If the houses were not to have been covered with siding, it would have been far better to have removed the bark, for the bark shrinks and curls, leaving pockets for rain water to get into. Removing the bark would have taken very little time, and it was a task that could have been entrusted to any sturdy boy. It would also be absurd to charge the builders of log houses with carelessness or lack of foresight in this regard. Almost every point at which we examine a log house we see that painstaking care and foresight based on long experience were used to insure long life and ease in maintaining the house. The removal of the bark would have been so easy that we can only assume that it was left on because the house was to be covered with siding.

It is also true that a log house which is not covered with siding on the outside and plaster or paneling on the inside can be very cold in the winter. A number of people who have bought log houses and "restored" them by stripping off the exterior siding and the interior plastering can testify to this fact. I have heard about a family that "restored" in the usual way a fine log house northeast of Bloomington. The first winter the house was so cold that water froze in the toilet bowl. I have heard of another family in a similar circumstance elsewhere who found the water in their pet's water bowl frozen on a number of occasions.

The reason why a log house with the logs exposed inside and out is cold involves a discussion of how large pieces of wood react to changes in the moisture content of the air. Most people are aware that green wood shrinks as it dries out, but they are not aware that wood will always expand across the grain as it picks up moisture from the air and contract as it loses that moisture. It does not matter how long a piece of wood has been cut, for it will always "come and go," as people in southern Indiana say, when the moisture content of the air changes. One illustration of this fact is that fine European antique furniture nearly 250 years old and in perfect condition has been ruined by one winter in the extremely dry atmosphere of an American home with central heating. The wood has shrunk far more than it ever had in its 250 previous years, and the wood has cracked or the piece has been damaged beyond repair in some other way. The moral here is that anyone who has European antiques made of wood in his home should make sure that he also has a humidifier to keep the air from getting too dry. No matter how old the wood or how many coats of finish on it, the wood will shrink if the air gets dry.

To return to our logs, they will expand across the grain when the air is damp and especially if rain water gets directly on the log, and they will contract in those relatively brief and few dry spells we have in southern Indiana. If the chinking is put between the logs while the logs are expanded, when they contract there will be a gap all along the logs between the wood and the chinking. If one puts the chinking in when the logs are contracted, when they expand they will squeeze some of the chinking out. Then when they contract again the gap will likewise be there. When the cold winds of winter blow, the cold air comes in those gaps all around the house, all up and down the wall, not in the form of a concentrated blast but as a series of gentle currents of cold air that permeate the whole house and defy the efforts of the best heating system. There are modern caulking compounds which can be forced into cracks from the nozzle of a caulking gun and which remain sticky and flexible for many years. With these it may be possible to seal the gaps effectively. No such material was available in the nineteenth century, however. People who lived in log houses then needed a good layer of siding on the outside and a good coat of plaster or paneling on the inside to keep them warm in the winter. Actually, a hewn-log house with good, solid wooden siding on the outside and good plaster on the inside is probably the best insulated house that could or can be built. The small gaps that open between the chinking and the logs are insignificant as long as the siding is in good condition and the plaster unbroken. The wind cannot force its way through these gaps then. The seven-inch thickness of nearly solid wood inside the walls is far better insulation than the three inches or so of material in the walls of the best insulated modern frame houses. Moreover, wood is a far more effective insulator than brick or stone.

Finally, the appearance of siding on a hewn-log house cannot be neglected. People in the nineteenth century especially must have felt that a log house without siding gave a very unfinished impression. Appearance and various attitudes towards craftsmanship, ways of life, and the like helped in the nineteenth century to dictate that a hewn-log house should be covered with siding. They also help to dictate in the mid-twentieth century that hewn-log houses should not be covered with siding. Nineteenth century homeowners were very concerned with appearances and the impression their homes made on people. It is very common to find that the facade of a house that faces the road and the rooms visitors are most likely to see are finished in a different and more expensive way than the rest of the house. For example, in a brick house the front side may have the bricks set in Flemish bond while the back and side walls are set in common bond. The stone foundation and other stone work in a masonry house will often be finer on the front wall than on the other walls. The windows on the front of the house may have large panes of glass while those in the rear may have smaller and less expensive ones. Sometimes this means the old windows in the front of the house were remodeled late in the century, but the differences in the stone and brick work can only be the result of original construction.

Inside the house, the parlor, dining room, and front hall are often finished better than the rest of the house. The mantelpieces will nearly always be more elaborate, the doors may be of the paneled type while doors elsewhere in the house may be the simpler board and batten type, and even the hinges and the latches may be more elaborate and more expensive than elsewhere. This innocent vanity was not, of course, confined to the nineteenth century. It flourished in earlier times and it still flourishes today. The front door of the house I live in has larger hinges and a larger and more elaborate latch and lock than other doors in the house. I tell myself it is because the front door is larger and heavier than the other doors, but I daresay there are other influences at work as well. The desire to present a more finished, more attractive appearance to the world probably also helped account for the use of exterior siding.

To sum up a lengthy discussion, then, it seems to me that the use of exterior siding on hewn-log houses evolved as the technology of building such houses evolved and as an integral part of the houses. Hewn-log houses were normally covered with siding. Just as we have seen that at least one individual builder chose to leave the chinking out from between the logs of his house, there may have been some builders who chose to leave the siding off their houses, but this was not typical. As the knowledge of how to build and maintain hewn-log houses declined, people in southern Indiana tended to confuse the round-log temporary cabins known primarily from written sources with the extant hewn-log permanent structures. The written sources said log cabins built by the pioneers did not have siding. The extant log buildings that had siding on them must have been built by pioneers and the written sources cannot be wrong, hence the siding must come off. As a result, hundreds of hewn-log houses have had the protective siding removed and the vulnerable logs exposed to decay. The restorers in this case have helped contribute to the decay of the houses they have tried to restore because they have confused round-log cabins with hewn-log houses.

A word remains to be said concerning the siding used, the way it was applied, and where it was obtained. The siding used on log houses is almost invariably of the type called weatherboarding in southern Indiana or clapboards. These are yellow poplar boards about five inches wide, one half inch thick, and of varying lengths. They may be sawed or hand planed so that they are slightly wedge-shaped in cross section, thicker at the lower edge as placed on the wall and thinner at the top edge. Occasionally they are not wedge-shaped in cross section but are of the same thickness throughout. In every case that I have seen, furring strips which are strips of wood about two inches wide by one inch thick have been used to nail the weatherboarding to. These furring strips run vertically up and down the logs providing a straight surface to nail to. Because the outside surfaces of the wall logs do not always present a true, straight line, it is sometimes necessary to cut a channel or groove in the surface of one or more logs for the furring strip. (See Plate 16, following page.) It is these channels for the furring strips that are visible on log houses long after the siding has been removed or fallen off.

Trim boards which are wider and thicker than the weather boarding are used at the bottom and top of the wall and sometimes at the corners. The weatherboarding is applied, starting at the bottom and working up the wall, so that each piece overlaps the piece below it (Fig. 4.8). As long as the weatherboarding remains in good condition, rain water cannot penetrate the wall except where the weatherboarding butts up against the door and window frames. Before caulking compound or putty was generally available, there was no practical way of making a tight seal at these butt joints. I am convinced that this fact helps explain why early houses seldom had doors or windows

Plate 16. Furring strips still in place after clapboards have been removed.

in the gable-end walls. The overhanging cornice on the long walls of the house, formed by the overhanging plate in log houses, kept most of the rain water from running down those walls and getting in around the door and window frames. No such protection could be provided on the gable-end walls.

To the casual observer the weatherboarding on a log house is indistinguishable from the weatherboarding on a frame house of the same period. Where did the people who built log houses get the sawed weatherboarding? They got it at the same place they got the sawed floorboards used on both floors of the houses, the sawed roof decking boards used underneath the shingles on the roof, the sawed boards used in doors, windows, and cupboards: at the local sawmill. These sawmills were driven by water power in the first half or perhaps three quarters of the nineteenth century and by steam power later. There must have been large numbers of them. One of the things that the earliest settlers in a region looked for was a suitable location for a water mill and mills were built and operated at an early date.

To complete this long discussion of the log walls and related topics, a description must yet be given of how the gable-end wall is

Plate 17. Barn with short logs in the tirangular space in the gable-end walls. The short logs are held in place by "purlins," heavy timbers that run from one gable end to the other and which support the roof. This construction feature is very uncommon in southern Indiana.

constructed above the point where the plate occurs. From this point up to the peak of the roof, the gable-end wall forms a triangle. Only one house of the many observed had this triangular space filled in with horizontal logs like the rest of the walls. Probably the reason why logs were not more commonly used here is that they were difficult to keep in place. There are, of course, no logs running at right angles to them to join at the corners and hold them in place. The interior of the house that had logs in this part of the wall could not be investigated so that it was impossible to tell how the logs were held in place. (See Plate 17.) All the other houses that I have seen have had this part of the wall filled in with vertical studs between the top log in the wall and the rafters. These studs are usually two by four or five inches in cross-section and spaced about two feet apart. Their lower ends are set in notches in the log below them and their upper ends are notched around the rafters. They are nailed securely in place. On their exterior surface weatherboarding is nailed, which is a continuation of the weatherboarding on the lower walls. In most cases the interior walls of the sleeping loft on the second floor of the house are not finished off with plaster. If this area on the second floor was indeed used as a sleeping loft in those houses where the interior walls are unfinished, it must have been very cold in the winter and hot in the summer.

THE ROOF

The roof construction in log houses is comparatively simple. There are always coupled rafters whose lower ends sit on the outer edges of the plates and whose upper ends are joined together at the peak of the roof. Rafters which have been observed have been made in five ways. Occasionally the individual rafters are simply round straight poles whose top sides have been flattened with a broadax or an adze. Rarely the rafters have been split from a log, resembling the famous fence rails split from logs by young Abe Lincoln. Their top sides have been flattened and made straight by hewing or adzing. Rare, too, are rafters which have been hewn into a timber square in cross section from a small log. Most frequent are rafters which have been sawed at a mill. These may be thicker at the lower end and taper towards the top end or they may be the same dimension their entire length. Either way, their average dimension in cross section is about three-by-five inches.

Where the bottom ends of the rafters rest on the plates, they are either pinned or nailed in place. Sometimes a notch is made in the plate for the end of the rafter to fit into. More commonly, the end of the rafter, cut to the correct angle, merely rests on top of the plate. At their tops where the rafters are joined together, they may use a halved joint or an open mortise and tenon joint with a pin driven through the joint (Fig. 4.10). More often they are merely nailed together at their upper ends. A ridge pole is rarely seen. Collar beams running between the two rafters that compose a pair are very common (Fig. 4.11). Collar beams are usually fastened to alternate pairs of rafters or every third pair of rafters. The ends of the collar beams may be joined to the rafters with an open dovetail joint (Fig. 4.12), or they may merely be nailed in place. The collar beams also serve to support the ceiling if the sleeping loft area is finished off with either plaster or paneling of some sort.

The pitch of the roof is, of course, determined by the rafters. In log houses the pitch of the roof is usually about forty degrees from the horizontal, slightly less steep than the roofs of most frame houses of the same period.

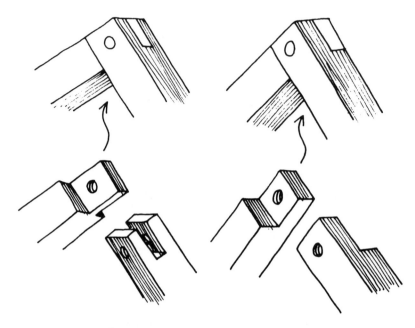

Fig. 4.10 *Rafters using open mortise and tenon joint, pinned (left).*
Rafters using halved joint, pinned (right).

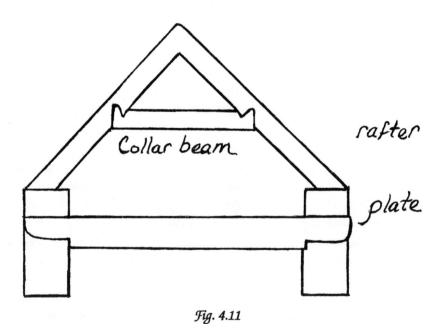

Fig. 4.11

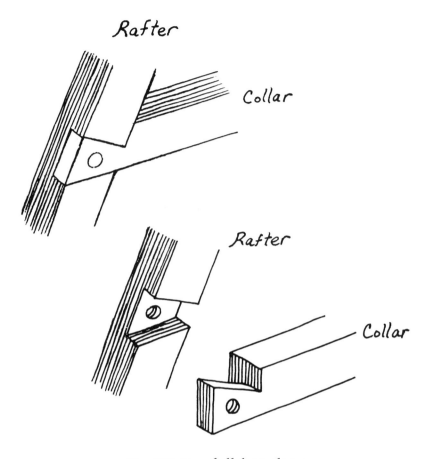

Fig. 4.12 Open half-dovetail joint.

In discussing the details of roof construction it is tempting to arrange features into an historical sequence. It would seem, for instance, that rafters made of round poles or from split rails are older than those sawed at sawmills. It would seem that rafters joined at their peaks with an open mortise and tenon joint with a wooden pin through it are older than rafters simply nailed together at the peak. Moreover, it would seem that collar beams joined to the rafters with an open dovetail joint are older than those beams simply nailed to the rafters. The difficulty in accurately dating log houses, however, makes it dangerous to assume that this historical sequence actually exists in Indiana. We are probably safe only in assuming that the hand-hewn rafters and the more complex joints are rough indicators of greater age than the sawed rafters and the nailed joints.

On top of the rafters, roof decking is laid consisting of boards running at right angles to the rafters and nailed to them. In order to extend from the eaves to the peak of the roof, several courses of boards are needed. A space of three or four inches is invariably left between the courses of boards, mainly because it is assumed that the shingles which are laid on top of the boards will last longer if air can reach their under sides to help dry them more effectively when they become rain soaked. In almost every case of a house that seems to have been built in the first half of the nineteenth century, the boards which have been used for roof decking are rough, unedged boards left just as they came from the saw. That is, the surfaces of the boards have not been planed by hand. Hence it is easy to see whether they have been sawed by a water-powered "up-and-down" saw which leaves straight saw marks at right angles to the long axis of the board, or by a later steam powered circular saw which leaves curved saw marks on the board. Moreover, on boards from the first half of the nineteenth century used in roof decking, the edges of the boards are usually left rough and untrimmed so that the board shows the outline of the log from which it was sawed. Since in the course of its history, a house from the first half of the nineteenth century will have been re-roofed several times, at least once every fifty years, the undersides of the roof decking will have great numbers of nails sticking through. Each time a new roof is put on, the old shingles are pulled off but most roofers did not bother to pull the old nails out of the roof decking.

Wooden shingles were nailed on top of the decking in order to complete the roof. While wooden shingles were almost universally used in the nineteenth century, it is extremely rare to find a log house today with wooden shingles forming its roof. Most houses have been re-roofed at least once in the twentieth century, and cheap substitutes for wooden shingles have been used throughout most of the twentieth century. These substitutes are, first, sheet metal and, later, composition roofing consisting of heavy paper coated with asphalt on which granules of slate or similar substances have been sprinkled. There can be no doubt, however, that throughout most of the nineteenth century wooden shingles were almost invariably used, for both written sources and oral accounts agree on this point. Moreover, in most extant nineteenth century log houses, some shingles will be found somewhere, tucked between the rafters and the roof decking or fallen between the wall siding and the logs. Three general types of wooden

Plate 18. Hand-split shingles still in good condition on a roof.

shingles were used, and in this case it seems safe to arrange the types in an historical sequence, for all older men I have talked to on this point agree with one another.

The earliest type was hand-split or rove (the form of the past tense of the verb "to rive" preferred in Indiana). These are usually called clapboards or, simply, boards in southern Indiana, but I will call them hand-split shingles. Hand-split shingles were usually quite long, between two and three feet, so the first step in making them was to get a log with straight grain and saw it into pieces or bolts of the proper length. According to most sources, oak, and preferably white oak, was the wood chosen for this purpose. Compared with other woods, oak splits easily and cleanly and at the same time is remarkably resistant to decay. (See Plate 18.)

To begin the splitting process, the ax and wedges were used to halve and then quarter the bolt, but the final splitting was done with a froe, a large, dull, knife-shaped blade with a handle at one end turned at a right angle to the blade. (See Chapter Six.) The froe was driven into the block of wood with a froe mallet or club and levered back and forth with the handle to produce accurate, straight splits. After the shingles (about one half inch thick and between about four and eight inches wide) were split from the bolt, any sapwood was trimmed off, since the sapwood decays more quickly than the heart-wood. Then the shingles were clamped in a shingle horse and shaved down with a drawknife so that one end was thinner than the other and so that there was a reasonably uniform taper from the thick end to the thin end. If the shingles were not to be used immediately, they were fastened together in bundles to keep them from warping.

According to traditional beliefs in southern Indiana and many other areas as well, shingles which were laid in the light of the moon (that is, nailed to the roof while the moon was full or nearly full) were likely to cup or twist and hence leak. Recent research on the effects of moonlight on growing plants and freshly cut plant materials seems to confirm the validity of this traditional belief. Moonlight is, of course, sunlight reflected from the moon and the number of hours during the day plant material is exposed to sunlight seems to be important regardless of the intensity of the sunlight.[4] While the traditional belief is probably valid as far as freshly cut shingles are concerned, it probably would not hold true for shingles which had been seasoned for a long time before they were put on the roof. In this case it seems likely that the traditional belief persisted into the era when factory-made shingles were used for roofs. These shingles were thoroughly seasoned by the time they were laid on the roof. Even though the seasoned shingles were not affected in the same way by moonlight, the belief persisted.

In only about a half dozen buildings have I seen this old style of shingle still on a roof. In one case these shingles were on a smokehouse and, though covered with moss, still in good condition. These shingles had been made in the 1930s by a man living alone on the family farm who had learned how to make them from his father. The other buildings observed which still had the long hand-split shingles on them were abandoned and the roofs were in bad condition. These long shingles were laid with about one foot "to the weather" or exposed (Fig. 4.13; see following page).

At some time probably shortly after the Civil War a different way of making shingles was developed. The device which made the new type of shingle was a large knife that slid up and down in a frame. This shingle machine actually bears a close resemblance to a small guillotine. The power to operate the machine came either from a sweep with a long beam to which a horse which walked in an endless circle was harnessed or from a lever pulled by one or two men. A block of

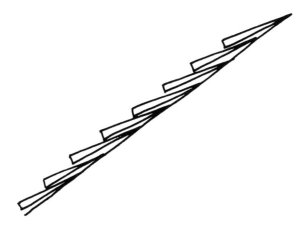

Fig 4.13 *Shingles as installed on roof.*

wood of suitable size was steamed or boiled ("cooked") in a large caldron for several hours. Then it was fished out and held on a table against a stop (or "fence") underneath the knife. Each time the knife came down it sheared or cut off a shingle. The fence was built in such a way that the shingle which was cut off tapered from about one half inch in thickness at the butt end to about one eighth inch thick at the top end (Fig. 4.13).

These cut shingles differed in several ways from the hand-split shingles. They were much shorter, no more than sixteen or eighteen inches, about half the length of the hand-split shingles. It was, of course, much easier to cut a shorter shingle than a long one because a longer knife and much more force would be required for longer shingles. Moreover, the cut shingles were made from wood that could be most easily cut whereas the hand-split shingles were made from wood that could be most easily split. The most common wood for cut shingles was yellow poplar, for this wood is relatively soft and cuts smoothly, especially after being cooked. Yet yellow poplar does not split well so that it was not normally used for hand-split shingles. Moreover, yellow poplar is resistant to decay and stands up well when exposed to sun and rain. Because they were so much shorter than the hand-split shingles, cut shingles were laid with only four or five inches "to the weather." Hence a roof made of cut shingles looks rather different than one made of hand-split shingles.

The third type of wooden shingle was made in the last part of the nineteenth century and in the twentieth century, still being available today. This type of shingle is sawed from blocks of wood in a large, complicated sawmill. These sawed shingles are currently available in southern Indiana but made elsewhere in the country of cedar wood and shipped in. I do not currently have information as to whether or not sawed shingles were ever made in southern Indiana of local woods. These sawed shingles are about the same size and shape as the cut shingles and are laid in the same way. After they have been on a roof for a few years and have turned a dark grey color, they are indistinguishable from cut shingles.

A note on shingles may be added for those who wish to examine extant log buildings. Many restorations, including those in museums, use what is called "hand-split cedar shakes" which are available at most lumber yards today. These shakes are split or rived by hand in parts of the country such as the Pacific Northwest where large cedar trees are cut. Their top surface is rough like hand-split shingles, and they are much thicker than shingles. Moreover, they are laid with more exposure to the weather than cut or sawed shingles and less than hand-split shingles since they are intermediate in length. It should further be noted that the introduction of devices to cut shingles did not mean an immediate end to splitting shingles by hand, nor did the importation of sawed shingles into Indiana immediately put an end to cutting or splitting them locally from native wood. There was considerable overlap in time with some people continuing to use the older methods. I have talked to several men who remember splitting large numbers of shingles with a froe to roof barns in the twentieth century, and I have talked to men who have used shingle cutters in the twentieth century.

One characteristic of roof construction in log buildings is that the roofs did not overhang the walls to any appreciable extent. At the eaves the shingles overhang the plate by only a few inches, and on the gable-end walls the shingles extend only a few inches past the vertical wall. Modern buildings usually have far more roof overhang than most nineteenth century buildings, especially those from the first half of the nineteenth century. Nineteenth century builders probably feared that high winds might tear off the overhanging sections of the roof and cause extensive damage. It will be recalled that the plate in log houses extends out over the front and back walls for several inches giving the same effect as a roof overhang and insuring that most rain water would not run down these walls. No provision was made, however, to keep rain water from running down the gable-end walls. There is, therefore, probably a connection between this aspect of roof construction and the practice of having the doors and windows in the front and rear walls and almost no doors and windows in the gable-end walls. Rain water cannot run down the walls and leak around the doors and windows unless, of course, it is driven against the front and rear walls by high winds.

THE FIREPLACE AND CHIMNEY

A major consideration that throughout history has had an important effect on the size, shape, and construction of houses is the location of the fire. The fire is the source of heat both for warming the house in cold weather and for cooking. At the same time, it is usually the source of light. The central, open hearth that served our ancestors for heating, cooking, and light during millennia, probably in Great Britain back at least to the Middle Ages, required a smoke hole in the roof directly above the fire. As a result, no house so heated could be over one story in height and no sleeping loft could be used above the living quarters under the roof. The room with the fire in it had to be open to the rafters. When the chimney as we know it came into use, it became possible to use interior space in a house more efficiently. The heat from the fire on the ground floor rose and warmed the sleeping quarters above the ground floor, and smoke inside the house was no longer a problem—as long as the fireplace was operating well. The size and shape of a room and hence of a house are also directly affected by the source of both heat and light. With a fireplace in one end wall—and I have never seen an original log house with a fireplace in any other position—a room cannot be much over twenty-four feet long and twenty feet wide. Otherwise it will be almost impossible to heat in the so-called temperate zone, which can get pretty intemperate at times. The dimensions, size, and shape of one-room log houses in southern Indiana are remarkably stable. Log houses of more than one room are seen to be simply two or more of the one-room houses hooked together end to end with a common roof. It is undoubtedly the fireplace and all that is connected with it as a source of heat and light that dictated this stability in size and shape. Later, when houses were built without fireplaces and with stoves as a source of heat, the same shape and dimensions were still used.

As stated, not only are fireplaces and chimneys always in end walls, in ninety-nine percent of the houses the fireplaces are in exterior end walls. In a one-room house, obviously, the end wall is at the same time an exterior wall, but this is not true in a house with more than one room on the ground floor. Yet I have seen only one house with more than one room where the fireplaces were not in the exterior end walls.[6] In a house in northwest Monroe County the two fireplaces served by one chimney are in the center of the house in the interior end walls of the two downstairs rooms. (See Plate 19.) End chimneys and fireplaces on exterior walls in multi-room houses are found mainly in the southern United States while central chimneys and fireplaces are found mainly in the northern United States. It must be emphasized that I am talking here about fireplaces with attached chimneys, not chimneys which serve stoves. It is not surprising that the fireplace and chimney in log houses in southern Indiana should conform to this general trend. There seems to have been no consistency as to which gable end was chosen for the fireplace. As one stands facing the front door, fireplaces are sometimes on the left and sometimes on the right. As far as I have been able to discover, too, it is not

Plate 19. *Two-room log house with fireplaces on interior end walls of the rooms so that the chimney is in the center of the house, an unusual arrangement.*

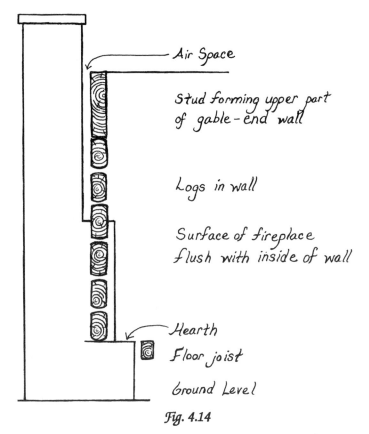

Air Space

Stud forming upper part of gable-end wall

Logs in wall

Surface of fireplace flush with inside of wall

Hearth

Floor joist

Ground Level

Fig. 4.14

Plate 20. *When a fireplace and chimney are built just inside an exterior wall of a house, the back of the firebox will extend through the wall and be visible from the outside.*

an orientation toward any particular point of the compass that affects the choice of which end of the house has the chimney in it.

I have stated that fireplaces and chimneys are in exterior end walls. Actually, they are more outside than in the walls. At least ninety percent of the fireplaces and chimneys conform to a consistent pattern. A large hole is cut in the end wall and the fireplace built in such a way that the inside surface of the fireplace is flush with the inside surface of the wall. Part of the masonry for the fireplace is then inside the wall but much of it is outside the wall. From the back of the pile of masonry comprising the fireplace the chimney rises in such a way that the chimney is completely outside the wall with an air space of three inches or more between the wall and the chimney (Fig. 4.14; see Plate 20). There probably are a number of reasons why fireplaces and chimneys were constructed in this way, but I will mention only two. First, they did not take up space inside a room. Second, there was no problem in building the roof around the chimney and trying to make a water-tight joint where the roof met the chimney because the chimney did not go through the roof.

The remaining ten percent of the fireplaces and chimneys were likewise at the exterior end wall, but placed in a slightly different way. The hole was cut in the logs in just the same way as for the other type of fireplace, but the back of the pile of masonry comprising the fireplace was flush with the outside surface of the log wall. (See Plate 21, next page.) The fireplace therefore protruded into the room about two feet and the chimney went up just inside the wall and, of course, passed through the roof at the peak (Fig. 4.15; see page 107).

In some log houses, notably large ones consisting of several rooms, there may be fireplaces on the second floor. These second-floor fireplaces are always much smaller than those on the first floor. Usually they are so tiny that one wonders how any fire large enough to give much heat could have been built in them. Probably the fires in them were not kept burning throughout the day but were only kindled when going to bed and on arising. Perhaps glowing embers were brought up from the downstairs fires rather than building a fire in them. Perhaps, too, the light they gave was as important as the limited amount of heat they gave. These second-floor fireplaces were built into the same masonry stack which serves for the downstairs fireplaces. I have never seen in southern Indiana two separate chimneys for fireplaces on the same end of a log house. Because they are built

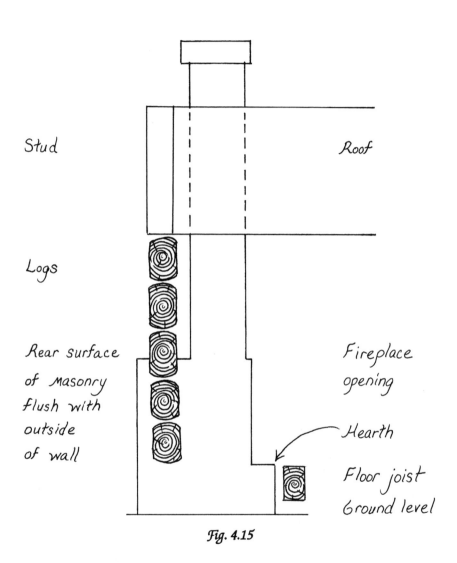

Stud

Roof

Logs

Rear surface
of masonry
flush with
outside
of wall

Fireplace
opening

Hearth

Floor joist
Ground level

Fireplace
opening

Fig. 4.15

Plate 21. A brick fireplace and chimney.

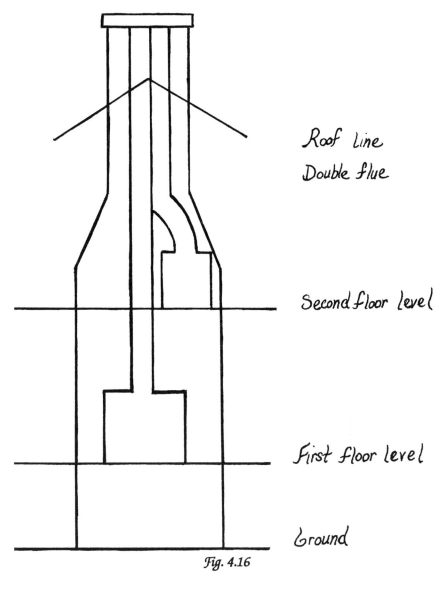

Roof Line
Double flue

Second floor level

First floor level

Ground

Fig. 4.16

into the same stack of masonry as the downstairs fireplace, they cannot be directly over the downstairs fireplace because they would then interfere with the flue for the downstairs fireplace. They are built off-center in the masonry stack and therefore have to be very small (Fig. 4.16).

Fireplaces and chimneys are usually built of rock (the term "rock" seems to be most commonly used in southern Indiana rather than "stone"). Brick is used for a complete fireplace and chimney only very rarely, but a combination of rock and brick is not unusual. (See Plate 22.) Sometimes the actual firebox will be lined with brick, but it is always possible that the brick lining was added after the original rock lining burned out. Occasionally all the masonry enclosing the firebox from ground level up to a height of about eight feet at the point where the pile of masonry narrows (the "shoulders") will be of rock with the actual chimney of brick. Sometimes only the part of the chimney above the roofline will be brick, but this may be because that part of the chimney had to be rebuilt.

The rock that was used in fireplaces and chimneys probably came in most cases from near the site of the house. Rock that could be gathered from creek bed or hillside or dug with simple tools from the ground was the only type that was generally available until large scale quarrying with heavy machinery began towards the end of the nineteenth century. By that time stoves were taking the place of fireplaces.

Plate 22. *A sandstone fireplace and chimney.*

It would seem that in most parts of Indiana, enough rock could be gathered or dug from the ground to build fireplaces and chimneys, but there was not enough available to build many complete houses of rock. Hence, most masonry houses in southern Indiana built in the first seven decades of the nineteenth century are built of brick. Even in the Bedford-Bloomington area, which since about 1875 has supplied limestone to build such enormous structures as the Empire State Building in New York City, early rock buildings are quite rare.

Since only locally available rock was used and since some kinds of rock can be used in some ways and some in other ways, it follows that there are regional patterns discernible in masonry work. In areas where there is limestone, chimneys and fireplaces are built of relatively small pieces of rock. They may be of carefully selected pieces used mostly as they have been gathered with a minimum of shaping with chisel and hammer, or they may have been worked into relatively regular blocks of the required dimensions. When building fireplaces with limestone, two special problems were present. The actual lining of the firebox could only be made of certain varieties of limestone, since some varieties crumbled quickly in contact with the intense heat of the fire and some varieties are said to actually explode in contact with intense heat. Constructing the arch over the opening of the fireplace was also a problem when rocks were used in their natural shapes. In all fireplaces the arch is very shallow, hardly rising more than a few inches in the center. In some fireplaces the builders found or made a shaped keystone to use in the center of the opening, but in others they relied upon a long piece of iron which spanned the opening and supported the rocks. (See Plate 23.)

In areas where sandstone (called "sandrock" in rural southern Indiana) is available, the fireplaces and chimneys present a different appearance. Although of the same size, shape, and location as the fireplaces and chimneys in limestone areas, the sandrock ones are of a different color and are made usually of much larger pieces of rock. The sandrock is found in large sheets at outcroppings. Each sheet is very nearly the same thickness, though some sheets may be quite thick and some only a few inches thick. By digging back from the surface a short way into the bank, it was possible to procure fairly large pieces of rock of uniform thickness. In many of the sandrock fireplaces, there will be a number of shaped pieces such as the large piece

Plate 23. *A limestone fireplace and chimney. The limestone has been shaped by hand into pieces of reasonably uniform size.*

spanning the opening of the fireplace and the specially shaped pieces forming the "shoulders" where the masonry stack narrows above the fireplace to form the base of the chimney. The actual chimney in sandrock areas is often built of pieces of rock from a sheet no more than two or three inches thick. Pieces are cut from this sheet of the required lengths and about a foot wide so that the four pieces stood on edge "make the round" or raise the height of the chimney a foot. (See Plate 24.)

Plate 24. *Note the space between the house wall and the chimney. There has been uneven settling here, and the chimney has leaned away from the house, creating the unusually large gap.*

All masonry used in fireplaces and chimneys, be it rock of different kinds or bricks, requires mortar. In every case that I have investigated a fireplace and chimney—and it must be remembered that for all practical purposes this means masonry work done before about 1875—the mortar has been simply mud. As far as I have been able to discover, if there has been any other substance mixed with the mud, it has gotten into it by accident. That is, if there was sand in with the mud, it probably was not put into pure mud on purpose but was there because the mud was taken from the bank of a creek and had sand in it already. The mud mortar always seems to be in excellent condition. When I helped take down the chimneys of a log house that I am convinced was built around 1840, the mud mortar stuck so tenaciously to the rocks that it was very difficult to remove. As a matter of fact, it seemed much harder to remove from the rocks than modern mortars would be. Rains tend to wash the mud mortar away from the exterior surfaces of the masonry, but seems to do little or no harm. The insects called mud daubers probably do more harm than rain does. Occasionally, of course, modern mortar has been used to replace the mud mortar that has been washed away from exterior surfaces, but the careful observer can usually find evidence of what the original mortar was.

As has already been indicated, the fireplace in a log house served many functions. As a source of heat in cold weather and as a source of light both before and after daylight, it must have been the center of family activity. In very cold weather people probably did not get too far from the fireplace for very long. Almost all the cooking done for a family must have been done at a single fireplace. It is possible that in very hot weather some cooking might have been done outside over an open fire and it is possible that some special kinds of cooking such as making apple butter were normally done outside, but day in and day out most cooking was done at the fireplace. It is very rare to find a separate summer kitchen with its own fireplace or a separate washhouse with its own fireplace near log houses in southern Indiana. I have never seen a log house in southern Indiana with a bake oven built into the masonry close to the fireplace such as is found in other parts of the United States. The amount of baking that can be done at an open fireplace is rather limited. Fried and stewed foods were probably far more common than baked foods. Undoubtedly, most fireplaces used for cooking had at one time some device to suspend a pot over the fire.

In only a very few fireplaces are there left cranes that were built into the masonry (Fig. 4.17, see Plate 25). The fact that most fireplaces were no longer used after stoves became common probably explains why cranes were removed from many old fireplaces. (See Plate 26.)

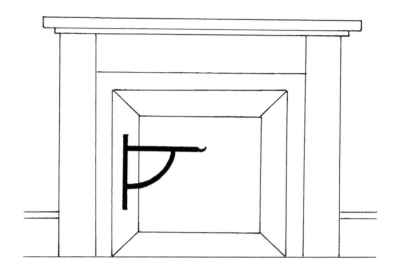

Fig. 4.17 Fireplace with crane. See also Plate 25.

Plate 25. Fireplace with crane.

Plate 26. *Fireplace from which the crane has been removed.*

At some time towards the end of the nineteenth century stoves became available in most of southern Indiana. In some parts of the area stoves must have been available at reasonable prices before that time, for it was overland transportation that made a heavy, bulky object like a stove so expensive. Some stoves were made in cities in Indiana such as Evansville, but transportation to rural areas was still costly. The spread of the network of railroads around Indiana was probably the decisive factor in making manufactured goods like stoves available in rural areas. As mentioned previously, converting from a fireplace to a stove also involved discarding the old pots and pans with their rounded bottoms and short legs. It also involved buying kerosene lamps, for the stove, unlike the fireplace, gives off no light. While again it is impossible to give exact dates, it seems as if log houses built after about 1875 usually are built without a fireplace. A stove does not need such a large chimney as a fireplace does. The large chimney for a fireplace is necessary to create a substantial draft to keep the fire from smoking, but in a stove the draft can be regulated and confined, and a smaller chimney is satisfactory. In many houses that originally had fireplaces, the fireplaces were blocked up when stoves became available. Often the same chimney was used, however, for a

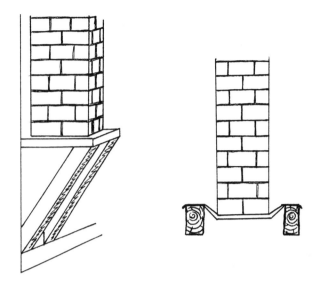

Fig. 4.18 *Flue for stove resting on a platform built against a wall (left). Flue for stove suspended between ceiling joists, resting on iron supports that are hooked over joists.*

section of stove pipe was run from the stove into a hole cut into the chimney above the fireplace. Sometimes, though, a new, small chimney was built to serve the stove. The fireplace and chimney in such cases were often pulled down, and the opening in the log wall for the fireplace was boarded up completely or converted into a window.

A small chimney for a stove is usually called a "flue." Whether the flue is added to an older house which originally had a fireplace and chimney or is part of the original construction in a later house, it is usually of brick rather than rock. Brick was probably more readily available at the later date when these flues were built. Certainly, a flue which is small in diameter can be built more readily from brick than from rock.

Three types of brick flues for stoves have been observed. One type starts at ground level, usually being built on a small foundation of rocks, goes all the way up through the house, and emerges through the roof. Another type rests on a wooden platform which is built against a wall about four or five feet above the floor level of the main floor. The inner edge of the platform is fastened securely to the wall while the outer edge is supported by timbers like two-by-fours which come out from the wall at an angle (Fig. 4.18). From the platform, of course, the flue rises and emerges from the roof. A third type of flue is built on a pair of iron supports whose ends rest on two ceiling joists.

This flue also rises through the attic or sleeping loft and through the roof. In all types a metal stovepipe passes through a hole in the ceiling and enters the flue above the ceiling. These small flues seem insecure and flimsy in comparison to the massive piles of masonry in the fireplaces and their chimneys. Nonetheless, many stove flues seem to have been in use for many decades and are still in good condition.

From a survey of stove flues, it would seem that they are usually built so that they can pass through the peak of the roof because in this way it is easier to build a roof which does not leak. Water cannot run down a roof and be caught behind a flue when the flue passes through the peak of the roof. This still leaves much latitude in the placing of the flue because the peak runs the entire length of the house. Some flues are located toward one end of the house, some more nearly in the center. The stove can be some distance from the flue because the stovepipe can be run for some distance. And as has been mentioned, log houses built after stoves became available were generally of the same size and shape as earlier ones with fireplaces.

When a log house was to have a fireplace and chimney, construction of the masonry work probably began as soon as the wooden portions of the house had been built. A place was marked out on the logs in one gable end of the house. Then the logs were sawed through and two timbers were pegged or nailed against the cut end of the logs just as was done in making an opening for doors and windows. An area of appropriate size and about a foot deep was dug out and large rocks were fitted into it as a foundation. On this the pile of masonry was started, allowing for a hearth which would extend into the room about two feet from the front of the fireplace opening. As the actual firebox was being built, the iron anchors for the crane were built into the inner wall, and the top of the firebox opening was spanned often with a heavy strip of iron to support the rocks above. Small blocks of wood were built into the surface of the masonry which faced into the room so that the wooden mantelpiece could be nailed snugly against this surface, the nails being driven through the mantelpiece and into the blocks of wood. At the height of about a foot above the fireplace opening, the pile of masonry narrowed down to form the chimney unless there was to be a fireplace on the second floor. If there was a fireplace on the second floor, the pile of masonry continued up with the same dimensions until a level shortly above the upper fireplace was reached, whereupon it narrowed down (Fig. 4.16).

The chimney itself usually extended about three feet higher than the peak of the roof. As has already been mentioned, the pile of masonry is one separate, independent structure and the wooden portions of the house are a second independent structure. The pile of masonry does not lean against the house, nor vice versa. Actually, the masonry does not even touch the wooden parts of the house, for there is always a small gap left between the masonry and the wood even though this gap may be filled with mud mortar. Should the pile of masonry, because of its great weight, sink into the ground a fraction of an inch, that settling will not affect the wooden structure. A gap may open between the masonry and the wood, but more mud mortar can be packed into the gap.

FINISHING DETAILS

While the basic structure of a log house has been described in detail, there remain to be discussed a number of features which are needed before a house can be lived in. Since these are not part of the basic structure, they can be removed and new ones substituted with relative ease. Such removable items as mantelpieces, doors, and windows, therefore, are less likely to be original than the basic structure of a house still in use today.

Once the roof was completed on a house, the windows probably would be installed before much further work was done in order to keep rain out of the interior of the house. The most common nine-teenth-century window sash seems to have been made up of six panes of glass, each ten inches high and eight inches wide, and two sashes were, of course, used in each window unit. Hence windows are usually about forty-six inches high and twenty-eight inches wide. The upper sash is fixed so that it cannot be lowered, but the lower sash may be raised and lowered. The wood used in the sashes is invariably yellow poplar and the bars and muntins, the strips of wood which hold the panes of glass in place, are much thinner in cross-section than are the bars and muntins in modern windows. Old window glass is usually thinner than modern glass and frequently has a large number of imperfections in it, such as bubbles and swirls. Exterior or interior shutters probably were very uncommon on log houses in the nineteenth century.

The finished floor was probably laid soon after the roof was completed and the windows installed, because doors could not be hung, nor could baseboards and much other trim be installed, until the flooring was down. The flooring for the first and second floors was alike except for two features. In many log houses the flooring for the first floor was of ash wood while that for the second floor was of poplar. Ash, of course, is a much harder wood than poplar and hence better suited to resist the wear of greater use on the ground floor. Although most log houses had wall-to-wall carpeting laid over a thick layer of straw on the floor during the winter, the straw and carpeting were often taken up for the summer and the floor left bare. Both ash and poplar are smooth woods which do not become rough or splintery from wear. Another difference between the first and second floors is that a decorative bead molding was often worked on the edges of the flooring for the second floor. This bead molding appears only on the bottom side of the boards. As mentioned earlier, the beams which supported the second floor were often left exposed so that when one stood on the first floor, one could see the under side of the flooring for the second floor. The beaded edges of the floor boards added a decorative finishing touch (Fig. 4.19).

The boards used for flooring were obtained from sawmills. Since the bottom sides of the boards for the first floor were seldom planed, the marks left by the saw show whether the boards came from an early water-powered sawmill or a later steam-powered mill. The long, straight "up-and-down" water-powered saw leaves marks which are

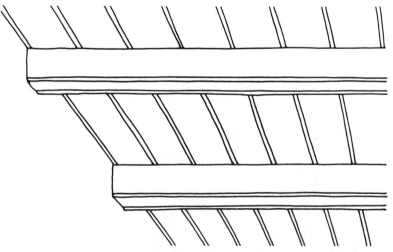

Fig. 4.19 First floor ceiling floor joists, showing bead molding.

straight and at right angles to the grain of the wood, while the steam-powered circular saw leaves marks which are curved. Wide boards of uneven widths such as are found in the floors of old houses elsewhere in the eastern United States have never been found in log houses in southern Indiana. Both ash and poplar expand and contract quite a bit with changes in the moisture content of the air. If wide boards, over a foot in width, for example, had been used, the space between the boards in dry weather would have been both noticeable and troublesome, for the wider the board is, the wider the gaps would be. Most floor boards are about six inches in width, and only very rarely are boards wider than eight inches used.

I have never seen an original floor in a log house which was of double construction, that is, a subfloor with another layer of finished flooring. Hence floorboards are nearly always one and one quarter inches thick in order to keep them from bending under the weight of furniture and of people walking on them. Each board is fitted to the one beside it by means of a tongue and groove joint so that small objects cannot fall down through the gaps between the boards and so that air cannot so readily come up through the gaps.

When the floors are laid, great care is taken to force the boards tightly together. When the flooring is removed in an old house, one can usually see that holes about one inch in diameter and two or three inches deep have been bored down from the top into the floor joists at irregular intervals. When the flooring was being laid, these holes were bored and a peg of suitable size was driven into the hole. Then wedges were driven in between the peg and the floor board in order to force the boards tightly together (Fig. 4.20, next page). In most houses the boards were fastened to the joists by driving nails in such a way that the heads of the nails were hidden in the tongue and groove joint. Special flooring nails which have very small heads were used (Fig. 4.21, next page).

The baseboards at the foot of the wall rest on top of the finished flooring. The baseboards are usually six to eight inches wide and decorated only with a simple bead molding on their upper outside edge. When the interior walls of a log house are plastered, as is frequently the case, it is possible to see that the baseboards were fastened against the wall before the plastering was put on so that the coats of plaster partially cover the top of the baseboard. In modern work it seems to be common practice to apply the plaster to the wall

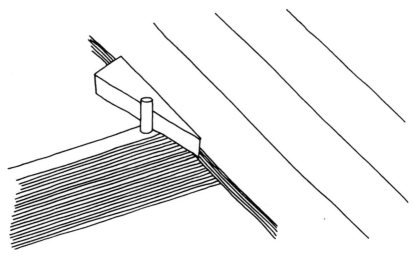

Fig. 4.20 Wedge and peg used to force floor board into place.

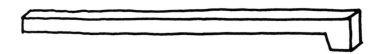

Fig. 4.21 Cut or "square" flooring nail.

first and to put the baseboard over the plaster. Plastered walls often have a strip of wood decorated with bead moldings which runs parallel to the baseboard at a height of about thirty inches from the floor. This strip, called a chair rail, was probably intended to keep the backs of chairs placed against the wall from denting the plaster. Around door and window openings strips of wood about four inches wide and decorated with bead moldings are fitted.

The fireplace is surrounded by a wooden mantelpiece. In its simplest form the mantelpiece consists of two boards along the sides of the fireplace opening, one board across the top, and a shelf along the very top. The mantelpiece is built as a unit and fastened against the masonry by nails which go into wooden blocks which have been built into the masonry. In actual practice, most mantelpieces seem to have had a considerable amount of decorative skill expended on them, for moldings of various kinds are worked into the design, molding which can only have been made by special molding planes. Because the wooden blocks to which the mantelpieces are nailed have to be built into the masonry as the fireplace is being constructed, it

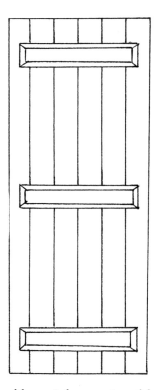

Fig. 4.22 "*Board and batten*" *door, as viewed from inside of the house.*

does not seem likely that log houses were originally built without mantelpieces. It is, however, always possible that a particular mantelpiece has replaced an original one. It seems likely, though, that many of the decoratively molded mantelpieces are original to the houses in which they are now found, thus demonstrating that the builders of the houses owned molding planes and were skilled in their use. If there is more than one fireplace in a house, the mantelpieces in that house will all be of the same design, but it appears as if each house has its own special mantelpiece design. It is, of course, possible that if so many old houses had not been destroyed, one might be able to see that houses in the same neighborhood had the same or very similar designs, but all available evidence indicates that a new design, albeit simple, was worked out for each house.

Doors of two types of construction were used in log houses (Fig. 4.22). The board and batten door, as it is often called, consists of vertical boards six or eight inches wide joined to each other with tongue and groove joints and with two or three horizontal boards four

Plate 27. A board and batten door. When the door is opened, it swings into the room.

to six inches wide fastened across the back. The vertical boards often have decorative bead moldings along their edges. The horizontal boards or battens have chamfered edges and are fastened to the vertical boards with many small nails. Much wider boards could have been used to make such a door because wide boards were readily available in the nineteenth century, but the effects of expansion and contraction with changes in the moisture content of the air would have been much greater with wider boards. (See Plate 27.)

The other type of door, the paneled door, is still being made and is sometimes used in modern houses. It consists, essentially, of a frame with vertical and horizontal boards joined together. Panels are fitted into grooves between the members of the frame in such a way that the panels can expand and contract in their grooves as the moisture in the

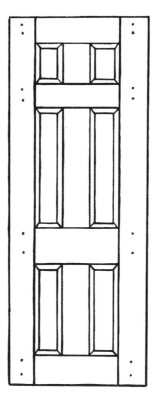

Fig. 4.23 Panelled door.

air changes without affecting the door. Early handmade paneled doors can be easily recognized by some obvious construction features. The tenons on the ends of the horizontal members of the frame extend completely through the two outside vertical members, so that if one looks at the very outside edge of the door, one can see the ends of these tenons. Usually, small wedges are driven in at the top and bottom of the tenons so that the ends of these wedges can also be seen on the very outside edge of the door. Moreover, wooden pegs are driven through the door so that they pass through the tenons and it is usually possible to see the ends of these pegs on the surface of the door even though the door may have been painted many times (Fig. 4.23).

Of the two types of door, the board and batten door is the easier to build, and many log houses have only board and batten doors in them. The paneled door, however, seems to have been more esteemed, so that it is not unusual to find both types used in the same house. If the house is a small one, the front door may be paneled and the rear board and batten. If the house is large, the downstairs doors may be paneled while those on the second floor may be board and batten. It may be that when both types of doors are found in a house, the paneled doors have been used to replace board and batten doors at some time after the original construction. Unfortunately, unless a house is being torn down it is usually impossible to tell what doors are original and what are replacements, and sometimes it is not even possible to tell then. I have been able to investigate a few large houses, however, in which I was able to find convincing evidence that both paneled and board and batten doors were used as part of the original construction.

A staircase of some sort is found in nearly every extant log house. The ladder to the sleeping loft mentioned so often in popular accounts of life in early Indiana must have been used only in temporary round-log cabins. The placement of the staircase depends upon the number of rooms a log house has and will be treated when floor plans are discussed. Some of the larger houses have fairly elaborate staircases, but this description will be confined to the most common log house which has a single room on the ground floor and a sleeping loft overhead. The staircase in houses of this type is usually quite narrow, not over thirty inches wide, with narrow treads and high risers. To make the staircase even more difficult to use, it almost invariably has a ninety degree turn in it, for it starts along one of the side walls and turns to go along the end wall beside the fireplace. Except for the bottom two or three steps, it is completely enclosed. That is, one side is against the outside wall while the other side has vertical boards against it which rise from floor to ceiling. A door is placed usually at the third step. When the door is closed, therefore, heat cannot rise to the sleeping loft. Underneath the staircase is the only closet in the house. In the loft, the opening in the floor for the stairs is against the wall on one side and the other side of the opening is protected by a simple railing. Otherwise there is usually no hand rail of any sort. Since the staircases are so difficult to ascend and descend, it would seem that younger people slept in the loft and older people slept downstairs. (See Plates 28, 29.)

Investigating the hardware used in log houses involves the usual problems of trying to determine what is original and what a later replacement. With hardware it is often possible to see that the item currently installed is not the original one, for the hole for the original

Plate 28. A staircase in a house with one room on the ground floor. Note the door closing off the staircase and the cupboard under the stairs. The fireplace has been closed and a stove installed.

door latch, for instance, may still be in the door beside the newer latch, or on a door new hinges may have been installed which do not exactly match the holes for the old ones. I will try to confine myself to hardware used in the first half of the nineteenth century since the closer one comes to the present time, the greater the variety of hardware used and hence the greater the difficulty of describing it.

In trying to determine what hardware was used in the first half of the nineteenth century, there is one significant technological development in the manufacture of wood screws. Between about 1775 and 1846, wood screws were made by machine, but they were blunt on the end and did not taper to a point. A hole of the correct diameter and depth had to be drilled in the wood to receive them. In 1846, however, a machine was patented which made pointed screws, and these pointed screws must have quickly superseded the blunt type. If it is possible to remove a wood screw, and if it proves to be of the blunt-ended type, it is quite likely that the piece of hardware involved is from the first half of the nineteenth century.

While handmade hinges of both iron and wood were used on barns and other outbuildings throughout much of nineteenth cen-

Plate 29. *Typical staircase with narrow, cramped treads.*

Plate 30. A handmade "strap" hinge on a barn door.

Plate 31. A wooden hinge on a barn door.

tury, it is quite rare to find handmade hinges on houses. (See Plates 30, 31.) Perhaps if I had been able to visit more log houses close to the Ohio River in the areas where much of the earlier settlement in southern Indiana took place, I would have found more handmade hinges, but most of the houses I have located are outside this area. One house is remarkable in this context because every door in it seems to have had handmade hinges. This is the Guthrie house near Leesville which almost certainly was built by a gunsmith who seems to have made all his own hinges. These are of the strap variety ranging from eight inches long to over two feet long, the smaller ones having been used on cupboard doors and the larger ones on full-sized doors.

Most houses of the first half of the nineteenth century, however, seem to have been supplied with cast-iron butt hinges fastened to the door and to the frame with wood screws. These butt hinges differ from their modern counterparts in several ways. They are smaller than modern hinges because they are often used on board and batten doors only about an inch thick. The leaf of the hinge which is fastened to the door frame has a pin permanently affixed to it, while the leaf attached to the door has a projecting part with a hole in it that fits down over the pin. Some early cast-iron hinges are made so that the leaves of the hinge are permanently fixed together.

While many of the old type of butt hinge remain in use because they are relatively inconspicuous, the same cannot be said for door latches. They are conspicuous and have often been replaced by more modern door knobs and their mechanisms. I have observed only a few door latches that appear to be representative examples of the type widely used in log houses in the first half of the nineteenth century. These appear to be of an early manufactured type, for the handles seem to be cast iron, and iron casting was not normally done by blacksmiths. All in all, though, they closely resemble handmade latches from the latter part of the eighteenth century. On one side of the door (the outer side if it is an exterior door) is a thin iron plate about eight inches high and two inches wide. To this plate is fastened a curved handle of cast iron about four inches high like a long, low staple. Above the handle the flattened part of a bar protrudes, convenient for the thumb to press down. The bar passes through the door so that when it is pressed down on the outside it raises a small bar, the latch itself, on the inside, and the latch is raised from a notched piece of iron attached to the door frame. On the inside of the door the bar protrudes and is curved downward. (See Plate 32.)

Built-in cupboard doors, which are not very common, mostly are supplied with small hinges like those used on larger doors and wooden cupboard turns held on with screws. No hardware seems to have been used on windows. The lower sash, the only one which is movable, probably was held open with a stick of appropriate length. The cranes built into fireplaces are described in the section on fireplace construc-

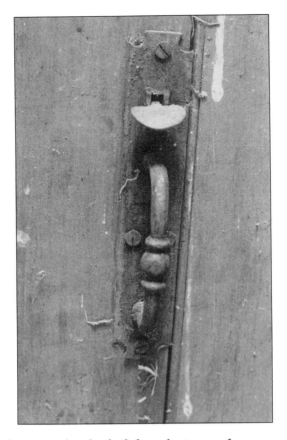

Plate 32. *A door latch of the early nineteenth-century type.*

tion. While door hooks and bolts were probably used in the first half of the nineteenth century, I have never found any that I could say with certainty dated from that period. Those expedients of the pioneer such as leather door hinges and wooden latches do not, for obvious reasons, appear on any extant houses I have seen, though wooden latches still can be found on many barns and other outbuildings.

As has been previously mentioned, a number of log houses have plaster on the interior walls. Unless a house is being demolished or is in a dilapidated state, it is usually impossible to determine whether or not the plaster is original to the house and what its composition is. When it has been possible to examine the plaster closely in a number of log buildings, it has appeared as if the plaster in many of them was originally in the house. The laths used in early work appear to have been split or "rove" with a froe from long blocks of wood. These laths are about three-eighths of an inch thick, one-and-a-quarter inches wide, and of varying lengths. They are usually nailed to the wall with small cut nails and run diagonally on the wall. If the laths ran horizontally, as they do in frame houses usually, there would be no place to nail them at the interstices between the logs. In later work, laths are of the same dimensions as the earlier ones, but have been sawed from logs at sawmills.

The plaster itself varies from house to house, of course, but it usually seems to be much coarser than modern plaster and often has hair from hogs in it. I have heard it said that lime for the plaster was made in the nineteenth century by burning limestone or mussel shells. It usually appears, too, as if many coats of whitewash have been applied over the plaster, but this was perhaps done over a period of many years.

I have been unable to obtain much information about the paints used on the interior of log houses in the nineteenth century. Most extant houses, of course, have been painted on the interior and many interior walls have been papered, but the detailed analysis involving the removal of layer after layer or the microscopic analysis of a cross section of layers has not been done. It does, however, appear as if whitewash was used in many houses. Sometimes wallpaper which has peeled off the walls of abandoned houses has revealed that the walls had been whitewashed many times before the paper was applied.

In a few houses I have found traces of an old brick red paint which has penetrated into the wood, somewhat like a modern stain penetrates into the wood, rather than forming a film on the surface as modern paints do. A location has been pointed out to me a few miles west of Bloomington where a deep reddish-purplish colored clay is found. The two older men who showed me this spot told me they had heard that people used to get this clay at this place for making paint.

It seems to have been a fairly common practice in the nineteenth century and probably into the twentieth century as well to use imitation wood graining on the woodwork of houses. This involves painting a base coat of one color on the wood and, after it has dried, applying a second coat of a darker color. While the second coat is still wet it is gone over with steel combs and other tools to imitate a wood grain pattern. Frequently yellow poplar wood is grained to make it resemble oak and if the work is well done only a close inspection will reveal the graining is painted on.

In one log house, the Ketcham house that stood about ten miles south of Bloomington until it was taken down in 1976, remarkable painted decorations were found on the walls under many layers of wallpaper. At the time I visited the house, most of the plaster had been torn away from the interior walls. Some, however, remained above the fireplace, and moisture had caused the wallpaper to peel off this section of the plaster. Painted directly on the plaster were large designs of a markedly "primitive" character in vivid shades of green, red, and black. Centered over the fireplace opening was a rectangular design about two feet long and one foot high, and to each side of it was a design in green of a stylized tree. The trees were each about three feet high.

When I saw this painted design, I picked up fragments of plaster which were scattered around on the floor. I found that most of them showed traces of paint of the same colors as used over the fireplace. Hence it is very likely that all the walls in that room at least had similar painted designs. When so painted, this room must have been very striking. While walls painted with designs are known elsewhere in the country, especially in old houses in New England,[7] this house was the first with such designs to be discovered in Indiana to the best of my knowledge.

Almost as many houses have the interior walls covered with vertical boards as have them covered with plaster, and in some houses some walls may be covered with vertical boards and some with plaster. In recent years it has become a common practice to call any type of wood covering applied to a wall "paneling." In the nineteenth century this term would not have been used for vertical boards nailed to the wall, for there are no panels involved in such a treatment. When vertical boards are used they are almost always yellow poplar wood about three quarters of an inch thick, joined to each other with a tongue and groove joint, and each board has a small decorative bead molding along one edge. Sometimes similar boards are nailed to the ceiling joists to form a ceiling for the room.

Chapter Five

Building Types

One-and-a-half Story Houses

The most common log house consists of a single room on the ground floor with a sleeping loft overhead (Fig. 5.1). Of the 296 houses investigated for this study, 192 or 65 percent were of this type. Large numbers of houses with a single room on the ground floor and a sleeping loft overhead were built over a period of centuries in Great

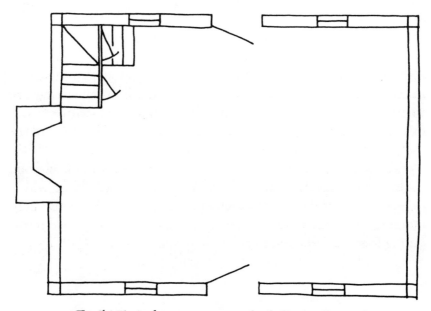

Fig. 5.1 Typical one-room, one-and-a-half story house.

Britain and in America by immigrants of British descent.[1] In Great Britain they were built of masonry or some type of wooden frame construction, while in America they might be of frame, masonry, or log construction, but they were all remarkably similar as to their general size and shape and the location of such features as doors, windows, staircases, and fireplaces. In southern Indiana the log houses of this type are almost invariably rectangular in floor plan in that they are longer (that is, the dimension parallel with the ridge) than they are wide. The average length of the houses of this type which were measured is 21 feet 6 inches while the average width is 17 feet 6 inches. Because there are somewhat more unusually small houses than there are unusually large houses, the typical house would be about 24 feet long and 18 feet wide. (See Plates 33, 34; Plate 34 on next page.)

The locations of the doors, windows, fireplace, staircase, and other features have been described in the preceding chapters. They will be briefly listed again, however, for the sake of clarity. There is one door in the center of the front wall and usually a door directly opposite it in the back wall. There are two windows usually in the front wall, one on each side of the door, and two windows in the back

Plate 33. One-room, one-and-a-half story house. The chimney and the front porch are recent, though the modern chimney replaces an old one. The siding has been removed recently.

Plate 34. *One-room, one-and-a-half story house. The extention of the roof on the gable end is unusual, as is the use of but one window in the long wall.*

wall directly opposite those in the front wall. The fireplace is centered in one of the short, or gable, walls. The staircase, which is enclosed or Indiana follow a consistent pattern. They are composed of a room which is rectangular in shape, having interior dimensions about 23 feet long by 16 feet wide. The thickness of the walls, of course, dictates that the interior dimensions must be about 1 1/2 feet less than the exterior dimensions. In addition, there will normally be a fireplace centered in one of the shorter walls, and there will be doors and windows in the longer walls with the door centered in the wall. It does not matter whether the house consists of one room on the ground floor or two rooms on the ground floor, or whether it is two stories or one story; each room will conform closely to the description given above. When a house has more than one room, however, each room will be shorter than 23 feet, more nearly square.

It would seem that the most compelling reasons for this consistency in form concern the way in which the room is heated, ventilated, and lighted. It must be true that a rectangular room of the dimensions given above can be adequately heated and lighted by a single fireplace located in the center of a short wall. Both heat and light radiate from a fireplace in a predictable way, and it will be noted by referring to the illustration (Fig. 5.2a and Fig. 5.2b) that there are two "dead spots" in the corners of the room (beside the fireplace) which the radiating heat and light will not reach. One of these is taken up by the staircase so that there is, in effect, only one "dead spot" in the room, and it is comparatively small.

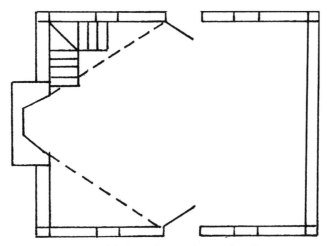

Fig. 5.2a Heat and light radiating from a fireplace in a typical rectangular one-room house.

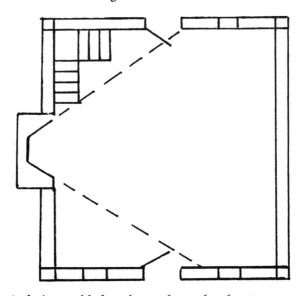

Fig. 5.2b Heat and light radiating from a fireplace in a square one-room house with the same amount of floor space.

Heat and light from the fireplace are, of course, most important in the winter when days are short and cold. In the heat of summer, when days are long, ventilation is of great importance in keeping a room cool. Windows and doors which can be opened, located in the long walls of the room, provide the best possible ventilation, usually referred to as "cross ventilation." Because the overhang of the eaves protects doors and windows located in the long walls from rain, they are normally in the long walls rather than the shorter walls. Moreover, the placement of the fireplace in one short wall makes it impractical to place doors and windows in that wall. In order to get true cross ventilation, therefore, the doors and windows must be in the long walls.

At all times of the year illumination by natural light is the best that is available during daylight hours. A rectangular room not much more than 18 feet wide will get the greatest amount of light in the interior if the windows and doors are evenly spaced on the long walls rather than being on the short walls. These houses were built in an era when grease, fat, and oils were in short supply, coming mainly from animals as a by-product of butchering, preserving, and cooking. They were the only source of soap, for soap was made by treating them with lye made from wood ashes. Consquently, artificial light such as from candles or Betty lamps was used as little as possible. People rose early in the mornings and went to bed early at night by modern standards to take advantage of natural light. It was important to have the best possible light in a room so that exacting tasks such as sewing and spinning could be done early in the morning and late in the evening, and on dark, cloudy winter days.

Let us look at some other alternatives to see why they would not be as feasible as the rectangular room described above. Why was the room rectangular rather than square? By referring to the illustrations (Fig. 5.2b) one can see that, in a square room with the same amount of floor space as the rectangular room, the "dead spots" where the light and heat radiating from the fireplace do not reach are somewhat larger than in a rectangular room. Moreover, the greater width of a square room with the same amount of floor space allows for less adequate natural light from the windows at the center of the room. In houses with two rooms on the ground floor, rooms are more nearly square, but they are the same width as in the one-room house, and hence have less floor space.

If radiating heat and light from a fireplace are so important, why was a fireplace not built in the corner as is done in many log buildings in Scandinavia? The heat and light radiating from a corner fireplace reach every point in the room so that there are no "dead spaces" such as are described above. It might be possible to build a corner fireplace so that it is partially inside and partially outside the house. In this way the chimney could pass up the outside of the house and not pass through the roof. Several logs at the corner of the house would have to be cut with such a fireplace, however, and the basic structure would be seriously weakened.

If a corner fireplace were set inside the walls as is done in Scandinavia, another problem would result. The chimney would have to pass up through the roof in such a way that, when it rained, water would leak into the room in substantial amounts (Fig. 5.3). As long as wooden shingles are used for roofing and as long as large sheets of thin metal are not available for flashing, there seems to be no way of avoiding such a problem. When one looks at the log houses in

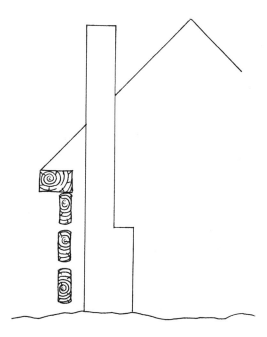

Fig. 5.3 Detail of how the chimney would pass through the roof if the fireplace were in the corner and within the walls. Note how rainwater running down the roof, would be trapped by the chimney to leak into the house.

Scandinavia, especially those old ones preserved in the Scandinavian folk museums, part of their charm is the roofs. Many of them are covered with sod which may be green and have flowers adorning it in the summer. What the casual observer does not notice is that under the sod there is a layer of large sheets of birch bark. The sod is there to hold the birch bark on the roof without the use of nails which would cause leaks. It might be noted, too, that the sod is a useful insulator and that, in the winter, it helps hold snow on the roof as additional insulation. To return to the subject of the birch bark, however, it may be seen that a sheet of it can be brought down the roof and curled up against the side of the chimney in such a way that water coming down the roof cannot run down into the room. In Indiana neither birch bark nor a suitable substitute was available, and people generally chose to avoid the problem of keeping rain water from leaking around a chimney which passes through the roof. In most log houses the chimney rises outside the exterior wall and doesn't pass through the roof at all.

It should be noted that a room which is not adequately heated, lighted, and ventilated cannot be fully utilized year round. Rooms on the ground floor in early log houses almost always have a fireplace and doors and windows. If there is no fireplace in a later log house, there is at least provision for a stove. It is a different matter with rooms on the second floor, if any, because such rooms were utilized primarily as sleeping quarters. Some two-story houses do, indeed, have fireplaces in the second-story rooms, but these fireplaces are so tiny that they could not have held a large fire. More rooms on the second floor did not have a fireplace, but they at least had windows so that the room could be ventilated during the summer. We must assume that second-story rooms without fireplaces must have provided pretty cold sleeping quarters during the winter. Some heat, of course, would rise from the downstairs rooms, but not much. In really cold weather, beds must have been provided with a large number of quilts, comforters, and blankets.

In one-and-a-half-story houses, it is very rare to find a fireplace in the overhead sleeping loft. Moreover, there are very few windows, usually no more than one very small one in each gable end. These sleeping lofts must have been uncomfortable both in cold weather and in hot weather. We have no way of knowing how much they were used in the winter and the summer.

As noted above, the most common log house in southern Indiana consists of a single room on the ground floor with a sleeping loft overhead (Fig. 5.4). The term "one-and-a-half-story," while frequently used, is somewhat imprecise. It is clear that a one-story house would have no living or sleeping space above the first floor though there might be storage space in the attic area under the roof. If there is no

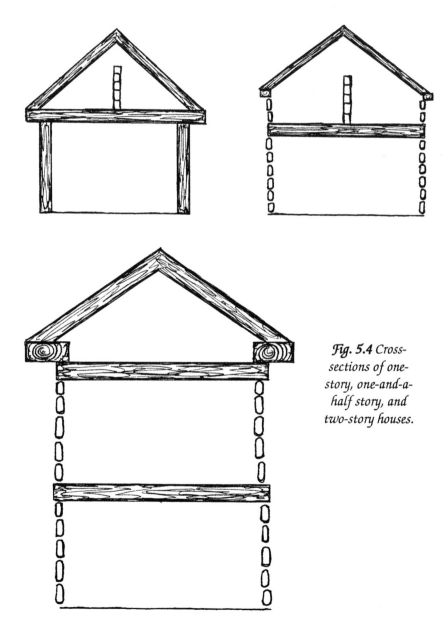

Fig. 5.4 Cross-sections of one-story, one-and-a-half story, and two-story houses.

stairway in a house, we would be justified in calling it a one-story house. This is a fairly common form in frame houses, but is rare in log houses. A true two-story house would have rooms on the second floor of nearly the same height as those on the first floor and, on the second floor, the ceiling would extend to the side walls without any break. Between these two categories, however, there are many possible variations. The side walls for the second-story rooms may be of almost any height, ranging from a few feet high to almost as high as the ceiling. Most log houses that are less than a full two stories have side walls in the sleeping loft that are between three and four feet high. The joists which support the floor of the loft and also form the ceiling for the first floor rest in notches that are cut into a log so that the ground floor is about eight feet high. Then there are usually two additional logs in the side wall plus the plate. Such an arrangement made an effective compromise between a one-story house and a two-story house. Beds were probably placed against the side wall and the occupants of the room could then stand upright towards the center of the room. The major drawback to this arrangement is that windows could not be conveniently placed in the side walls for the sleeping loft. Not only would they have to have been very small and close to the floor, but they would have been blocked by the beds.

For the purposes of this study, I have classified houses which do not have windows in the long, or side, walls for the second floor as one-and-a-half-story houses whether the side walls for the sleeping loft are only a few feet high or nearly the full height. It would seem to be splitting hairs to try to distinguish between, let us say, one-and-a-quarter-, one-and-a-half-, and one-and-three-quarter-story houses. If, on the other hand, the side walls are of substantial height and have windows in them, I have classified the house as a two-story house.

It should be borne in mind that almost all log houses have staircases, indicating that the loft was used for sleeping rather than solely for storage. In a small house where every square foot of floor space is utilized, it would seem unlikely that a space-consuming staircase would be built if the loft were intended only for storage. Hence, there are practically no log houses which should be classified as one-story houses.

The second most common log house type, though far less common than the one-room, one-and-a-half-story house, is the two-room, one-and-a-half-story house. Of 296 houses investigated, 46 (or 15.5

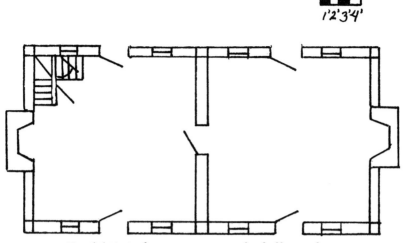

1'2'3'4'

Fig. 5.5 *Typical two-room, one-and-a-half story house.*

percent) are of this type (Fig. 5.5). The average length of these houses is 31 feet and the average width is 18 feet 3 inches. Because there are some relatively small houses but none that are unusually large, the typical two-room house is about 36 feet by 19 feet. The partition which separates the two rooms is almost always of logs, though some few are of frame construction. The partition divides the house exactly in half so that each room is the same size. Almost always each room has its own front and back doors, and each room has a fireplace on the exterior end wall. The logs which make up the long walls almost always run the full length of the house and it must have required special effort to find twelve or more trees which would yield logs 36 feet or longer, to hew them, and to raise them into place. Normally these houses have but one staircase which is located beside the fireplace in one of the rooms. (See Plates 35, 36, on following page.)

TWO-STORY HOUSES

The next most common house type is a two-story house with two rooms on each floor. I located 22 of these, or 7.4 percent of the whole. The dimensions of these houses are slightly larger than the one-and-a-half-story houses with two rooms on the ground floor, for the average size of the two-story houses is 33 feet by 19 feet and the typical house is 36 feet by 20 feet. Most of what has been said for the one-and-a-half-story house with two rooms concerning the size of the rooms, the

Plate 35. *Two-room, one-and-a-half-story house. At the time the house was built, a lean-to addition of frame construction was built across the back; hence, there are no windows in the log wall in this back side of the house. The old fireplaces and chimneys have been removed.*

Plate 36. *Detail showing how the logs forming the partition between the rooms are fitted into the front and back walls of a two-room house.*

doors, and the fireplaces may likewise be said of the two-story houses with one exception. In a number of cases where I was able to examine the interior of the house, there were two staircases to the second floor, one in each room, and there was no door in the partition separating the two rooms on the second floor. If one were in one of the bedrooms on the second floor and wanted to get to the other bedroom, he had to go downstairs and go up the other staircase. I was unable to enter many of these two-story, four-room houses because many of them are still lived in and because the owners were not home when I visited the houses. I cannot, therefore, offer figures as to how many houses use this seemingly awkward arrangement, but it does seem to be common in southern Indiana. On the basis mainly of infrequent and random field trips in states other than Indiana, it seems to me that this two-staircase pattern is a relatively common feature in the southern part of the United States in early houses.

A writer drawing upon statistics that must have been compiled by the National Park Service in 1935 has this to say of the log houses in the Blue Ridge area that became Shenandoah National Park:

> Most of the houses were of ax-hewn logs, though often covered outside by weather-boarding in various stages of decay.... The 465 homes left in the park area in 1935 averaged 3.9 rooms each, and a few had six rooms or more. There was nearly always a private bedroom for the parents, and often another occupied by a grandparent or another elderly relative. The children generally slept in attics; the sexes were separated by a solid wall and used independent entrance . . . from different rooms downstairs.[2]

A native of Philadelphia visiting Bloomington, Indiana, in 1822 or 1823 commented on many aspects of life which were different from what he was accustomed to and which he therefore considered crude and backward. Those things he found to be familiar to him from his past experience, of course, he thought to be signs of civilization and progress. Like most travelers before and since, however, he noticed mostly the unfamiliar. At any rate, he visited a large brick house built in Bloomington by Dr. David H. Maxwell. The Philadelphian, Baynard Rush Hall, wrote in his usual supercilious manner years after his visit:

> From the [two] rooms [on the ground floor] doors apiece opened into the street; and as these were very rarely ever shut, summer

or winter, the whole house may be said to have been out of doors. In fact, as the chimneys were awfully given to smoking, it was usually as comfortless within the rooms as without. But in each of the small rooms a large space was cut off in one corner for a staircase; each stairway leading to separate dormitories in the fractional story--the dormitories being kept apart, as well as could be done, by laths and plaster. Often wondering at this dissocial wall upstairs, I once inquired of Mrs. Sylvan [Mrs. Maxwell] what it was for, who answered,

"Oh! sir, I had it done *on* purpose--"

"On purpose!--it wasn't accidental, then?"

"Law! bless you, no!--it was to keep the boys and girls apart."

Now where, pray, had modesty in the far east ever built for her two staircases and a plastered wall, and to the discomfort of a whole family? Yet, vain care! The boys had perforated the partition with peep-holes; but these were kept plugged by the girls on their side with tow, so that their own consent was necessary to the use of said apertures. Still I was told the syringes from the shop were often used on both sides of the wall, to give illustrations and lessons in hydraulics, little perhaps to edification, but very much to the fun of both squirters and squirted: proof that even among Hoosiers and all other wild men, "love laughs at locksmiths."[3]

Elsewhere in his descriptive comments, Hall cites examples of what he considers immodesty, such as the necessity for men and women staying in a one-room log house with no sleeping loft to undress in the same room. If it is different from what he is accustomed to, it is either modesty or immodesty depending on the whim of the observer. Different customs cannot be viewed as simply different and often the outcome of conditions which are purely physical; the observer must give a value judgment. In the instance of the separated rooms, Hall does not feel it worthwhile to report that sleeping on the girls' side there were probably some servant girls not blood members of the family, and sleeping on the boys' side there were probably some servant boys likewise not blood members of the family. The parents sleeping downstairs probably felt much more comfortable about the situation with a partition between the rooms. Note, too, that the house, although of brick, is a one-and-half-story structure with two rooms on the ground floor, each with its own fireplace and each with its own front door. As I have said elsewhere in this work, log houses in southern Indiana are generally of the same shape and size and have the same characteristic patterns as do houses of masonry and frame construction. Note, too, that Hall, in this early use of the word "Hoosier," gives it what undoubtedly was its original meaning, namely, "wild man" or backwoodsman.

Almost as common as the two-story house with two rooms on each floor is the two-story house with only a single room on each floor. There are 19 of these houses, or about 7 percent of the total. They average in floor plan 24 feet by 18 feet 9 inches. The room on the ground floor is exactly like the standard room described before as regards the fireplace, staircase, doors, and windows. The room on the second floor likewise has usually a fireplace in the end wall and windows on the long walls. For obvious reasons, however, it has no front or back door. (See Plates 37, 38; plate 38 is on following page.)

Log houses of this type present a somewhat unusual appearance, being taller and with less mass than one is accustomed to. However, building them presented a logical and relatively simple solution to the

Plate 37. A two-story house with one room on each floor.

Plate 38. *Two-story house with one room on each floor.*

problem of gaining additional space in a log house. There are, of course, a number of ways of building a log house with more than one room. One way that some builders chose was simply to find extremely long logs to build two rooms on the ground floor as in the house types described above. Another way was to build two separate and distinct log structures and to join them with some sort of frame connector as will be described below. A process much simpler than either of the above solutions was to build the usual structure with one room on the ground floor and then to continue adding logs to the side and end walls until the walls were a full two stories in height. In this way no extra long logs were needed and there was likewise no need to build a rather complicated frame connector between two complete and separate log structures. Hence it is not surprising that a number of builders chose the two-story house with one room on each floor.

OTHER HOUSE TYPES

A log house type common in the southern part of the United States and frequently mentioned in literature on log buildings[4] is the so-called "dog-trot" house. This house type consists of two independent log structures with an open space between them but with a common roof. They are built in such a way that there is a log room on each side of a central breezeway (Fig. 5.6). I have found only seven log houses which approximate this plan. Four are one-and-a-half-story structures and three are two-story. They average 44 feet by 19 feet in floor plan. I do not, however, believe that it is appropriate to call these Indiana buildings dog-trot houses, even though the term has a pleasantly quaint aura about it. Superficially they resemble the dog-trot house in that, on the ground floor, there are two log rooms separated from one another by about six feet. When it is borne in mind that most Indiana log houses were covered with siding from the time they were built, it will be realized that we actually have a large two-room house with a central hallway. It is only when the siding has fallen off or been taken off such a house that it resembles a dog-trot house.

In these houses there are fireplaces in the exterior end walls, and each room has windows in the long walls, but there is only one doorway in the long walls. One entered the house via the hallway and doors to the two rooms opened off the hall. The staircase to the second floor is also normally in the hallway. In other words, there is little difference in floor plan between these large log homes and large frame or masonry houses of the same era. With siding covering the

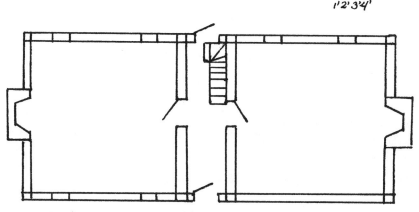

Fig. 5.6 Two-story, central-hall ("dog-trot") house, or log I-house.

whole house, the casual observer would mistake it for a large and impressive frame house. It is probably safe to say, too, that this is the way the builders of the house wanted it to be. They may not have wanted passers-by to think that they lived in a "log cabin," but they probably wanted the strength, solidity, and superb insulation of log construction.

Students of folk architecture have long used the term "I-house" for a two-story house with two rooms on each floor, usually with a central hallways.[5] The older examples often have fireplaces and chimneys on the exterior end walls and a one- or two-story ell at the rear. Either in frame or masonry construction, these houses are commonly found in the central and southern parts of the eastern United States and in areas westward where settlers from those regions moved. Indeed, I-houses of frame or brick construction are common in southern Indiana both in the countryside and in towns. The Indiana houses of log which have just been described can best be called log I-houses if they are two-story, and a useful, though somewhat cumbersome, term for the one-and-a-half-story examples would be one-and-a-half-story log I-houses. When the log examples are in good condition with the usual siding intact, it would be very difficult to tell them from frame I-houses of the same period. (See Plate 39.)

Plate 39. Log I-house. The siding had been removed from this house a few years before the photo was taken.

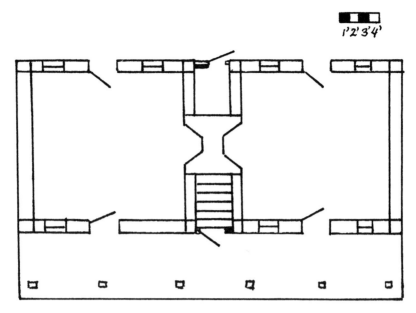

Fig. 5.7 Typical saddle-bags house, built in two stages.

Another log house type common in the southern United States and frequently mentioned in literature on log buildings has been called the "saddle-bags" house, though I have not heard this term in Indiana. This type is relatively uncommon in southern Indiana, however, for only three were found for this survey. They average 41 feet by 18 feet. This house type has two basically separate log structures which share a common chimney stack and a common roof (Fig. 5.7). An examination of the three houses showed that in each the two log rooms must have been built at different times, for the workmanship on the logs was markedly different in the two rooms. We may assume that a person living in a one-room, one-and-a-half-story house wanted more living space and decided to build another room. Rather than adding on at the end away from the fireplace, he added on at the end with the fireplace in it. This demanded a complex piece of masonry building, for each fireplace requires a separate fire box and a separate flue. None of the three houses has a door in the walls between the two rooms, but each room has a front and a back door and the houses all have front porches. In order to get from one room to the other, one used the porch as a hallway.

Four houses were found in which two separate log structures were built with the gable ends directly against one another. The average

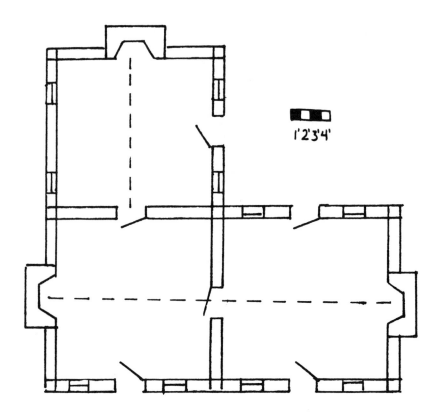

Fig. 5.8 L-shaped log house. Dotted lines show peak of the roof.

dimensions are 41 feet 6 inches by 18 feet. In each case it appeared that the two log structures had been built at different times even though they shared a common roof. The fireplaces were on the exterior ends and the rooms duplicated one another in respect to doors and windows.

In two houses the same complex form of construction was used, for they were "L" shaped, each with three rooms. One was 36 feet by 34 feet while the other was 32 feet by 31 feet. The floor plan (Fig. 5.8) will best explain the construction method, but it may be noted that a large number--about thirty--of unusually long logs were required in each house. These houses are about fourteen miles from one another as the crow flies, and one wonders if they were not

Plate 40. *L-shaped house. All of the fireplaces and their chimneys had been removed and windows built into the openings thus left.*

built by the same person or the same family, for they are certainly unusual. (See Plate 40.)

Only one house is unique in the survey. It has two rooms on the ground floor, but one half is two-story while one half is one-story. It appears that it was built that way at the beginning and was not the result of remodeling.

Of the houses investigated, ten had log rooms attached so as to form an extension at the rear of the main house. There seemed to be no observable pattern involved. Some of the houses were large two-story structures with two rooms on each floor so that the log room at the rear added a fifth room, usually serving as a kitchen. Some of the houses, however, were one-and-a-half-story, one-room houses so that the additional log room doubled the space available. Always, however, there was some framed connecting construction between the main house and the extra room.

OTHER BUILDINGS

In addition to the houses which have been described in preceding chapters there are other kinds of log buildings in southern Indiana such as churches, smokehouses, and barns. The construction features of these other buildings are basically the same as for houses. The logs are shaped in the same way and joined together at the corners in the same ways, for example. In treating these other buildings, therefore, their sizes, shapes, and floor plans will be described, but construction features will be discussed only when these differ in some significant way from those of the houses.

CHURCHES

A number of log churches were built in the nineteenth century. Indeed, some rural congregations have built churches of log construction in the twentieth century, but since these are usually of round poles, their construction differs markedly from those of hewn logs, and they will not be described. A fair number of nineteenth-century hewn-log churches have survived to the present. People are not so apt to destroy a church as they are to destroy a house. Moreover, in the countryside the land on which a church stands has often been dedicated for church use and there is often a cemetery partially surrounding the church. There is, therefore, little likelihood that the land will be used for agriculture so the church is allowed to stand.

Often these churches are found in rural areas which once were well populated, but people have moved away, farms have been deserted, and woods have now reclaimed many of the fields. Often it is only the churches and their cemeteries which remind the casual visitor that he is surrounded by a once-thriving farming area. Probably in most cases the church was once viewed as the center of a farm community, not a community in the sense of a town but a community of people held together by bonds of friendship and family relationships.

Many of these churches are used today only occasionally. There may be a service every other week or there may be only special services once or twice a year attended by the descendants of families that once lived in the area. At any rate, these churches and their cemeteries are maintained and are usually in reasonably good condition.

Rural churches in Protestant regions of southern Indiana are usually not large and elaborate buildings. Often if one compares the log churches with their nearby counterparts of frame construction one will find they are essentially the same in size, shape, and floor plan. Since the log churches are often covered with horizontal clapboards painted white, they look very much like the frame churches.

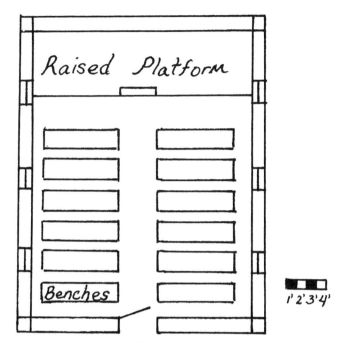

Fig. 5.9 *Typical log church with one front door.*

The log churches average about 30 feet long by 24 feet wide. They might be said to be simply large one-room log houses from the standpoint of their construction, except for two important details.

First, their doors are never in the long walls as they are in log houses, but are instead in one of the gable-end walls (Fig. 5.9). Usually the gable-end of the building with the door, or doors, in it faces the road. The interior lay-out of the churches seemingly dictates this door placement. The pulpit is at one end of the church, usually on a slightly raised platform that has space for a choir. Rows of benches occupy the floor in front of the pulpit. It is convenient, therefore, to have the entrance to the church in the wall behind the benches. In this way the seating arrangement is not broken up and late-comers to a service can enter the church at the rear without disrupting the service. Some churches have a single door in the center of the gable-end wall while others have two doors in this wall. In those churches with two doors the sexes were separated during the services. (See Plates 41, 42; see next page.)

The second way churches differ from houses is that no log church that I have ever seen in southern Indiana has ever had a fireplace. Most of them now have a stove with a long metal pipe leading to a

Plate 41. *Church with one front door.*

Plate 42. *Church with two front doors.*

small chimney, but they never show any indication that they ever had a fireplace. The absence of fireplaces raises some puzzling questions when we bear in mind that stoves do not seem to have been used in rural areas in southern Indiana before about 1875. Were services simply not held in really cold weather? Many churches were served by circuit-riding ministers who may not have made their rounds in the depth of winter. Were people able to obtain stoves for churches long before they used stoves in their homes? There were tin footstoves available before 1875, but they would not keep one very warm for very long. It is possible that church records contain the answers to these questions, but most church histories I have been able to read are silent on the matter of how early churches were heated or if they were.

BARNS

A large number of log barns must have been built in southern Indiana in the nineteenth century. Often, in talking with the owners of barns of frame construction, I have been told that they can remember or their fathers have told them how the old log barn was torn down and replaced by the frame barn. Log barns were well adapted to the subsistence type of farming whereby each farm grew mostly the crops and raised the animals needed to sustain the family and sold or traded very little of their produce. As the nineteenth century progressed and most farmers began to concentrate on producing larger quantities which could be sold, the log barns often proved to be too small for their needs. Larger frame barns were built, but they in their turn have proved to be inadequate to the needs of large-scale mechanized farming. They, too, are now being neglected or torn down. It is mainly in those regions in southern Indiana where the terrain makes large-scale mechanized farming unfeasible that log barns are still found. Some are still in use, though they are ill-suited to store modern farm machinery, but still more are falling into decay because they are not used.

The most common log barn consists of a single set, or pen, of logs surrounded by sheds of frame construction. Fifty-nine barns of this type were located. The average length of the log pens was 21 feet 6 inches, the smallest being 16 feet long and the largest 40 feet. The average width was 18 feet 6 inches with the smallest 13 feet and the largest 30 feet. The fact that most barns have frame sheds on all four

Plate 43. Single-pen barn.

sides means that the overall dimensions of the barns are considerably larger. (See Plate 43.)

The construction of these log pens is relatively simple when compared to a house, for almost always they have only a dirt floor and comparatively few openings cut into the logs. The log pens are usually five or six feet higher than a log house. It appears as if animals were stabled in the frame sheds while the central log portion of the barn was used for the storage of hay and grain. Abandoned log houses have often been turned into barns, but the presence or absence of an opening for a fireplace cut into the end log wall indicates the original use of the structure. In this study houses which have been turned into barns have been treated as houses and have not been included in the tabulation of barns. In all barns the interstices between the logs are normally not filled with chinking but are left open to facilitate circulation of air.

Many barn builders must have considered the single pen barn to be inadequate to their needs. They built barns consisting of two log

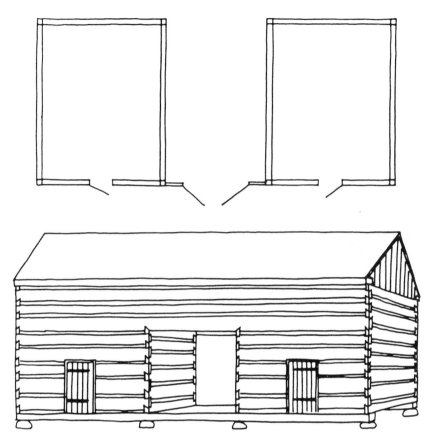

Fig. 5.10 *Double-crib log barn. Sheds on all four sides not shown.
Main doors and other details omitted to show log portions more clearly.*

pens with a central passageway between them. At a height of about twelve feet, the two pens are joined together by two or three logs and a plate which span the entire structure (Fig. 5.10). These barns are often of imposing dimensions. Of the 35 examples located, the average overall length of the log portions was 49 feet, but one was as long as 72 feet while five were over 60 feet long. The average width was 22 feet 6 inches, the largest being 26 feet. When one realizes that wooden sheds on all four sides may extend the total length and width by as much as 30 feet, it can be seen that some of these barns are really large. In many barns, too, the four or six logs and the two plates that run the entire length of the barn are in unbroken lengths. The longest of these timbers that I have ever seen came from a barn that had been pulled down a few years before I visited the site, but the two plates were still lying on the ground. They were 72 feet long. The trees from which these two plates came must have been very straight and free of branches for at least 72 feet, but the virgin forests in Indiana contained many remarkable specimens.

Most of these double pen barns have a dirt floor in the passageway between the log pens. The farmer was able to drive his loaded hay wagon into this passageway and pitch the hay up into the large lofts over the log pens. When these areas were filled he could move timbers across the top of the passageway and use that area for hay storage as well. Six of the thirty-five barns, however, had wooden floors in the passageway. These floors, which are sometimes called "tramping floors," could be used for threshing. Wheat and other grain stored in one of the log pens could be pitched out onto the wooden floor and threshed from time to time as needed. Usually one of the log pens was used for stabling animals, and the frame sheds surrounding the log portions of the barn were used for miscellaneous storage. In about two-thirds of these barns the log pens are of about equal size, but in about a third of them one of the pens is quite small, seemingly built as a corn crib.

SMOKEHOUSES

Even if we did not know it from other sources, we could still determine that pork was an important part of the diet in the nineteenth century in southern Indiana from a study of the architecture. Almost every farm in the area has a smokehouse or once had one. Hogs are still raised and slaughtered for home consumption, but most people on farms today have their butchering done at slaughtering plants and store their meat in freezers. Consequently, the smokehouses still standing tend to be used for miscellaneous storage. Originally they were used for smoking the meat and storing it. Hams and bacon were first cured for a period of time with salt and sugar. Then they were hung from hooks in the rafters and ceiling of the smokehouse and a small fire was built on the floor in an old iron kettle or something similar. The fire was kept small so that it would produce smoke instead of flame. Hickory and sassafras were the most favored woods for the fire. After a week or two of the smoking process, the meat would keep for a long time. It was usually simply left in the smokehouse hanging from the hooks. Other foods were likewise stored in the smokehouse. Hence this building was usually located near the house, the house facing the road and smokehouse behind it. Six of the smokehouses seen were built over fruit cellars, making a combined food storage unit under one roof.

Smokehouses may be of frame or of log construction. A very few are built of brick. Whatever the type of construction, they are all very similar to one another in size and shape. Twenty-eight log smokehouses were found. They varied in length from 11 to 16 feet, the average being 14 feet. Their widths ranged from 7 feet 6 inches to 14 feet with an average of 11 feet 6 inches. It can, therefore, be seen that there is a marked consistency in the sizes of log smokehouses when compared to houses and barns. Not only are the dimensions quite consistent but other features are also. Almost all the smokehouses (26 of the 28) had doors in one of the gable ends and the plates and the roofs were built in such a way that they extended out over the gable end with the door in it. While this extension of the plates and the roof protected the doorway from rain, it also in earlier times was used to hang up meat during the butchering or curing process. (See Plates 44, 45; plate 45 is on next page.)

Plate 44. *Smokehouse of wooden-frame construction.*

Plate 45. *Smokehouse of log construction.*

There seems to be little need for the overhanging roof in the slaughtering routine as followed in the twentieth century, for the animal is killed early in the morning and the butchering completed during the day. In earlier times, however, the routine differed. In the evening of one day the hog was killed and the bristles removed, and it was gutted. The carcase was then hung up and left overnight. The next day the actual butchering, sausage making, and lard rendering were done. The overhanging roof of the smokehouse provided an excellent place to hang the carcase overnight, protecting it from dew and any rain that might fall. In some regions in England where smokehouses are not common, it was customary to hang the carcase overnight in the porch of the church.[7]

CORNCRIBS

Eight log corncribs were located in the course of fieldwork for this study. They are relatively narrow structures averaging 18 feet long and 7 feet wide. No chinking is used between the logs in order to allow air to circulate freely through the stored corn, and there are usually small doors at each end (See Plate 46, next page). One double log corncrib was seen with two log cribs under a common roof with a driveway between.

Plate 46. Corncrib.

MISCELLANEOUS STRUCTURES

Twelve miscellaneous storage buildings of log were seen which can probably best be called sheds. They were usually small, under 20 feet in length, and about half of them appeared to have been built of logs salvaged from other structures.

Other structures of log included two large houses which may have been inns, two small maple sugar houses, four granaries, two gunsmith's shops, and a blacksmith's shop. (See Plates 47, 48, 49, next two pages.) One log house was seen which had once had on its second floor a harnessmaker's shop. It is perhaps noteworthy that no log schoolhouses were located, although early written records mention such buildings and a number of people interviewed remembered them.

It is quite possible that there are still standing in southern Indiana towns log buildings which were once used as stores, craft shops, offices, and the like. It is certainly true that occasionally when old buildings are torn down in towns and cities it is discovered that parts of them are of log construction. It is usually impossible to tell whether such structures were originally houses or whether they were other types of buildings. In the mid-1960s, for example, a structure was torn down in Spencer. Part of it was built of hewn logs, and a number of people believed that this part was the original log county court-

Plate 47. *Granary.*

Plate 48. *Maple sugar camp.*

Plate 49. *Log building once used as a gunsmith's shop.*

house. The central part of a building only two blocks from the Indiana University campus in Bloomington is a log structure that probably was originally a house. These log buildings in towns and cities have usually been so modified by additions and other changes that it is impossible to recognize them for what they are.

SPECIAL TYPES OF CONSTRUCTION

There is a remarkable consistency in southern Indiana in the ways in which structures are built of horizontal, hewn logs, as has been shown. A few variations, however, are worthy of comment. The first of these concerns special features found in log buildings in two areas which are predominantly German-American. One of these is mostly in Dubois County, though the German-American settlement area extends into other counties to the south and west of Dubois County. The area, then, includes most of Dubois County except for the northeast part, and parts of Warrick, Spencer, Perry, Crawford, and Pike counties. This area has been investigated with reasonable thoroughness so that valid generalizations can be made about the log buildings there.

The second area is in Franklin County, centering around Oldenburg. This area has not been investigated so thoroughly so that less can be said with certainty about the log buildings there. In both of these areas a large proportion of the population is Catholic. Most of the immigrants to these areas from Germany came during the 1840s and later.[8] It should, perhaps, be mentioned that the German settlers were not Pennsylvania Germans. The German immigrants to Pennsylvania came, for the most part, at an earlier date and were mainly of the Protestant faith.

For the Dubois County area, data on 13 log houses, 20 log barns, and 15 other log structures are available for this study. A number of other log buildings have been observed in this area and their general characteristics noted, but detailed records have not been compiled for them. Almost all the log buidings resemble those found in other parts of Indiana in a number of ways. In particular, the ways in which the logs are shaped by hewing and the ways in which they are fitted together at the corners are the same. Moreover, the logs are fitted in such a way that interstices of various sizes are left between the logs to be filled with chinking in houses and left open in barns, as in other areas. Too, the outsides of log houses are almost invariably covered with horizontal siding. So similar are these features in the German-American and the British-American areas of southern Indiana that one must assume that the German immigrants to the Dubois County area learned a great deal about building with logs from the British-Americans among whom they settled. It is unlikely that these aspects of log construction were almost exactly the same in those areas of Germany from which the immigrants came.

There are, however, a number of ways in which the log buildings in these two German-American areas differ from those in other parts of southern Indiana. The most striking difference concerns a structural detail in which one log in each short or gable wall extends forward from the wall for several feet. These logs support an extension of the roof which forms a front porch for houses and a protective roof overhang on barns (Fig. 5.11, next page). Sometimes the same log extends from the back wall so as to support the roof for a shed extension on barns and houses. Sometimes one log in each wall extends to the front and one to the rear. At any rate, this feature is very common in the Dubois County area and has been observed in the Franklin County area. I have not seen it in any other part of Indiana. (See Plates 50, 51, second page following.)

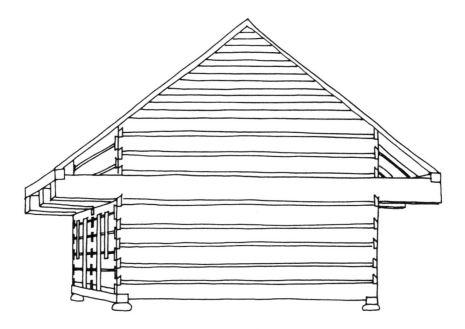

Fig 5.11 *Log house from Dubois County area. Details omitted to show logs clearly.*

The most common log house in British-American areas of southern Indiana consists of but a single room on the ground floor while the second most common house has two rooms of equal size on the ground floor. Houses with but a single room on the first floor, however, are very rare in the German-American areas, for only one of the thirteen houses measured was of this type. The houses in these areas almost all have two rooms on the ground floor, usually of unequal size. It follows, then, that the German-American houses are larger than one-room British-American log houses but not as large as British-American two-room houses. The average size of the log houses in the Dubois County area is 29 feet by 18 feet 6 inches. Most of these houses have two front doors, one for each room.

Almost all log houses built in British-American parts of southern Indiana have fireplaces. It is only relatively late log houses, those from the last two decades of the nineteenth century and the early twentieth century, that do not have fireplaces but use stoves for heating and cooking. On the other hand, fireplaces are relatively uncommon in the German-American areas. In the Dubois County region in particular only two log houses were found to have fireplaces. Houses built at

Plate 50. *Double-pen barn in Dubois County with the "porch" roof supported by projecting logs.*

Plate 51. *One of the projecting logs supporting the "porch" roof.*

a reasonably early date, seemingly in the 1850s, for instance, were built without fireplaces.

It would seem that the German immigrants who came to the Dubois County area were accustomed to having stoves in their homeland. Stoves must have been difficult to obtain and expensive in the Dubois County area. Some newcomers from Germany built fireplaces, not like those of their British-American neighbors which are always on an exterior end wall, but on the interior of the house, against the partition that separated the two rooms. This is probably the way they remembered them from their homeland. Most of the German immigrants, however, went to the trouble and expense of obtaining stoves. It should be borne in mind that fireplaces and stoves not only are used to heat a house but also are used for cooking. The ways of cooking at a stove and at a fireplace are rather different, and different kinds of utensils are needed. It would seem that the immigrants from Germany who had become accustomed to stoves did not, for the most part, want to change to fireplaces.

In sum, then, it may be said that the German immigrants to the two areas seemingly learned much about how to hew logs and join them together for buildings from the British-Americans among whom they settled. The houses and barns they built, however, incorporated some features which must represent an architectural inheritance from Germany. These features include a special way of supporting extended roofs in houses and barns, and, in houses, included a special floor plan and a strong preference for stoves for heating and cooking.

A single house was seen that used a type of construction markedly different from any others found in southern Indiana. This house, located near Patricksburg, has horizontal hewn logs for its walls, but the logs do not interlock with one another at the corners. Instead, there is a large, squared vertical post at each corner. On the appropriate two sides there are large grooves cut into this vertical post. Each horizontal log has a large tongue cut on its end which fits into this groove. Large wooden pins are driven through the post and the tongue to keep the horizontal logs in place (Fig. 5.12, next page). The horizontal logs do not fit closely upon one another. Instead, there are interstices between the logs which are chinked in the usual way. (See Plate 52, second page following.) The entire house was originally covered with horizontal siding.

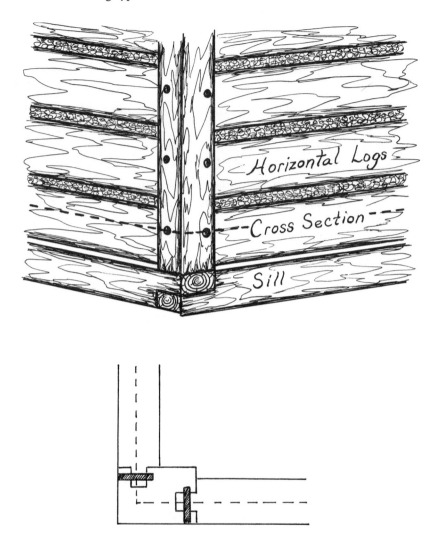

Horizontal Logs

Cross Section

Sill

Fig. 5.12

This house, therefore, represents an interesting combination of many features of true horizontal log construction with some features from heavy frame construction. This form of construction seems quite rare for it has not been described in written sources to the best of my knowledge.[9] However, several years ago Henry Glassie showed me a few houses built in this way which were located near Dillsburg, Pennsylvania, in a predominantly Pennsylvania-German area. In the vicinity of Patricksburg where the Indiana example is located there

Plate 52. Log-and-corner-post construction.

must have been a substantial number of Pennsylvania German set-tlers. There are still standing in the area a number of barns of the type found in the German areas of Pennsylvania, and barns of this type are found in Ohio, Indiana, and westward where Pennsylvania Germans settled.[10] It would seem possible that some Pennsylvania German settler built this log and corner post building near Patricksburg, so different in many ways from other log buildings in southern Indiana.

Chapter Six

The Tools Used in Building Log Houses

IT WILL be convenient to list here the tools which were used in constructing the log houses which have been described in such detail in preceding chapters, even though some mention of tools has already been made. By listing all the tools we can not only better understand the buildings but we can also gain some insights about the craftsmen who built them and about the general conditions that prevailed at the time they were built. Because tools changed rapidly after the Civil War, thanks to the growth of factories, I will restrict myself to tools used in the first half of the century in southern Indiana. By reading histories and visiting museums that portray life in the area in that era, one gets the impression that life at that time was pretty simple and crude and that people had only a very few tools.

Trying to discover what tools were used in building the log houses that still stand in southern Indiana revealed that the available accounts are inadequate. One of the two kinds of written sources comprises the reminiscences of people who actually lived in Indiana in the early nineteenth century and who described log buildings. But these accounts describe the construction of the round-log *cabins* that were hastily built, temporary dwellings; no building of this type survives in southern Indiana. Although these writers often mention much more carefully built, hewn-log houses for the same period as the round-log cabins, they do not describe the building of hewn-log houses, the type that survives in southern Indiana. The accounts of the building of round-log cabins are often confusing and contradictory with regard to the tools used. While one writer says that these cabins were built with "an axe and a frow,"[1] another mentions "sawing" blocks from a white oak log and "boring holes," tasks requiring a saw and an auger.[2]

Another kind of source is recent writing describing log buildings. In the past decade two excellent surveys of log buildings have been published in the United States. C. A. Weslager's *The Log Cabin in America*[3] covers the entire United States but concentrates on the eastern part of the country for historical reasons, while Hutslar's "The Log Architecture of Ohio"[4] concentrates on one state rich in log buildings. Both works make it clear in a general way that there is a difference between the hastily constructed cabins built of round logs and intended as temporary shelter and the more carefully built hewn-log buildings intended to be more permanent. Because most of the round-log cabins have disappeared in the areas where these writers worked, they know of them mainly through historical accounts of various kinds. Their works are profusely illustrated with photos of extant log buildings, most of which are built of hewn logs. Each work devotes some pages to the tools used in constructing log buildings. While they do not emphasize this fact, the tools they list, very few in number, are the tools which might have served to build an extremely crude round-log cabin without, for instance, any windows or much of a door. The casual reader might well come away from these works with the mistaken notion that all log houses were built with a few simple tools. The extant hewn-log buildings which are illustrated in these works could not possibly have been built with the few tools listed. While both works distinguish between the round-log cabin and the hewn-log house in some ways, they tend to lump them together in listing the tools needed to build them. What seems to have happened is that the writers have used historical accounts of various kinds in describing the tools which they feel are appropriate both in kind and in number to the pioneer period. They have then ascribed the log houses which they illustrate in their works to this pioneer period. They conclude that the houses must have been built with the few tools they list. It would seem to be a safer process to examine the buildings themselves and to try to ascertain what tools were used in building them, especially since no detailed accounts seem to have been left by the builders or their contemporaries.

I have, therefore, relied mainly on fieldwork, examining four hundred log houses, most of them built in the first half of the nineteenth century. Many were tumbling down, making it possible to examine almost every detail of their construction. I have helped take apart five log houses, noting the details of their construction. My list of tools is based upon this experience.

Tools often leave characteristic marks, such as those left by an ax, a plane, or saw teeth. More often, I had to rely on a general knowledge of how tools are used and of the tools demanded by specific tasks. This general knowledge came from several sources, beyond my own craft experience. I interviewed older craftsmen who still use older tools or who learned about them from their fathers. I also examined collections of old tools, many in private hands. I have used works that describe older tools and their use, especially Henry C. Mercer's whose research began, as he says, "in the carpenter's tool chest of one hundred years ago."[5]

To illustrate how a general knowledge of the use of tools leads to inescapable conclusions, I give one example. Every log house that I have examined had wooden floors. True enough, accounts of round-log cabins mention dirt floors, but it is inconceivable that a hewn-log house could be built with a dirt floor and later have a wooden floor added. Hewn-log houses in southern Indiana always sit well up off the ground, upon stones at each corner. Without a wooden floor, they would have been uninhabitable. In every case, an original first-story floor was made of boards six to eight inches wide and about one and a quarter inches thick. The top surfaces of the boards had been planed smooth. The hidden bottom surfaces still showed the marks left by the saw that cut them from the log. The boards were always joined to one another by tongue-and-groove joints, and the boards were held down by nails driven diagonally through the tongue edge of one board so that the nailheads were hidden by the groove edge of the next board.

From field examination of floors, I can state positively that a sawmill cut the boards, that a jack plane smoothed the surfaces of the boards, that a tongue plane and a plow plane made the joints, and that nails held the boards down. Several other tools were certainly used in making such a floor, tools whose marks are not obvious on the finished floor, but whose use can be safely assumed from a general knowledge of how work had to have been done.

The use of planes raises the question of how a board is held while being planed. A board cannot be planed while it is lying flat on the ground without extreme discomfort. A board cannot conveniently be placed across sawhorses and planed, for the thrust of the plane will push the board off the horses or knock them over. Some kind of workbench, no matter how crude and simple, is required to support the board while it is being planed, and the workbench must be supplied with some device, such as a vise, to hold the board to the bench. A plane that is used constantly soon becomes dull. The bit of the iron must be honed fairly often on a whetstone and occasionally sharpened on a grindstone.

The boards that come from a sawmill must be cut to length at the building site, so that a handsaw certainly was used. Moreover, a square and a marking device, either a scratch awl or a pencil, is needed to make a mark for the saw to follow. Some boards in a floor had to be narrower than the rest to fit the space exactly. To cut a board lengthwise requires a rip saw, a handsaw and a rip saw not being interchangeable. The mark on the board for a rip saw to follow was probably made with a marking gauge. Saws that are used constantly must have their teeth sharpened and reset from time to time, implying saw files, a saw set, and a saw vise. Finally, a hammer drives the nails into the floorboards, and a nail set is needed to sink the head of the nail below the surface of the wood. These tools will be described in more detail and even more tools were needed in laying a floor, but at least this discussion shows how an examination of a building leads to inescapable conclusions concerning tools used in building it.

In compiling the following list I have confined myself to tools that were probably used in the first half of the nineteenth century, even though hewn-log houses were built in southern Indiana throughout the nineteenth century and well into the twentieth century. American life during the second half of the nineteenth century saw many changes, and that is true of tools. Woodworking tools that had changed little for centuries were still being used in the early nineteenth century, but shortly after the Civil War, factory-made tools began to supplant the older forms. The fairly common practice for the early nineteenth-century craftsman was to procure the metal parts of his tools from a blacksmith and to make the wooden parts himself. If he needed an ax, for example, the craftsman got the handmade head from the blacksmith and made the handle to suit himself. After the Civil War, however, factories produced more and more of the tools and tool parts, and many parts that had previously been made of wood were made of metal, even though the basic tool shapes remained largely unchanged. Many patents for factory-made tools were issued in the late nineteenth century.⁶ Many of the older types of tools continued, however, to be made and used in the late nineteenth and twentieth centuries. Older types of tools continued in use because they were still in good condition, because many craftsmen preferred the older forms of tools, and because it was still often cheaper for a craftsman to make a tool for himself.

I can vouch for only the tools used in building the hewn-log houses of southern Indiana. Those who are familiar with the log houses of other parts of the country can judge for themselves whether the same features and marks are present in the houses familiar to them. If they are, the same tools were used. Some tools have different names in other parts of the country. The tool commonly called a "drawshave" in New England is called a "drawknife" in Indiana. The same holds true for some building terms. Horizontal, overlapping siding used on the exterior of a house is called "clapboards" in New England; in Indiana, it is called "weatherboards." Insofar as possible, I have used the names and terms common among older craftsmen in Indiana.

THE TOOLS

TOOLS FOR FELLING, SPLITTING, AND SAWING LOGS

1. The *felling ax*, so familiar as scarcely to need general description, felled the trees used to build a log house and was used in a number of other tasks, such as supplementing the work of the broadax when the logs were hewed and to shape the corner notches that held the horizontal logs together in the walls of the house. I have never seen a hewn-log building of any kind in southern Indiana where any tool other than an ax was used to shape the notches. When a log building is dismantled, one can closely examine the notches, and the marks left by tools are especially obvious. Even in parts of the notch where a modern carpenter would almost certainly use a handsaw, the nineteenth-century builder used only an ax.

A century and a half ago, ax heads were generally made by local smiths from wrought iron with inserted steel bits. The owner made the handle, or helve, to suit himself. Axes made elsewhere in the country were also available in southern Indiana. In Bloomington, Indiana, in the 1830s, a local smith made axes that "brought in real cash, one dollar beyond any patent flashy affairs from New England, done up in pine boxes and painted half black, while their edge-part was polished and

shiney as a new razor."[7] Even today, several patterns of axes are made, usually named for some locality or part of the country: e.g., Michigan pattern and Western pattern. In turn-of-the-century hardware catalogs, I have found twenty-four pattern names, not brand names but names of specific shapes. Several different companies made Michigan pattern axes, for example. No writer has, to the best of my knowledge, explored the origins, significance, and ages of these names. A recent book on the American ax ignores the question altogether.[8] At any rate, a Hoosier pattern ax was made and sold for a number of years by a large hardware firm in Louisville, Kentucky.[9] In the light of what is known about other tools and implements, I assume that local smiths in southern Indiana developed an ax of a special size and shape adapted to the kind of tree to be felled and the kind of work to be done in the area and that, when factories began to produce axes in quantity, they retained this special shape.

2. The *froe* is a heavy, thick, dull-edged knife, usually at least a foot long and two inches wide, with a short handle rising at a right angle through an eye at one end of the blade; the cutting edge is *froe*, or away from, the handle. The froe served in carefully controlled splitting, or riving. Splitting that requires no great accuracy can be done with wedges as in making rails for a worm fence or in splitting firewood. Very small pieces can be split with such a tool as a pocket knife, but the froe served when most of the materials for a log house were rove out (*rove out* seems to be the most commonly used term in southern Indiana). When making shingles, an appropriate length of oak log was cut with a cross-cut saw. This section was roughly split into smaller pieces, or billets, with wedges and a maul. The sap wood, which is found just under the bark of the tree and which decays more rapidly than the heart wood, was then split off. Then a billet was stood on end in a froe horse, and the froe was beaten down with a froe club into the top end of the billet. When the blade was buried in the wood, the handle protruded on one side and part of the blade protruded on the other. By clubbing the end of the blade and prying the handle back and forth, a slab about the size of a shingle was riven off. The froe also served in riving out the lath to be nailed to the interior walls to hold plaster, and it seems that pieces of wood riven to the appropriate size served as the basis for the chinking between the logs.

Compared to other tools, the froe must have presented a relatively simple task for a blacksmith. The blade should not be particularly sharp ("dull as a froe"), for it is meant to split, not to cut. Many a froe that I have seen has for a handle only a short length cut from a branch of appropriate size. The tool often appears to be clumsy and crude, but in the hand of a good workman, it was very effective.

3. The *froe club* drives the froe into the billet. It is frequently nothing more than a section of a branch about four inches in diameter and eighteen inches long with one end whittled down to a comfortable size for the hand. Some especially hard and tough wood, such as hickory, would be used if possible, but clubs soon became so battered that they were discarded and new ones made.

4. The *froe horse*, which holds the billet upright while the froe is driven into it, usually consists of a large forked branch. It may be raised off the ground by legs, or it may be supported at a comfortable working height by a stump.

5. The *shingle cutter*. See Chapter IV, section on "The Roof."

6. *Wedges* were used for various kinds of rough splitting, such as preparing the billets from which shingles were either rove or cut. An iron wedge was usually used to start the split, and a wooden wedge, a *glut*, was used to finish it. I have never found any evidence that wedges were used to split or otherwise work the logs used in the walls of a house, for these were hewn with a broadax.

7. The *maul*, a large wooden hammer, drove the wedges; a hammer with an iron head would soon have battered the top of the wedge so badly as to make it useless. Mauls served other purposes, such as driving large wooden pins into their holes or driving two timbers together. Mauls were made in several ways, but the continued currency of *knot maul* in southern Indiana indicates that the heads were often made from a knotty piece of wood or one with intertwined fiber, such as a burl.

8. The *sawmill*, driven mostly by water power, must have been in wide use in early nineteenth century southern Indiana because I have never seen a house of log or of any other type in the area from that period that failed to include many boards sawed by a water-driven sawmill. The blade in such a mill was long and narrow, something like a two-man cross-cut saw, and moved up and down while the log was moved against it. It left vertical, straight scratch marks quite unlike the curved marks left by the steam-powered, circular saws of the later nineteenth and twentieth centuries. Although carpenters planed away any saw marks that would have been exposed to view, they often left

the saw marks in such hidden places as the undersides of floor boards on the ground floor. Strange though it may seem at first to term a sawmill a tool, it is one in the broadest sense and was used to produce the boards that made the floors, staircases, mantlepieces, doors, windows, purlins, siding, trim, and frequently, such smaller timbers as rafters and the joists that supported the floor for the sleeping loft or second floor.

9. The *pit saw*, or *whip saw*, consists of a long, narrow blade like that in a water-driven sawmill, but with a handle at each end. A log having been rolled over a pit or raised on trestles, two men, one above and one below the log, sawed boards from it. Such saws were certainly used in southern Indiana at one time, for some examples have been found in the area and are displayed in museums, such as that at Spring Mill State Park near Mitchell, Indiana. How common they were is impossible to say. I have never seen a board in any early house that I can say with certainty was sawed with a pit saw, but its mark is straight, slanting saw scratches.

10. The *cross-cut saw* has a long, narrow blade, but is used to cut a log or large timber to length, rather than to cut it into boards. Such saws may be one-man saws, relatively short, with a handle on only one end or two-man saws, longer, with a handle on each end. Cross-cut saws seem not to have been used to fell trees in the early nineteenth century, the felling ax alone being used in that task. The logs used in the wall of most log houses were cut to length with a cross-cut saw, for the ends of such logs do not show ax marks. The smaller handsaw may have been used for this purpose because cross-cut saws would have been costly. The manufacture of the blades for pit and cross-cut saws and for sawmills required facilities not available to most local blacksmiths.

TOOLS FOR MOVING AND MEASURING

11. *Chains* and *hooks* of some sort must have been used to drag logs from the woods to the site of the house or to the mill and to move them about generally. I have been unable to discover exactly what types of chain were in use in the era under consideration, but the chains and hooks would have been forged by local smiths. Oxen, supposedly common at the time, were probably used more for this type of work than were horses.

12. A *sled* may have been used to support the front end of a large log as it was hauled, and smaller logs may have been piled on a sled.

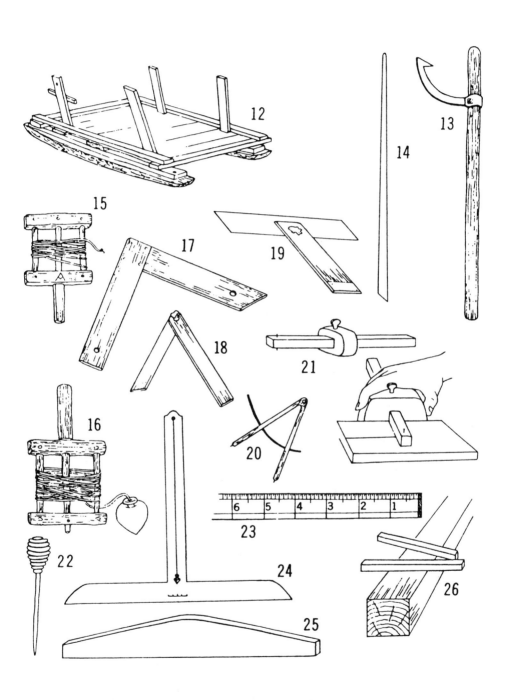

Sleds were probably used more than wagons because it is far easier to load logs onto a sled, and there is far less danger of the sled's tipping over on uneven ground. Sleds of relatively simple construction were often home-made with runners of some very hard, smooth wood, such as dogwood.

13. The *cant hook* has a sturdy wooden handle four or five feet long, about one foot from the lower end of which a curved, iron arm with a spur is hinged so that it can move freely. With this device, a log can be rolled over with relative ease by one or two men.

14. The *crow bar*, a metal rod three or more feet long, with one end either pointed or flattened, served in prying up heavy timbers and logs and in shifting them a few inches at a time. A wooden pry bar might have been used in its place, but the greater size of a wooden bar made it more awkward and restricted its use.

15. The *chalk line* is simply a length of stout string rolled for convenience in carrying on a reel or spool. The string is pulled over a lump of chalk and held firmly at two points on a board or log; then it is pulled up vertically at its center and allowed to snap back, marking a straight line in chalk between two points. I have seen in a few old barns the 150-year-old mark left by a string that was probably soaked in a reddish-purple fluid, such as pokeberry juice, rather than rubbed with chalk. The chalk line, used especially to mark straight lines on logs before they were hewed, would have served in a variety of ways in building a log house.

16. The *plumb line* is a heavy weight (the *plumb bob*) at the end of a string used to establish a truly vertical line or to test whether a wall is vertical. The weight was often a piece of lead.

17. The *square* is used continually in marking boards to be cut square, in testing whether timbers meet at a right angle, and in other ways. Several types of square were used in the first half of the nine-teenth century. In building a log house, probably at least one large *framing square* and a small *try square* would have been indispensable. Some squares of the period are homemade of wood, while some are of iron, both probably used in southern Indiana.

18. The *miter square* is so constructed that a forty-five-degree angle, or miter, can be marked on a board, permitting the craftsman to make matching cuts on two boards in a right-angle joint. Although a miter square is used far less frequently than a square, it is hard to imagine how without one a mantelpiece could be made or how trim

could be fitted around doors and windows.

19. The *bevel* somewhat resembles a miter square, except that the two arms can be set at a chosen angle and the ends of a number of rafters, for instance, marked at the same angle. During the era that we consider, bevels were often simply constructed by riveting two strips of wood together so that they could be moved, but would remain in position once set.

20. The *dividers* consist of two sharply pointed legs that may be set at appropriate distances apart by means of a quadrant wing projecting from one leg and passing through the other (or passing through both). Some dividers have set screws to hold the leg position by friction on the wing. They may be made of metal but in early nineteenth-century southern Indiana were more probably made of wood. They can, of course, be used to lay off circles and arcs, but they have another important use. When the edge of a board is to be fitted up against an irregular surface, the board is held close to the surface. The dividers are opened an appropriate distance and drawn along so that one leg follows the irregular surface while the other leg scribes a matching line on the board. When cut along the scribed line, the board will fit against the irregular surface.

21. The *marking gauge* consists of a bar of wood with one or more metal points set in it; the bar passes through a block of wood, or head, that can be set at any distance along the bar from the metal point. The head may be set with a wedge or a thumb screw of wood or metal. The purpose of the marking gauge is to scribe a line on a board, the line being parallel to one edge of the board. As the head is slid along the edge of the board, the metal point in the bar scribes the line. Marking gauges are of many different sizes and shapes. Some having two metal points and used to lay out mortises are *mortise gauges.* Those eighteen or more inches long are *panel gauges.* A carpenter who needed to lay off many lines always the same distance from an edge could have made a non-adjustable gauge of the right size so that he would always have it ready to hand.

22. The *scratch awl,* a thin metal rod with a convenient handle on one end and a sharpened point on the other end, is used for many sorts of marking, but especially to draw along the arm of a square to mark where a board is to be cut. Pencils, though expensive, were available at this time. When old buildings are torn down, boards occasionally show pencil marks, such as simple arithmetical computa-

tions, but the scratch awl, which once sharpened rarely needs resharpening, has an important advantage over a pencil, namely greater accuracy.

23. The *rule* was constantly used for measuring, and rules of many kinds were available in the first half of the nineteenth century. Let us assume, however, that our builder of a log house had only the simplest of instruments, a foot-long wooden rule with one-eighth of an inch as the smallest division and numbered from right to left, rather than from left to right as in modern rules. With this rule he could construct a ten-foot rule, or ten-foot pole, from a suitable strip of wood notched or pencil-marked at needed intervals. We sometimes hear that an ax handle was a frequently used measuring device in earlier days, and it may well be that an ax handle was used roughly to gauge the length of logs or for similar tasks, but a more precise rule was certainly needed for many measurements in building a log house.

24. The *level* is, of course, a tool used to establish a true horizontal line. Spirit levels with a bubble in a curved tube were available in the early nineteenth century, but were probably uncommon and expensive. Much more likely to have been used was a device consisting of a straight strip of wood two or more feet long with an arm extending upwards from the middle of it, at a right angle, so that a small plumb bob attached at the top of the arm could dangle down. When the string coincided with a line scribed on the arm or when the point of the bob rested over a mark on the strip of wood, the work was level. Levels of this sort could be constructed in a number of ways as far as the shape of the arm is concerned, but the basic principle was always the same.

25. The *straight edge* is any object known to have a truly straight-line edge. It may be several feet long with one straight side and a back edge of greater width at the center to keep it from bending. A straight edge may also be a narrow board planed so as to have two straight parallel edges. It was used in many ways, such as to extend the line established by a level or a square or to test the surface of a board or timber to detect irregularities.

26. *Try sticks, trying sticks,* or *wind sticks* are two short straight edges. When the craftsman sets the sticks across a timber at some distance from each other, he can sight over the tops of the sticks and tell whether the timber is plane and true or whether it has a wind (twist) in it. They are especially useful when a board that is being planed is clamped flat on the workbench.

TOOLS FOR HOLDING AND GRIPPING

27. The *workbench* is a multi-purpose tool, using the word in a broad sense, for holding and supporting work in a number of ways. It is, however, almost indispensable in holding boards for planing, and great numbers of planed boards were used in a log house. Workbenches can be of many kinds, but a craftsman building a log house surely had a bench to use, no matter how simple and crude it might have been, together with most of the devices used with a workbench.

28. The *vise* that was attached to, or built into, a workbench, was almost entirely of wood in the first half of the nineteenth century, including the vital, wooden bench screw. Although the vise is very convenient, a board could be held on the bench with other devices.

29. The *holdfast* is a stout, L-shaped iron device with one long, round arm and one short arm flattened at least on the under side of its outer end. When a board is laid on the bench and the long arm of the holdfast is driven down through a round hole in the bench top, the short arm pressing down on the board binds the long arm in the hole so that the board is held firmly to the bench top. The hold of the holdfast is released by pounding the lower end of the long arm upward. The holdfast could easily have been made by a blacksmith.

30. The *catch*, or *bench stop*, is a short, rectangular iron plug with a projecting, notched tip on its upper end. When driven into a hole in the top of the work bench so that the lip is a short distance above the surface, it can snag a board forced against it. When the surface of the board is planed, the catch will hold the board steady, yet leave the surface of the board unobstructed. A wooden plug can also be used.

31. *Sawhorses* are simply made, wooden trestles, generally used in pairs, to support boards or small timbers that are being sawed. Sawhorses can be quickly moved from place to place in and around a house that is being built. Moreover, a plank laid between a pair of sawhorses provides a platform on which the craftsman can stand.

32. *Clamps* come in various kinds. The *handscrew*, commonly made entirely of wood and using wooden screws, is very convenient for holding small pieces of work. A *bar clamp*, or *door clamp*, is almost indispensable when a door or window sash is being assembled.

33. The *hook*, or *hook pin*, is shaped like the figure 4. The shank can be driven into the previously bored hole of the joint where two timbers, such as rafters, are fitted together to test the fit of the joint.

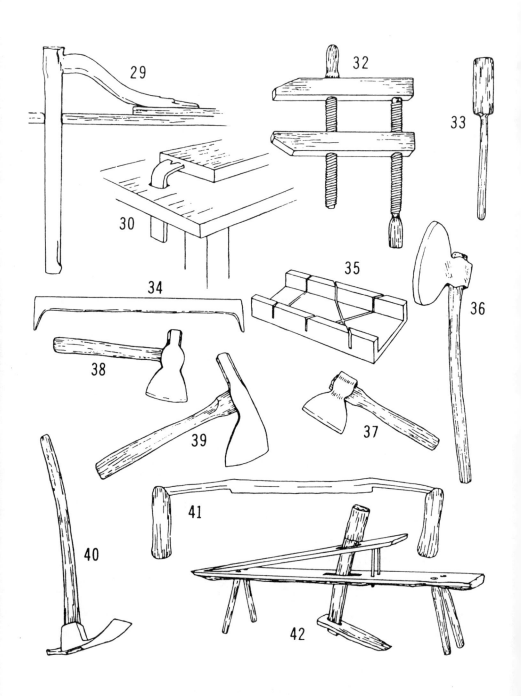

The pin can be removed by prying up or hammering up on the underside of its protruding head.

34. *Dogs* are large iron staples. When a small timber is being hewed, one end of the dog can be driven into the timber and the other end into the block of wood on which the timber rests in order to hold the timber steady.

35. The *miter box* is made of three boards forming a bottom and two sides. The sides have accurate forty-five-degree saw cuts (kerfs) in them so that if a piece of molding is held firmly against the inside of the box, a saw worked in the kerfs will cut the molding at a forty-five-degree angle. Two such mitered pieces fit so as to let them form a right-angle joint.

TOOLS FOR SURFACING, CHOPPING, AND PARING

36. The *broadax.* See Chapter Four, section on Walls and Logs.

37. The *broad hatchet,* or *hewing hatchet,* a small version of the broadax, has a bit about five or six inches wide. The hatchet, used with one hand, is especially useful in working on smaller timbers or for removing wood from a timber already in place in a house where using the ponderous broadax would be awkward.

38. The *shingling hatchet* is actually a multi-purpose tool very convenient for the workman who is shingling the roof and who finds it awkward to carry several single-purpose tools. With the shingling hatchet, he can drive nails into the shingles, for the one end of the head is shaped like a hammer; he can split or pare down shingles to fit certain spots, for the other end is a sharp hatchet; and he can pull misdirected nails because a nail slot is cut into the side of the hatchet face. Frequently, too, the handle is marked with a notch letting the shingler measure the correct distance between courses of shingles.

39. The *lathing hatchet* resembles the shingling hatchet, except that it is flat across the entire top so that it can be used to nail lath along the top of a wall, near the ceiling. Many log houses had one or more plastered walls. The laths that I have examined from log houses of the first half of the nineteenth century have almost always been split, undoubtedly with a froe, from larger blocks of wood. They are, like modern lath, about three-eighths of an inch thick, about one and a quarter inches wide, and of various lengths. The ends of the laths have never been sawed, but have been cut with a hatchet.

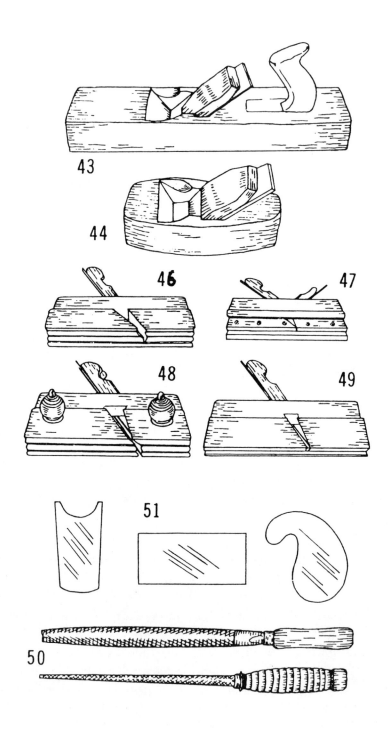

40. The *foot*, or *carpenter's, adze* is shaped somewhat like an old-fashioned garden hoe, except that the head is much heavier, the blade longer and much sharper, and the handle shorter. Unlike the ax, the cutting edge of the blade is at a right angle to the handle. The foot adze was probably used to true the surfaces of floor joists and timbers once they were in place. I have never seen marks on the logs in the walls of houses that could be identified with certainty as adze marks, and no older craftsman has told me of using the adze for finishing house logs. Nonetheless, because old examples seem very common at farm sales in southern Indiana, foot adzes were available and used. Although neither the early catalogs nor the reference works that I have consulted use it, the term *foot adze is* most common among older men in southern Indiana.

41. The *draw knife* is a sharp, straight, knife-like blade, from eight to twelve inches long, with a wooden, right-angle handle at each end placed such that the tool cuts as the blade is drawn toward the craftsman. Drawknives may also have longer, shorter, or curved blades. The drawknife serves well where there is more material to be removed than can be done conveniently with a plane, but not enough to warrant using a broadax or adze. One important use was thinning the upper end of a shingle after it had been "rove" out with a froe.

42. The *shaving horse* is built in such a way that a workman sitting astride it can clamp a shingle on a surface before him by pushing down with his foot on a lever under the bench. He can then shave thin with a drawknife the end closest to him. The shaving horse was used almost exclusively with a drawknife.

43. The *jack plane* of the era that we consider is a rectangular block of wood about sixteen inches long, three inches wide and three inches high. Near the center of the block, a slot pierces it, tapering from top to bottom and sloping down toward the front in such a way that with a wooden wedge a steel-tipped blade, or iron, can be wedged into the slot. Such a plane iron is about two and a half inches wide, six inches long, and one-eighth of an inch thick. When set for work, the iron's bit protrudes slightly from the bottom of the block of wood, and the entire iron inclines at about a forty-five-degree angle towards the back of the block. A handle is fastened on top of the back of the body of the plane.

Because each of the several kinds of plane has its specific purpose, a craftsman building a log house would have needed a number of different planes. Each kind of plane usually leaves its characteristic mark so that one can tell with reasonable certainty what planes were used. The jack plane removes relatively large amounts of wood as the first step in planing a board to remove the sawmill's marks and to bring the board down quickly to near the finish size. The jack plane's iron is slightly convex so that it protrudes most in the center and cuts a slight trough into the surface of the board. With other planes, the ridges between these grooves are removed from surfaces exposed to view, but they were sometimes left on the backs of boards, such as those used in mantlepieces, that were wanted to be straight and true, but which would not be exposed.

A craftsman in southern Indiana in the early nineteenth century could well have made the wooden parts of his planes himself and gotten the irons from the blacksmith. Planes were specifically mentioned as produced by the Bloomington smith, Austin Seward, during the 1820s.[10]

44. The *smooth*, or *smoothing, plane* is about half as long as the jack plane (that is, about eight inches long). Some versions are narrower at the front and rear than in the middle, and the most common type has no handle. The bit of its iron is straight across, unlike the jack plane, and it is used mostly to remove the ridges left by the jack plane.

45. The *jointer plane* is twenty-eight inches or more in length. Its iron is straight across, and the plane has a handle. The jointer plane makes an especially straight surface and the edges of boards, such as floor boards, so finished can fit closely together. Other long planes include the *trying plane* (22 to 24 inches) and the *fore plane* (18 inches). The jack plane can serve as a jointer plane if its iron is exchanged for a straight one.

46. The *rabbet*, or *rebate, plane*, narrower and shorter than a jack plane, is so constructed that its iron cuts a notch along one edge of a board. Rabbet planes would have been especially useful in building door frames and window frames into which the sashes fit.

47. *Tongue and plow*, or *match, planes* were usually made in pairs that made tongue-and-groove cuts that fit together, or match. They are shorter and narrower than a jack plane. The tongue plane's iron has a notched bit that cuts in one operation the familiar tongue of a tongue-and-groove joint. The plow plane's iron has a narrower bit that cuts the groove. The match plane illustrated combines two planes into one. One side cuts the groove. When the plane is turned end for

end, the other side cuts the tongue. Every log house that I have seen had tongue-and-groove flooring. If the flooring was made in the first half of the nineteenth century, the joints were almost certainly made with tongue and plow planes, for no other tools could very well have made them.

48. The *sash plane* is another specialized plane used to shape the wooden parts of a sash that actually hold the glass panes. Although the work can be done with a rabbet plane and a molding plane, a sash plane is more convenient. The early nineteenth-century log houses that I have seen as they were being disassembled or that were falling into decay, seem to have had windows in them since they were first built.

All of my evidence points to the making of window sash at or near the site of the house. The same may be said for doors, mantelpieces, and other finish items. Even though these items are today commonly made in specially equipped mills, I have never found any documentation that mills of this sort operated in the area in the era that we consider. Long distance shipping of a fragile piece, such as a window sash, or a bulky piece, such as a door, would have been prohibitively expensive. Panes of glass could have been properly packed and shipped. They were very early stocked by stores in southern Indiana.[11] I have closely examined sashes, mantelpieces, and doors from early houses and have carefully disassembled doors to see how they were made and what tools were used. They were all made with hand tools and, I am convinced, by local craftsmen.

49. *Molding planes* are of many different sizes and make many different shapes of molding. One plane normally makes one size and shape of molding, though complicated moldings result from combining the shapes formed by different planes. In some log houses, several different planes were used to make fairly elaborate mantelpieces, doors, baseboards, and the like, while in other log houses very few molding planes were used. One molding shape, however, in almost every log house is the bead molding, which is in cross section one-quarter or one-half of a circle. The edges of boards and timbers that can be seen in the inside of the finished house almost never have sharp edges, but have bead moldings of different sizes worked upon them.

50. The *woodrasp* is a file-shaped, metal tool with coarser teeth than a file. It was used to smooth the cut ends of boards and to remove small amounts of wood in fitting joints together.

51. The *scraper* is a piece of thin steel, usually rectangular in shape and not much larger than four by six inches. Scrapers were often cut out of worn-out saw blades. When properly sharpened and drawn with the grain, a scraper will remove a tiny amount of wood and leave a smooth surface. Scrapers were often used for the same sort of task for which a modern carpenter uses sandpaper, but sandpaper would have been scarce and expensive.

Tools for shaping and fitting

52. The *handsaw* used during the first half of the nineteenth century was very similar in shape and size to contemporary ones. It was in constant use to cut boards and small timbers to length, that is, across the grain. The handsaw commonly has eight pointed teeth per inch.

53. The *rip saw* looks very much like the handsaw. Close inspection reveals that its teeth are slightly larger and chisel-shaped. The rip saw is used to cut boards lengthwise, with the grain. Forging the blade of a saw would have been a difficult task for a blacksmith. Most handsaws and rip saws were probably imported into southern Indiana.

54. The *compass saw* has a much narrower and shorter blade than the handsaw. The walls of a hewn-log house were commonly built up of solid logs and openings for doors, windows, and the fireplace cut only later, using a saw with a narrow blade in the gap between two logs. Once a narrow-bladed saw, perhaps the compass saw, had begun the cut, a handsaw could finish it.

55. The *tenon,* or *dovetail, saw,* a smaller variety of the handsaw, has a blade made of such thin steel that the blade must be stiffened with a thick, brass or steel rib along its top. Consequently, it cannot make a deep cut, but its smaller size, finer teeth, and thinner blade fit it for such fine work as shaping the tenons for the joints that held window sash together.

56. The *firmer chisel,* a long, narrow blade sharpened on one end and with a wooden handle on the other end, is a general purpose chisel used to cut, pare, and trim in a number of ways. It may be pushed by hand or driven with a mallet. A craftsman building a log house probably had several firmer chisels of different sizes.

57. The *paring chisel* is usually longer and of lighter construction than the firmer chisel, being pushed by hand pressure only. It is kept very sharp and used for light paring in fitting joints and similar work. A very large paring chisel with a blade two and a half inches or more in width is a *slick,* or *carpenter's slick.*

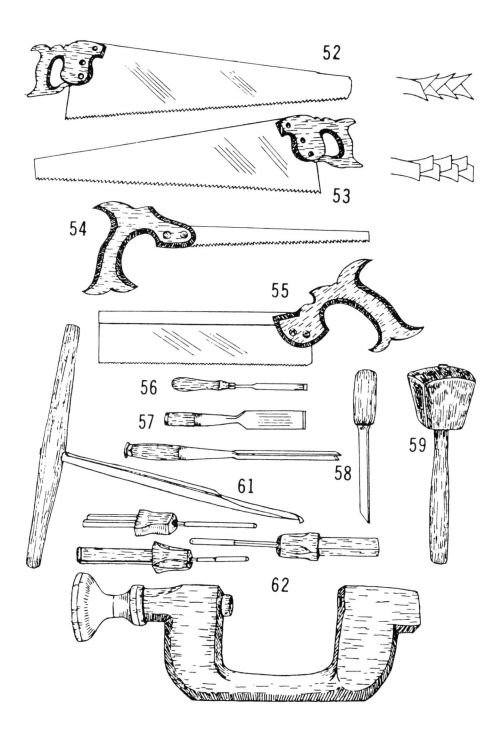

58. The *mortise chisel* has a much thicker blade than the firmer chisel and is driven with a mallet. In making mortises, chisels of several different sizes were used, depending on the size of the mortise. A special type of mortise chisel that is L-shaped in cross section is a *corner chisel*. It was used especially to square-cut the corners of the mortises.

59. The *mallet* is a lump of wood with a handle of convenient size, usually about a foot long. They were made in a number of shapes. Sometimes the head and the handle are made from one piece of wood. They are used especially to drive chisels because the wooden head of the mallet will not destroy the chisel handle as would the metal head of a hammer.

60. The *brad awl* is a small steel rod flattened and sharpened on one end with a wooden handle on the other end. By pushing the sharpened end into the wood and turning it back and forth, the brad awl makes a small hole into which a nail may be driven. If a nail is driven in near the end of the board without this preliminary hole, the board may split.

61. The *auger,* or *gimlet,* is a metal rod with one end shaped so as to cut a round hole in wood and with a wooden handle attached to the other end at right angles to the axis of the rod; turning the handle turns the shaft of the auger, making it cut the hole. Augers were made in a number of ways in the early nineteenth century. The *twisted auger* with spiral flutes was just coming into use at the beginning of the century; but because its manufacture demanded equipment not available to the average smith, it was probably not widely used in southern Indiana in the first half of the century.

Even though the twisted auger bores a deep hole rapidly across the grain of a piece of wood because the flutes carry the chips up and out of the hole, it cannot bore a hole lengthwise, with the grain, into the end of a timber. In building a log house, many holes were bored into the ends of logs where openings were cut through the walls for doors, windows, and fireplaces. At these openings, a heavy plank was set against the cut ends of the logs, a hole an inch or more in diameter bored through the plank and several inches into the end of the log, and a wooden pin was driven through the plank and into the log. Augers (other than spiral twist augers) must have been used for this task, but their exact form is unknown. The most likely form is the *pod auger* in which the cutting end of the rod is shaped into a short, cylindrical trough that tapers, thins, and curls to the right. A blacksmith can make a pod auger.

Augers were used to bore large holes from one inch to three inches in diameter, but the largest bored holes usually made in a log house were the two-inch holes bored through the plate and into the log supporting it at each outside corner of the house so that a large wooden pin could hold the plate in place. Gimlets are tiny augers used in one hand.

62. The *brace and bit* makes holes smaller than those of the auger and larger than those of the brad awl, roughly diameters between one-quarter inch and one inch. The brace commonly used in the early nineteenth century, while having generally the shape of the familiar modern tool, was made of wood. Bits of several different types and in a variety of sizes could be made by smiths, but the spiral bit was probably not common.

TOOLS FOR FASTENING AND UNFASTENING

63. *Nails* were used in large numbers in a hewn-log house, and although I may seem to extend the meaning of the term to classify them as tools, I follow Mercer.[12] The handmade *wrought nail*, laboriously produced one by one by the smith at the forge, was superseded about 1800 by the *cut nail* that was quickly stamped by machine from a thin sheet of iron and that had its head formed by another machine. It is very unusual in my experience to find any wrought nails in an early nineteenth-century, southern Indiana hewn-log house. The machine-made cut nail, which is rectangular in cross section and today often called a "square" nail, was used throughout the log house. Some are headless or nearly so in order that they can be driven beneath the surface of a board, such as floor boards or baseboards; others have noticeable heads; and some are large spikes and some tiny brads; even so, they are essentially alike. Hundreds of nails were used to shingle the roof, and the log houses that I have seen were originally roofed with wooden shingles nailed on. Hundreds more were used elsewhere in the house. Whether there were nail-making machines in southern Indiana or whether the nails were imported readymade, I cannot say. The illustration shows two cut nails and a modern wire nail for the sake of comparison.

64. The *claw hammer*, used both to drive and to pull nails, hardly needs to be described, for the early nineteenth-century claw hammer looks very much like the modern one, except that the head of the early hammer does not have the deepened eye (the hole that the handle fits

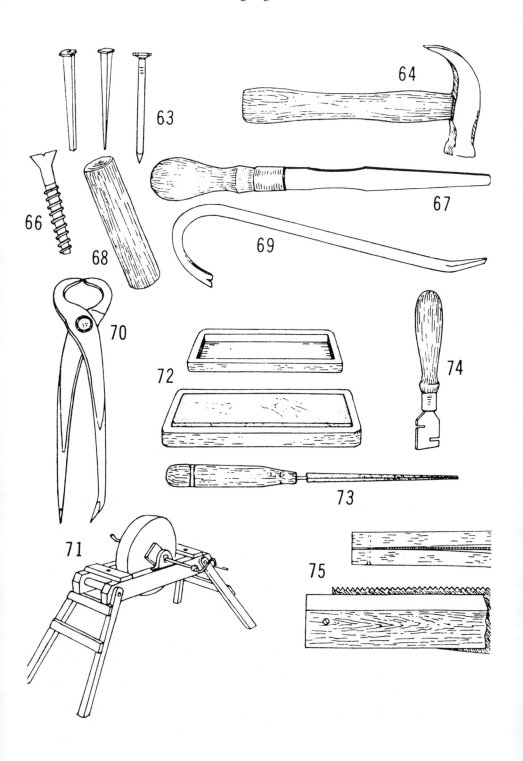

in) of the modern hammer. The heads of claw hammers were probably made by local smiths in earlier times, and the owners made the wooden handles.

65. The *nail punch,* or *set,* is a short, steel rod tapering at one end to a blunt point. It is used to sink the heads of nails below the surface of the wood in floor boards, baseboards, and the like.

66. The *wood screw* was used in a log house to hold door hinges, latches, and such. Those that I have been able to remove from their places in early nineteenth-century log houses usually appear to be machine-made; but, unlike modern screws, they are blunt-ended. A machine to make pointed wood screws was patented in 1846, and pointed screws quickly superseded the notched to interlock at the corners were held in place by their own weight and needed no fasteners, but pegs were used to secure planks against the cut ends of logs at window and door openings, to hold the plate at each corner to the log beneath, to hold the butt ends of rafters to the plate, and elsewhere. As time went on, more spikes and fewer pegs were used so that, in later houses, the butt ends of rafters were spiked to the plate. Even in late log houses, however, the plates are nearly always held to the logs beneath them by pegs a foot or more in length and two inches in diameter. Iron spikes large enough for this task seem not to have been available. Every peg that I have seen removed for examination from its hole was hand made, whether a tiny peg from a window sash or a large trunnel from a plate. They seem first to have been "rove" out from a straight-grained piece of wood, usually oak, and then trimmed, the small ones probably with a knife, the large ones with a drawknife, to a roughly cylindrical shape. Many are more or less octagonal in cross section while some are nearly square, but none is smooth and round in cross section as if machine-made or turned in a lathe. The rough shape insured that the peg would stay tight in the bored hole into which it was driven. The word *peg* seems to be in wide use in southern Indiana, and the barns with heavy frames are often called "pegged barns."

69. The *claw,* or *wrecking bar* (as it is often called today), is an iron rod perhaps an inch in diameter and two feet long. At least one end of the rod is flattened, tapered, and notched so that it can be slipped under a nail-head, around the nail shank, and pry out the nail. The rod is usually bent near one end, sometimes into a half circle, to provide more leverage. Even though the claw hammer pulls nails

effectively, the common early nineteenth-century type had a much shorter eye than the modern one, and the head could not be so strongly affixed to the handle. Frequent nail pulling with the claw hammer would have loosened the head, and pulling a large nail might well have broken the handle. A claw, commonly kept on hand to pull large nails, could easily be made by blacksmiths.

70. *Pincers* are a plier-like tool having wide, sharply tapered jaws. Pincers can be used to pull headless nails and brads where a claw hammer or claw cannot be used. They were frequently made by blacksmiths.

TOOLS FOR SHARPENING

71. The *grindstone* is a thick disc of carefully selected sandstone. It is pierced by a horizontal axle that is set in a frame so that the stone can rotate when the axle is turned by a crank. Some arrangement, such as a container above it from which water drips, keeps the surface of the stone wet while it is being used. Almost all edged woodworking tools require rough sharpening from time to time. The whetstone and the file will produce a finer edge and can touch up the edge between grindings, but they could not fully take the place of the grindstone, especially for sharpening axes.

We might pause to wonder how the pioneer, so frequently described in historical accounts as moving into a heavily forested area with not much more than an ax, managed to survive.[14] On the one hand, he had constantly to use his ax to clear trees from his land and to build all sorts of things, including a log cabin, so that his ax would need continually to be sharpened. On the other hand, a grindstone large enough to be of any use would have been very difficult to bring with him. It seems unlikely that the average pioneer could count on finding suitable stone or have had the skill to make a grindstone even if he had found suitable raw material, because a grindstone that is not round and that does not run true is nearly useless. If he used his neighbor's, where did his neighbor get one? It seems that the average pioneer was better provided with tools and equipment than many have believed.

72. The *whetstone* is a small piece of fine-grained sandstone with at least one flat surface. When this surface is moistened with water or oil, it can put a fine edge on chisels, plane irons, axes, and the like. Very small or specially shaped stones were needed to sharpen some tools, such as augers. Frequently used stones often sat in lidded wooden boxes to protect them from being chipped and to keep them clean.

73. The *file* is needed to sharpen the teeth of saws. While other shapes might be used on the large teeth of the cross-cut saw, only a file which is triangular in cross section can be used on the smaller teeth of handsaws, rip saws, compass saws, and tenon saws. Files were probably imported into southern Indiana because making them was a highly specialized craft.

74. The *saw set*, or *wrest*, is a thin metal blade having notches of various sizes in it. For a saw to cut properly without binding, the teeth must be bent out to each side, one to the left and the next to the right. The teeth then cut a groove, or kerf, in the wood, which is wider than the blade and which keeps the blade from binding. During use, the teeth of the saw tend to lose their outward bend, and from time to time, they must be rebent, or set, with the saw set.

75. The *saw vise*, or *clamp*, holds the saw with the teeth uppermost while the saw is filed and set. The vise can be made in a number of ways and may be of wood, but it must be made to hold the blade firmly just below the teeth, else the saw will chatter, or vibrate, and quickly dull the file.

OTHER TOOLS

76. The *ladder*, while Mercer does not mention it, would certainly have been used in building a log house, and probably several ladders of different lengths were used.

In conclusion, it should be obvious that a large number of tools were used in building a hewn-log house during the first half of the nineteenth century, far more than most writers would lead us to believe. Some of these tools, admittedly, were of the type that might have been made just for the job of building the one house and might have been discarded when that job was completed. Examples of disposable tools would include the long measuring stick and the trying sticks. Most of the tools, however, were of the permanent type which would be used over and over again on job after job. It seems unlikely that the average farmer would have owned all of the tools needed to construct a house. He certainly would have owned axes, hatchets, saws, hammers, wedges, and other tools, for he would have needed them in day to day work about the farm. The more specialized tools such as molding planes, however, probably would have been owned only by a few men in any community or comparable rural area. These men would have been carpenters as well as farmers. In the first half of the nineteenth century in any rural area, there would have been craftsmen of various kinds who farmed in addition to practicing their crafts and who helped their neighbors when their special skills were needed. In return, their neighbors helped them at harvesting, hog-butchering, or maple sugaring. It was probably these carpenters who made the window sash, the mantlepieces, and other parts of a house which need special tools and special skills and who, aided by the owner of the house and perhaps other neighbors, built the rest of the house. It also was a common practice in earlier times to borrow and lend tools and other implements so that a large copper kettle, ostensibly owned by one family, might make the rounds among neighbors at apple butter-making time. At any rate, the tools and the skills necessary to use them must have been readily available in earlier times, for large numbers of solid, well-built log houses were constructed in southern Indiana in the first half of the nineteenth century and, while many have disappeared due to neglect or destruction, many are still in use today.

If there has been a tendency to believe that the tools needed to construct a log house were simple and few in number, this tendency may be the result of two factors. First, the simple, round-log cabin, intended for temporary shelter, has been confused with the hewn-log house, intended as a permanent dwelling. In southern Indiana, at least, the temporary cabins all seem to have disappeared if they were, indeed, as common as historical accounts would lead us to believe. The hewn-log houses remain in fair numbers. The average observer thinks of them as "pioneer log cabins," and, recalling the accounts in history books, assumes that they were constructed with a few simple tools. Writers on log buildings have, for the most part, helped to perpetuate this misconception. The second factor is the general notion that life in "pioneer times" was very simple and crude. Life in the first half of the nineteenth century was certainly much different than it is today, but the evidence derived from a close inspection of log houses demonstrates that there were far more tools available and in use than is generally assumed and that life was perhaps not so crude as we have been led to believe.

In listing the tools used in the first half of the nineteenth century, I have mentioned several times that craftsmen in that era often made their own tools, sometimes with the aid of a blacksmith. A survey of tools found in southern Indiana bears out this generalization, but it also shows that craftsmen usually owned some tools which they must have bought.

In comparison with other artifacts made in the first half of the nineteenth century, woodworker's tools are unusual in that they are often clearly marked with the name of the maker and usually the name of the town or city where he worked. Wooden planes, for example, often have such marks stamped on their front ends. Cincinnati, Ohio, seems to have been an important center for tool makers who supplied Indiana craftsmen, for large numbers of tools have been found which were made in that city. A few names of makers who were almost surely making tools in Cincinnati before 1850, names which have been found on tools from southern Indiana, include G. Siewers, E. F. Seybold, G. Roseboom, and S. Sloop. Far fewer tool makers seem to have worked in southern Indiana, for only a few tools by early Indiana makers have been located. A few who worked in New Albany are S. P. Woodruff, J. Gilmer, and T. Stout.[15]

Chapter Seven

Afterword

THOSE LOG buildings that were built in southern Indiana in the nineteenth century are a valuable testimony to a vanished way of life. They were built at a time when careful hand craftsmanship and cooperative labor were parts of daily life. The buildings survive into an era when neither is common. It is not surprising, therefore, that these log structures excite wonder, admiration, and affection today.

As we have seen, the log buildings of southern Indiana are built in a special way of carefully hewn timbers, flat on each side, joined at the corners in such a way that the corners are flush, chinked between the timbers, and covered on the exterior with horizontal, lapped siding. These elements, the hewn logs, the flush corners, the chinking and the siding, belong together and form a definite complex of traits which are interdependent. We may say that the logs are flat on the outside so that siding can be used over them, that the corners are flush for the same reason, that it is possible to use chinking of clay because it is protected from rain by siding, and that the siding is used to protect the logs and the chinking from rain damage. The individual elements work together to make a practical and aesthetically pleasing whole. It is practical because a structure using this complex is superbly insulated and because, as long as it is kept in good repair, it will last indefinitely. It is aesthetically pleasing because the builders must have thought that a structure built of logs and not covered with siding looked rough and unfinished. Uncovered logs might have seemed suitable for barns and other utility structures, and even barns were usually sided, but a house should have a more finished appearance.

It is probable that some builders chose not to use siding on their houses because they lacked the time to carefully plane so many boards or because the boards themselves were not readily available or were too expensive. Perhaps these builders hoped in years to come they could complete their houses by putting on siding, but, like some modern builders, they never got around to finishing the job.

There has been a strong tendency on the part of other writers to disregard this complex of traits, which I have called "hewn-and-chinked construction," and to attempt to deal instead with individual traits, especially the type of corner notching. But the specific type of corner notching, be it the single dovetail or the V-notch, is of less importance than the fact that both types of notches produce flush corners making it possible to cover the building with siding. It would seem that the time is ripe to realize the importance of the interdependence of the individual traits in the construction technology and concentrate on the complex as a whole.

It is impossible at this time, due to a lack of reliable information, to decide where and at what time this construction complex originated and how it spread. It is certainly true that the use of siding on log houses is, and was, widespread in the eastern United States. Many writers on log construction, however, have ignored the presence of siding on log houses under the misapprehension that it was a late addition. Time after time, too, when a house was abandoned the siding was stripped off so that it could be used on some other structure. A tremendous amount of time-consuming, demanding, and highly skilled work went into making the siding, for it all had to be planed laboriously by hand. Water-powered sawmills could saw out the boards, but no machinery was available to plane them until the end of the nineteenth century, at least in Indiana. Who, then, can blame the owners if they decided to salvage the siding and use it on some other structure once the old log house was no longer to be used?

It is also noteworthy that, when a family gathered and a photograph was wanted, the members of the family might well pose before the old log house even though the siding had been removed from it. For these and other reasons it is impossible to determine with accuracy how widespread the use of siding was.

One point, however, should be made in this connection. The builders of log houses that I have been able to examine in other eastern states as well as in Indiana were first-rate craftsmen. They were certainly as skilled as those others who built furniture, made baskets, wove coverlets, made iron artifacts, and produced a host of other useful, well-designed, and carefully made things in the pre-industrial era, things that delight collectors and students of crafts alike. The maker of a chair, to cite but one example, chose designs that would be comfortable, durable, light in weight, and sturdy. He carefully chose woods that were the best available for his purpose, he made the members of the chair of such dimensions that they would be adequately strong yet not cumbersome or needlessly heavy, and he joined the members together so that they would remain solid for generations. Surely, anyone who has ever carefully examined an early handmade chair must admire the craftsmanship of the maker and realize that the design, the construction techniques used, and the materials chosen are parts of a complex, each trait working together with the others.[1]

Why, then, can we not give the same respect to the craftsman carpenters who built log buildings? Are we to assume that they carefully hewed the logs, joined them at the corners with flush joints, carefully planed the floorboards and joined them side by side with tongue-and-groove joints, built fine mantelpieces, fine doors and windows, and then left the exterior walls uncovered so that rain water could wash away the clay chinking and rot the logs? If we think that carpenters did that, then we must think they were remarkably shortsighted, and it is obvious that other kinds of craftsmen were not shortsighted.

Certainly, the craftsman carpenters who put their houses up on rock pillars at the corners so that the lower timbers would not decay and who hewed four-square floor sills to rest on those corner pillars of such dimensions that the floors could not sag, these craftsmen were not guilty of shortsightedness. Why, then, should they be shortsighted in other ways?

It will not do to say that the carpenters could not put siding on log houses because boards were not available. Anyone who looks carefully at a typical log house of the eastern United States can see that sawed boards were used for flooring, for roof decking, for mantelpieces, staircases, doors, and windows. If sawed boards were available for these important features of the house, why not for siding? All in all, if we consider what craftsmanship entails, we must conclude that siding is a normal part of hewn-and-chinked-log construction.

It is impossible to say whether this construction complex originated in Europe, although many of the traits that make up the complex are found in various parts of Europe. Horizontal timbers joined at the corners are found in many countries in western Europe, horizontal siding is used in many countries, including England, on buildings of frame construction, and clay is commonly used to fill in between timbers, whether vertical or horizontal. On the other hand, the specific corner joints used in almost all Indiana log buildings are seemingly unknown in Europe. The V-notch has never been described in Europe nor has the single-dovetail notch, even though the full-dovetail notch has been. Indeed, the full-dovetail joint is the common property of woodworkers of all kinds everywhere. The use of clay chinking between logs is found in a few areas in Europe, but it is hard to believe that any influence from those areas could have been exerted on early American carpenters.

Even though some of the individual traits are undoubtedly of European origin, the complex itself seems to have been an American invention. When and where the invention occurred, it is impossible to say. It is conceivable that early builders in New England took the idea of using horizontal logs joined with flush corners and covered with siding from those builders who worked near sawmills in coastal areas where sawed logs, or timbers, were available to them. When other builders who were not near sawmills wanted to build comparable log houses, they adapted a technique that was familiar to them that had long been used in Europe. They hewed the logs with broad axes just as timbers for frame houses and barns had been hewed for centuries. They filled the gaps between the logs with clay just as the gaps between timbers in frame houses had been filled. Finally, at some point some builders discovered that the half-dovetail worked just as well as the full-dovetail and was easier to make, while other builders evolved the V-joint.

All this, of course, is the purest speculation. What is not speculation, however, is the fact that hewn-and-chinked-log construction was well known in states to the east of Indiana before the first settlers moved into Indiana in the early 1800s, for these early settlers were familiar with the technique and used it often. What is also clear is that the buildings thus built were solid, permanent, and well insulated so that a surprisingly large number of them have survived until today.

It is also clear that log construction is remarkable for its consistency in southern Indiana. It is true that temporary shelters built of round logs which were not covered with siding were built by some settlers who did not have the time, or perhaps the ability, to build more permanent structures. None of these structures, however, has survived into the last quarter of the twentieth century as far as I know. Some crude buildings of round logs have likewise been built in the twentieth century by people who either wanted to build cheaply or who wanted to imitate the pioneers. Most of the log houses that were built in the nineteen century, however, used the hewn-and-chinked-log method. This is true even for those log buildings erected by or for German immigrants who moved into the state in the 1840s and following, even though they came from a country whose log buildings use a different technique. It is buildings using hewn-and-chinked logs that have survived in substantial numbers. Their builders were not building for temporary shelter. They were building houses to last for generations, and they devoted their skills in using a well-developed construction complex that they knew would produce a comfortable, durable house.

Not only was the building method remarkably consistent, but the layout of the houses and other buildings was also notably consistent. The majority of the houses were what I have called "The Basic Anglo-American House." They had a single room on the ground floor with a sleeping loft overhead and with a fireplace and chimney on one of the gable-end walls. They had a front door in the long wall that faced the nearest road, and they had two windows, one on each side of the door. They had a steep, cramped, boxed-in staircase in the corner on one side of the fireplace. They built houses such as this for many reasons, including such practical considerations as the size of room that can be heated by a single fireplace and illuminated by the light coming from that fireplace, the need for daylight to illuminate the house coming from windows spaced logically in the long walls, and the ventilation that windows so placed and centrally located doors could provide.

Some of the reasons may have concerned the desire for the symmetrical and balanced appearance that a façade with a central door and windows on each side could provide. It should be noted, however, that a house of but a single room built before the use of stoves always had a huge pile of masonry—the fireplace and chimney—at one end and hence could never really present a balanced appearance. Certainly, the love of symmetry never drove a builder of a single-room house to place the fireplace and chimney in the middle of the house and never drove him to build a fireplace and chimney on each end of the house to achieve a balanced appearance.

It is difficult for us today to accept the fact that a family could consider a house with but a single room and a loft adequate to their needs. The evidence from southern Indiana and, indeed, from other parts of the United States as well as from Great Britain is clear and incontrovertible: Before the Industrial Revolution, the majority of people lived in houses of this size. Although information is lacking for the Middle Ages and earlier, it would seem logical to assume that, the further back in history one goes, the higher the percentage is of families living in one-room houses.

In the twentieth century Americans, at least, have come to feel that different family activities require distinct spaces and, usually, separate rooms. So, for example, sleeping requires a separate space, preferably one bedroom per person, while eating requires separate space, preferably a dining room; cooking requires a kitchen; entertaining, a living room; relaxing, a family room. This feeling is undoubtedly connected with the need for special furniture and equipment for each activity, beds for sleeping and a large table for dining, and the inconvenience of moving large pieces of furniture from place to place. Closely allied to the need for special furniture and equipment is a feeling for propriety. Most housewives in the United States today would feel it improper to entertain many guests in the living room if a bed were also in the room or to serve a formal dinner if a sewing machine were out on a table in the room. Close relatives and close friends might be exposed to such sights, but for someone such as a minister it would be different.

Other factors that affect modern notions of house size and the number of rooms include feelings about personal space and privacy. Americans today, for the most part, feel a need to keep a certain amount of physical distance from others, even members of their own family. So, for example, chairs in any room in a house should not touch one another because that would mean that people sitting in them would be "too close for comfort." While the husband and wife may share a double bed, most families would consider it ideal if each other family member had his or her own bed. Moreover, while family members are expected to be together during meals and at other times, there is a feeling today that each member of the family is "entitled to a little privacy" and hence should have a certain amount of private space, preferably a private bedroom to which he or she can retire.

Finally, it should be borne in mind that it is such modern conveniences as central heating systems and electric lights that make such a large house with so many rooms feasible. If it were necessary to keep a roaring fire going in a fireplace in each room all day and part of the night for both heat and illumination, many families today would undoubtedly find that they could get by after all with a smaller house with fewer rooms, especially if each family were responsible for cutting and splitting its own firewood.

But what about the pre-industrial era? How did most families get by with one room and a sleeping loft? It is clear that many activities had to be carried out in roughly the same space. The family ate, worked, relaxed, and entertained in the same room while some family members, probably the adults, slept in the same room. Of course, certain activities were confined largely to certain parts of the room. Cooking was done at or close to the fireplace while the bed was in the corner of the room and the dining table in the center. In cold weather, at any rate, chairs were pulled up close to the fireplace and any activity such as sewing that required light was likewise done at or near the fireplace after dark or near a window during daylight.

It is also true that families in the pre-industrial era had fewer personal possessions, including furniture, than families have today. If all the furniture from the average modern house were crammed into the average one-room plus a loft house of the earlier period, there would be no space left for people. Indeed, the one-room house would probably resemble the interior of a packed moving van. It is true that the family in the earlier era needed a considerable amount of equipment that the modern family not only has no need for but would probably not even recognize, such as a flail, an apple butter stirrer, and carding combs for wool, for many processes were carried out in and around the house that today are mostly memories, and indistinct memories at that. At the same time, of course, the modern family has a host of equipment and appliances, many of which require considerable space and are permanently fixed in place, which would bewilder and amaze their ancestors.

Much furniture in the pre-industrial era was collapsible, portable, or multi-purpose so that space within the one-room house could be used more efficiently. Quilting frames were collapsible and could be taken apart and stored away when not in use, for a full-size quilting frame would use a significant part of the interior space in a house. This fact helps account for the popularity of the quilting bee. A quilting frame could be set up, a number of quilters gather around and complete the quilting in one day, and then the frame could be taken apart and put away. Looms were likewise large and bulky and, when set up, must have taken up much of the floor space in the room. There is certainly no indication that most families in earlier times had any special building or attached room where a loom could be placed, and the heat and light provided by a fireplace would have been necessary for weaving during many months of the year. Most looms, we know, were collapsible, so that it is possible that the weaver in the family, the mother or grandmother, most likely, waited until adequate amounts of thread were prepared, then had the loom set up and wove many hours each day until an adequate supply of cloth or rugs was woven so that the loom could be taken apart and put away again. Certainly, life in the house must have been cramped and strained while the loom was up and in use.

Much furniture in the earlier era was much lighter in weight than its modern counterparts so that it could be easily moved about the room for different uses or pushed against the wall or into a corner out of the way. Chairs are a good example. The family that lived in a one-room house in southern Indiana owned no heavy, bulky, upholstered "easy" chairs that took up much space and needed two people to move. Most chairs were lightweight slat-backs with hickory bark seats or "bottoms" that could be used for many purposes and easily moved. The height of luxury as far as seating is concerned was the slat-back rocker with hickory bark bottom obtained from the nearby chairmaker.[1]

Much furniture, too, was certainly multi-purpose. There was probably only one large table in the house and it was used for cooking, for eating, for work such as sewing, and in a host of other ways. I should say that I have never seen in southern Indiana as family heirlooms any of the ingenious multi-purpose hutch tables, as they are called today by antique dealers, which could serve as a table but whose top could be tilted back so that it could also be used as a chair.

Families in an earlier era also had different notions of propriety concerning their houses and entertaining than we have today. They would not have hesitated to entertain anyone, even the visiting preacher, in the one room of the house with its bed in the corner. They may well have spread their best quilt or coverlet over the bed before the visitor came, and it is partly for this reason that so many lovely quilts and coverlets were made in earlier days. At the same time, there could have been no feeling that guests should be shielded from the final preparation of the meal, for it simply would not have been possible. We need, perhaps, not examine the ways in which the occasional overnight guests were accommodated with a place to sleep nor with the arrangements worked out when it was time to undress for bed or dress in the morning. It is only necessary to say that different notions of propriety prevailed.

It is clear, too, that different notions prevailed as to the need for privacy and the amount of personal space required. Information on such matters is, for the most part, lacking, but it is obvious that members of the family must have been in close physical contact much of the time, especially in bad weather when people were confined to their houses. More than one person usually slept in each bed, certainly, and it must have been impossible to avoid seeing other members of the family partially or totally unclothed. Finally, many activities or occurrences that today are removed from the house were not in earlier times. Most people were born and died in the one room of their house, for instance.

When a family needed or wanted a larger house, they built in units almost identical to the one-room house, that is, they built two such units end-to-end and sometimes built four units, two on the ground floor and two above on the second floor. Some went even further and added a unit to the rear in the form of an ell.

Why is it that most families found a single room with a loft quite adequate to their needs while a few families wanted at least five times as much space? There is no doubt that the families that felt a single ground-floor room was adequate must have been concerned about the time, energy, and resources needed to build a larger house and aware of the amount of fuel needed to keep a constant fire in more than one fireplace.

Those families that built multi-room houses, however, must have had some special motivation. I doubt that they were so different from their neighbors that they felt that each member of the family should, if possible, have a private bedroom. This motivation may well be a powerful one in the twentieth century, but nothing I know of indicates that it was prevalent in the pre-industrial era in southern Indiana.

I would like to suggest that the motivation to build a multi-room house was a more altruistic one, namely, hospitality. Some desire to impress one's neighbors may also have been present, but when a family joined with neighbors to hold quilting bees, apple-butter makings, hog butcherings, corn shuckings, flax scutchings, and a host of other communal work gatherings, how could a family hope to impress their neighbors by building a big house? Wouldn't their neighbors be more likely to be offended rather than impressed by ostentatious display? It seems to me that hospitality was the important factor.

We know that visiting between friends, relatives, and neighbors was an important feature of life in the pre-industrial era. We should bear in mind, however, that the difficulties of travelling had a powerful effect on visiting. If people came to a house to visit, they almost had to come and return by daylight. People trying to find their way home after dark over rough roads or where there were no roads, fording streams, passing through dense woods where, if one wandered from a path, one might not find it again until morning, were exposing themselves to very real dangers. Moonlight would, of course, sometimes help, but it could never be counted on. Hence most visits had to be made during the day and the visitors had to leave well before nightfall. Some families, however, wanted a large house so they could entertain friends after dark without jeopardizing their friends' lives and limbs. It was a source of great contentment to a family to know that they could invite visitors to stay overnight and that there would be enough rooms and enough beds for them.

There is a passage interesting in this context in the diary of Samuel Pepys. It is true that Pepys lived in seventeenth-century London, not in nineteenth-century Indiana, and that the dangers of travel after dark in the London of that era came more from thieves and cutthroats than from the natural terrain. Nonetheless, the hazards and difficulties of travel after dark placed a premium on hospitality in the original sense of the word, of giving lodging to guests. It was an ideal that one could give lodging to guests, and, it is clear, Pepys is mightily proud of himself that he has a house large enough to be truly hospitable. He wrote in his diary for March 2, 1669, after an evening at his house that included much music, dancing, and feasting that lasted "till two in the morning,"

I did lodge my cozen Pepys and his wife in our blue Chamber; My cozen Turner, her sister and Theophilia Turner in our best Chamber; Bab., Betty, [daughters of cozen Roger Pepys, aged eighteen and twenty] and Betty Turner in our own Chamber, and myself and my wife in the maid's bed, which is very good. Our maids in the coachman's bed; the coachman with the boy in his settle-bed, and Tom [a servant] where he used to lie. And so I did to my great content, lodge at once in my house, with the greatest ease, fifteen, and eight of them strangers of quality. [In the grand total of fifteen, Pepys includes himself, his wife, and his five servants, both male and female.]

The huge houses of the nobility and the gentry in England and of wealthy people in the United States must have been admired by those less financially fortunate. A family must have longed for a house with many rooms partly, of course, because such a house was a tangible symbol of position and wealth, but partly because it meant the family could be truly hospitable and lodge guests. Only by having rooms for guests could a family feel free to invite them to a party or to a ball that lasted until after dark.

This interpretation of the uses to which rooms in a large house were put helps explain the reason why a family in southern Indiana might build a house with perhaps six rooms when each room had a fireplace and the amount of wood needed to keep six fireplaces burning day after day would tax the ability of the males in the family to cut and split enough firewood. Some time ago I cut down a tree and cut it up into firewood using a buck saw and ax. I found that I spent over forty hours producing enough firewood to keep a small fire going less than a month. While I am sure that someone accustomed to such work could produce more firewood in less time than I did, nonetheless, keeping a house supplied with firewood in cold weather must have been time consuming. In cold weather most of the rooms in a large house would not be used except when guests were staying overnight and hence the fireplaces would only have a fire in them at those times.

An examination of log buildings can not only tell us a great deal about how individuals and families lived, but it can also tell us something about general social conditions at the time the buildings were constructed. For example, every log building investigated for this survey had window sash at the time it was seen and must also have had window sash at the time it was built. This fact tells us that window glass must have been available at an early date. It was undoubtedly expensive by today's standards, but it was available. The size of the window sash is dependent on the size of glass produced by the glass factories, for whole pieces of glass were used just as they came from the factory. Usually six of these panes were used for each sash. The holes cut into the log walls were always of the correct size to take these window sash of stock size. Had the holes in the walls been made for wooden frames covered with thin animal skins as is often thought, it seems unlikely that these crude windows would have been of exactly the same dimensions as the sash using six panes of glass.

Not only does the use of window sash with glass tell us that the glass must have been available, but also that skilled craftsmen well supplied with specialized tools were present in southern Indiana in considerable numbers at an early date. The making of window sash requires woodworking skills of a highly developed sort, not the type of skill the average farmer was or is likely to possess. Moreover, the making of sash requires several specialized tools such as special planes.

The use of window sash in early log houses, therefore, tells us that among those early settlers who moved into the area there were many highly skilled craftsmen, carpenters, and joiners in this case, a far cry from the rough backwoodsman in coonskin cap with an ax over his shoulder so frequently pictured in popular accounts of the early days in Indiana.

Indeed, the examination of log houses and the way in which they were built provides us, on the one hand, an enhanced appreciation of the qualities of the buildings themselves while, on the other hand, it helps correct a number of historical stereotypes that have long prevailed.

When one examines the houses themselves closely, one cannot but be struck by the skill, the foresight, and the traditional knowledge that produced them. Great skill as well as a large number of tools were needed to hew logs, lay floors, and make window sash, mantelpieces, staircases, and a host of other features. But even more impressive, and almost always overlooked, is the foresight and traditional knowledge responsible for every feature of the construction. Everywhere we look at a log house, we see that there has been some good, sound, practical reason for every feature. A combination of sound reasoning, practical experience, and transmitted knowledge has been at work. The earliest builders of log houses of the type found in Indiana, whoever they were, worked out a number of details, the solutions to problems they produced were tested by the years as the houses they built aged, and the knowledge thus produced passed from one generation to the next. The builders of southern Indiana's old log houses were, then, true craftsmen, using inherited skills honed by long practice, a variety of specialized tools, and an inherited knowledge to build solid, durable, and comfortable structures for themselves and their neighbors.

The construction features that have led me to these conclusions are detailed throughout this book. Let me, in this concluding chapter, cite but one example. It is important to keep rain water from running down the long walls of the house, for in those walls are the doors and windows. In order to have the roof protrude above those walls, the builders placed at the top of the walls a plate consisting of a heavy timber hewn four-square which overhung the wall by several inches and on which the ends of the rafters could rest. To support this plate they had to have a log in each end wall whose ends projected so that the plate could rest on those protrusions. One might say that this is a relatively minor matter and that any normally intelligent person could figure out such a solution. Perhaps it is a relatively minor matter in some respects, but let us remember first, that virtually every log house uses this feature which shows that it is a solution that was worked out long ago and had become a standard practice by the time Indiana log houses were built, and, second, that modern builders, because they cannot always be guided by tradition, are occasionally unable to solve problems of no greater difficulty.

The log houses of southern Indiana are often presented and regarded as examples of the crudity that prevailed because of the harshness of pioneer life. It is hoped, however, that future viewers of such houses will, instead, admire them as the monuments to traditional craftsmanship that they actually are and can cherish them for the skill, foresight, and inherited knowledge that produced them.

And what can these houses tell us about the general state of society at the time they were built? In other words, how can an examination of the houses lead us to a better understanding of the society that produced them? One point is abundantly clear. The people who built these houses were not the hardy souls who set forth into a trackless wilderness alone to build far from other human habitations a crude cabin using an ax and no other tools. It may be that there were some such lone individuals among the early settlers who moved into southern Indiana. If there were, though, it is important to note that they made no lasting impression on the landscape, and they left no buildings behind them to last into the twentieth century.

The people who built the log houses that have survived and who, therefore, made a lasting impression on the land were of quite a different sort. They were highly skilled, intelligent, though probably largely unschooled, equipped with a number of tools, and they had the attitude that anything they did should be done well. While it is true that they were independent and self-sufficient in many ways, it is also true that they were accustomed to rely upon their neighbors for many kinds of help and, in turn, expected to help their neighbors. It is certainly true that they depended upon their neighbors to help them build their houses, barns, and other structures, especially upon the skilled carpenters in their communities. They had, therefore, a highly developed sense of community, and they depended upon the community for the very necessities of life and they in turn supported the community in every way. The "rugged individual" who "asked no help from anyone" could not have been part of one of these rural communities. Cooperation was all-important; rugged individualism and competitiveness were undesirable traits. Certainly, it was cooperation that built the log houses and barns that still stand. Any structures that might have been built by individuals who prided themselves on their independence and scorned the help of their neighbors have long since rotted away. One lesson the study of log buildings can teach, then, is that working together with others and heeding the communal knowledge passed down from preceeding generations produces lasting results. Individual effort, independence, scorn alike for one's neighbors and for traditional knowledge produce transient and insignificant results.

And what did log construction mean in the pre-industrial era in southern Indiana, or what was people's attitude toward it? Generally speaking, their attitude, as far as we can tell, was a purely pragmatic one. Log construction was one way of building, of course, but there were others. Of the other alternatives, very few people chose to build in stone simply because in most places there was not enough stone to build an entire house. Chimneys and fireplaces could be built of available fieldstone or creek stone, and there must have been men in every community with the skills and tools for this purpose. Many people chose to build of brick, or they chose wooden frame construction. It is possible that they made these choices because most houses were built in these ways in the area they had come from "back East."

The availability of suitable trees for construction also must have played a role in determining what kind of house would be built. Most log houses were built in the countryside, where plenty of straight trees of appropriate size were to be found. In towns, a far larger proportion of brick or frame construction was used. Log houses were, of course, built in towns, but much less commonly than in the countryside.

In sum, it would appear that people in that earlier era considered log buildings to be solid, practical, comfortable buildings, easy to maintain and well insulated against the heat of summer and the cold of winter. It must have been because of an appreciation of their practical virtues that so many were built.

It is certain that people in southern Indiana in the nineteenth century did not think log walls were attractive by themselves. They covered the logs in their houses both on the inside and the outside. They felt that they had to cover the logs on the outside for practical reasons, but if they had found the logs attractive, they would have left them uncovered on the inside, and they usually chose to cover them. We must assume, therefore, that people regarded the logs as part of the basic fabric of the house, just as the heavy beams that held up the first floor were part of the basic framework, but that in a well-finished house, the logs and the beams were covered. Perhaps a log house without siding would have seemed to them very much as a modern frame building which did not have siding on the exterior of some sort would seem to use today. That is, the house would be habitable for some time, but it would not be finished.

As the nineteenth century wore on, and especially in the twentieth century, a new attitude began to develop toward log houses. Of course, this attitude was not confined to southern Indiana alone, and it is quite likely that outside influences were largely responsible for the attitude in southern Indiana. At any rate, the "log cabin" began to take on special associations and meanings. Thanks, probably, in part to the "Log Cabin and Hard Cider" campaign of Harrison in 1840, log cabins came to be directly associated in people's minds with the pioneer period and with all the virtues of the pioneers—honesty, bravery, independence, self-reliance, and a host of others. People saw in the pioneers the traits that they themselves admired and that they thought to be characteristic of America and Americans. So the log cabin came to be not only a symbol of pioneer times but also of the "true American" character. It especially became prestigious to have been born in a log cabin as the Lincoln campaigns demonstrate. So, in the twentieth century, many Americans dreamed of owning a log cabin in the woods as a vacation home and some actually acquired one. Very few Americans, it would seem, wanted a log cabin as their primary home in cities, towns, or suburbs, for sophisticated, "gracious living" would be impossible in a log cabin.

A special situation developed in southern Indiana where a number of log structures actually existed. On the one hand, people who had left the farm or whose parents had left the farm and moved to towns and cities tended to romanticize and misunderstand log buildings. They admired log cabins as symbols of the pioneer period and a special way of life. At the same time they thought that well-built, carefully finished, hewn-and-chinked log houses were crude log cabins. If they were able to acquire such a structure they immediately stripped the siding off. It seems strange that they could sit in a log house with carefully planed and fitted floorboards, a mantelpiece, and a staircase and say to themselves, "This is a crude pioneer log cabin built by a pioneer with only an ax," but such seems to have been the case.

On the other hand, those people in southern Indiana who remained on the farm and who owned log buildings that had been built by their ancestors had a rather different attitude. Log houses to many of them seem to have represented poverty and backwardness. Many of them built "modern" frame houses and moved out of their log houses. Even though the log houses were more solid and certainly better insulated, it was fashionable to live in a frame house and unfashionable to live in a log house. Perhaps I need not point out that clothing styles demonstrate clearly that if one has the choice between being fashionable and uncomfortable or unfashionable and comfortable, fashion and discomfort win out. At any rate, the abandoned log houses were used for miscellaneous storage, frequently for corn, and allowed to deteriorate to the point that many have simply rotted away.

So the era of the hewn-and-chinked log houses, together with the fine craftsmanship that was responsible for their construction and the pragmatic attitude that appreciated their true values, are all part of the past. Let us hope that those log buildings still remaining from the nineteenth century will be preserved, not as monuments to the crudity of the pioneer era, but as examples of early craftsmanship and as testimonials to a way of life that persisted for centuries and flourished in southern Indiana until drastically changed by the Industrial Revolution.

Appendix

Log Buildings by County

County	Houses	Barns	Other
Bartholomew	6	-	1
Brown	21	5	3
Clark	1	-	-
Clay	3	3	2
Crawford	3	-	1
Daviess	1	-	1
Decatur	1	-	-
Dubois	13	19	16
Franklin	5	2	-
Greene	47	11	6
Gibson	2	-	1
Harrison	1	-	-
Jackson	4	4	1
Jefferson	1	-	-
Jennings	4	-	-
Lawrence	42	18	11
Marion	1	-	-
Martin	4	2	3
Monroe	56	15	14
Morgan	3	3	-

County	Houses	Barns	Other
Ohio	1	-	-
Orange	8	3	2
Owen	37	14	6
Parke	3	-	1
Pike	10	3	2
Posey	8	1	-
Putnam	2	-	-
Ripley	-	-	1
Scott	1	-	-
Spencer	-	1	-
Switzerland	1	-	-
Vigo	1	-	-
Warwick	1	-	-
Washington	1	-	-
TOTAL	294	103	72

Please refer to the text for an explanation of the relative quantity of buildings listed in this appendix for various counties. The numbers found reflect the amount of fieldwork done. Generally speaking, the closer a county is to Bloomington, the more fieldwork was done there.

There are slight discrepancies in the totals between the figures used in the text and those given in the appendix. In several instances I found a house which had been converted into a barn or a shed of some sort. If it was possible to discover the type of house it once was, it was included in the totals in the text where house types are discussed. In this appendix, however, it has been listed as a barn.

For those counties in which a large number of buildings were found, the townships are given below:

LOG BUILDINGS BY TOWNSHIP IN SELECTED COUNTIES

County	Township	Houses	Barns	Other
Greene	Beech Creek	11	8	1
	Center	9	-	1

	Highland	12	2	2
	Jackson	3	-	1
	Richland	3	-	-
	Other Townships	9	1	1
Lawrence	Guthrie	3	1	1
	Indian Creek	3	-	-
	Marion	1	-	2
	Marshall	4	3	-
	Perry	3	2	-
	Pleasant Run	12	8	4
	Shawswick	12	3	3
	Other Townships	4	1	1
Monroe	Bean Blossom	8	-	1
	Benton	6	1	2
	Bloomington	3	-	-
	Clear Creek	3	2	1
	Indian Creek	4	3	2
	Perry	4	-	1
	Polk	13	4	7
	Richland	2	2	-
	Salt Creek	3	1	-
	Van Buren	7	2	-
	Washington	3	-	-
Owen	Clay	14	4	-
	Franklin	6	-	-
	Harrison	2	1	-
	Jefferson	2	2	1
	Lafayette	5	-	1
	Marion	6	1	-
	Washington	-	2	2
	Other Townships	1	4	2

THE COUNTIES IN SOUTHERN INDIANA

Numbers indicate the total number of buildings investigated in a given county.

NOTES

Preface to the Second Edition

1. Betty Lawson Walters, *Furniture Makers of Indiana, 1793 to 1850* (Indianapolis: Indiana Historical Society, 1972), p. 16.

2. *Stone* 4, no. 5 (September 1891): 128–29.

3. Cited in *The Magazine Antiques*, (May, 1977), p. 957.

4. Writing in *Antiques* (Dec. 1986), p. 1240, Louise Conway Belden, "a research associate at the Henry Francis Du Pont Winterthur Museum," stated that, at the end of the eighteenth century, hostesses of moderate means [!] used a footed bowl called a *compotier* as a centerpiece. The *compotier*, she says, held a compote or fruit or a dessert creme. Sometimes, she adds, the same hostesses of moderate means used *compotiers* in pairs or in fours. We might well ask how many of Benjamin Franklin's farmers Belden is talking about.

5. Bloomington *Telephone*, May 3, 1884.

6. R. B. Wood-Jones, *Traditional Domestic Architecture of the Banbury Region* (Manchester: Manchester University Press, 1963), p. 72.

7. Henry Glassie, *Passing the Time in Ballymenone* (Philadelphia: University of Pennsylvania Press, 1982), p. 395.

8. Gerralt D. Nash, "Up At Dawn," *Folk Life*, 27 (1988–89), pp. 57–59.

9. A. L. Cummings, *The Framed Houses of the Massachustts Bay, 1625–1725* (Cambridge: Harvard University Press, 1979), *passim*.

10. Dell Upton, *Three Centuries of Maryland Architecture*, (Annapolis: Maryland Historical Trust, 1982), p. 45.

11. Dean Nelson, in a pamphlet prepared for the Vernacular Architecture Forum meeting in Newark, Delaware, 1983.

Chapter One

1. Howard W. Marshall, "The 'Thousand Acres' Log House, Monroe County, Indiana," *Pioneer America* 3 (1971):48–56. John Vlach, "The 'Canada Homestead': A Saddlebag Log House in Monroe County, Indiana," *Pioneer America* 4 (1972):8–17.

2. C. A. Weslager, *The Log Cabin in America* (New Brunswick: Rutgers University Press, 1969).

3. Donald and Jean Hutslar, "The Log Architecture of Ohio," *Ohio History* 80 (1971):171–271.

4. Henry Glassie, *Pattern in the Material Folk Culture of the Eastern United States* (Philadelphia: University of Pennsylvania Press, 1968.). Fred B. Kniffen, "Folk Housing: Key to Diffusion," *Annals of the Association of American Geographers* 55 (1965):549–57.

5. Terry Jordan, *Texas Log Buildings: A Folk Architecture* (Austin: University of Texas Press, 1978).

6. Warren E. Roberts, "Some Comments on Log Construction in Scandinavia and the United States," in *Folklore Today: A Festschrift for Richard M. Dorson*, eds.

L. Dégh, H. Glassie, and F. Oinas (Bloomington: Research Center for Language and Semiotic Studies, Indiana University, 1976), pp. 437–50.

CHAPTER TWO

1. For Swedish examples of round-log buildings, see Sigurd Erixon, *Svensk Bygnads Kultur* (Stockholm: Aktiebolaget Bokverk, 1947), 21–35, especially p. 34. For other Swedish examples, see Henry C. Mercer, *The Origin of Log Houses in the United States* (Doylestown, Pa: Bucks County Historical Society, 1976), pp. 29–30. This pamphlet has been reprinted from *Papers, Bucks County Historical Society* 5 (1926):568–83. The paper in essentially the same form was also published in *Old-Time New England* 18:1 (July 1927):2–20 and 18:2 (Oct. 1927):51–63. For German examples, see Konrad Bedal, *Historische Hausforschung* (Münster: F. Coppenrath Verlag, 1978), p. 67.

2. Bedal, *Historische Hausforschung*, p. 67.

3. Mercer, *Origin of Log Houses*, p. 2.

4. Roberts, "Comments on Log Construction."

5. R. W. E. Perrin, *Historic Wisconsin Buildings* (Milwaukee Public Museum, 1962), pp. 10–11.

6. Henry Glassie, "The Types of the Southern Mountain Cabin," in Jan H. Brunvand, ed. *The Study of American Folklore*, 2nd ed. (New York: W. W. Norton, 1978), p. 401.

7. Jordan, *Texas Log Buildings*, p. 24.

8. Heinrich Franke, *Ostgermanische Holzbaukultur* (Breslau: 1936), plate 19.

9. Personal communication, June 5, 1980.

10. Terry Jordan, "Alpine, Alemannic, and American Log Architecture," *Annals of the Association of American Geographers* 70 (1980):165.

11. Jordan, *Texas Log Buildings*, p. 35.

12. Ibid.

13. Richard Candee, "Wooden Buildings in Maine and New Hampshire: A Technological and Cultural History" (Ph. D. Dissertation, University of Pennsylvania, 1976), chap. 5. See especially the map on p. 267.

14. John I. Rempel, *Building with Wood and Other Aspects of Nineteenth Century Building in Ontario* (Toronto: University of Toronto Press, 1967), p. 18.

15. Mercer, *Origins of Log Houses*, pp. 12–13.

16. See Candee, "Wooden Buildings," p. 342, where a builder's contract for a house built in 1677 is quoted. It specifies that the walls of the house are to be clapboarded. On p. 316, Candee states that in another early log house attic floorboards consisted of re-used sheathing.

17. Donald and Jean Hutslar, "Log Architecture of Ohio," p. 183.

18. Henry Glassie, *Folk Housing in Middle Virginia* (Knoxville: University of Tennessee Press, 1975), pp. 125–29.

19. "Cameron Plantations Tour," a booklet prepared for the Vernacular Architecture Forum, April 3, 1982.

20. Peter O. Wacker and Roger T. Trindell, "The Log House in New Jersey:

Origins and Diffusion," *Keystone Folklore Quarterly* 13 (1968):255–56. The authors cite a survey made before 1939 that found a number of houses built in this way, but they were able to find only one still standing in the 1960s. While this house was in an area of possible Swedish influence, it had a gable-end fireplace and chimney, widely recognized as an English trait, while "early Swede-Finns universally built houses with interior corner chimneys" (p. 265).

21. Ebenezer Robinson moved from Massachusetts to a farm near South Reading, Vermont, and built a hewn-and-chinked-log house there in 1778 (Herbert Wheaton Congden, *Early American Houses for Today* [Rutland, Vt.: Charles E. Tuttle Co., 1963], p. 60). In the Shelburne Museum near Burlington, Vermont, there stands a hewn-and-chinked-log house that was moved to the museum site from nearby Charlotte. Built before 1800, the house was sided with clapboards originally. When the house was reconstructed at the museum, the siding was left off the walls under the erroneous assumption that early log houses were never covered with siding (R. N. Hill and L. B. Carlisle, *The Story of the Shelburne Museum* [2nd ed. Shelburne, Vt.: The Shelburne Museum, 1960], p. 88).

22. Much of New York State was settled by people from New England, and many of these early settlers built log houses (Jared van Wagenen, Jr., *The Golden Age of Homespun* [new ed., New York: Hill and Wang, 1963], pp. 18, 95). Using the earliest statistics available to him, van Wagenen states that "as late as 1855 we had more than 17,000 New York State families living in log houses" (p. 54). The statistics do not differentiate between round-log and hewn-and-chinked-log houses, but van Wagenen testifies on the basis of his own observations that the latter type was common in the state. The earliest reference van Wagenen was able to find concerns three log houses built in Ithaca in 1758. They were built by settlers from Kingston, New York, which is near the Massachusetts border (p. 37).

Frank A. Scheuttle has recently done extensive fieldwork in Erie County in northwestern New York State. He found over twenty log houses, most of which were still in use. Most of them were solid, well built houses of hewn-and-chinked logs covered with siding. He was also able to locate records showing that log houses had been built by settlers from New England (Frank A. Scheuttle, "Log Architecture in Erie County, New York" [M. A. thesis, Cooperstown Graduate Program, 1978], pp. 81–87).

23. To show that some, at least, of the New Englanders who settled in Ohio were familiar with log construction, a documented example may be cited. Major John Burnham of Essex, Massachusetts, was hired in 1790 by an agent of a company that owned large tracts of land in Ohio. In his letter to Burnham concerning the log houses Burnham was to build, the agent said that instructions were unnecessary because Burnham already knew how to build log structures. Because we connect pioneers with rude log cabins, we might expect that round-log structures would have been built in such a place at such an early date. Nonetheless, this Massachusetts carpenter-soldier built hewn-and-chinked-log houses, for a visitor to the town in question in 1793 wrote, "The houses were all built of square logs" (Donald and Jean Hutslar, "Log Architecture of Ohio," pp. 184–85).

24. Cora Greenaway, *South Shore: Seasoned Timbers* (Halifax, N.S.: Heritage

Trust of Nova Scotia, 1974), p. 122. Further information on log houses in Nova Scotia was given in 1923 when Henry Piers, the President of the Nova Scotia Historical Society, wrote to Henry C. Mercer as follows: "Log houses . . . were common in Nova Scotia from the earliest date; that some still survive in Nova Scotia, and that this manner of building was taught to the first English settlers coming to Nova Scotia from England, by officials and others from New England" (Mercer, *Origin of Log Houses,* p. 7). Unfortunately, Piers does not cite the evidence upon which he based these statements.

The log architecture of the former province of Upper Canada (now part of the province of Ontario) has been extensively documented by John I. Rempel. He points out that the predominant architectural influence in this area came from the "United Empire Loyalists" who came mostly from New England and New York State. He provides many references to log houses built by these people before 1800 or shortly thereafter. It is clear from the evidence cited that many of these houses used hewn-and-chinked-log construction (John I. Rempel, *Building with Wood and Other Aspects of Nineteenth Century Building in Ontario* [Toronto: University of Toronto Press, 1967], pp. 3–5, 23, 28, 32, 41, 50, 64, 65, 69–72, 72–75, 76).

25. Fred Kniffen and Henry Glassie, "Building in Wood in the Eastern United States: A Time-Place Perspective," *The Geographical Review* 56 (1966):65.

26. Weslager, *The Log Cabin in America,* p. 155.

27. George E. G. MacLearen, *Antique Furniture by Nova Scotian Craftsmen* (Toronto: 1961), pp. 2–3.

28. Weslager, *The Log Cabin in America,* pp. 137–45. See especially p. 147 n. 22, and p. 203 n. 6.

29. "Letters from John Stewart to William Dunlap," *The South Carolina Historical and Genealogical Magazine* 32 (1931):17, 85, 97. Cited by Weslager, *The Log Cabin in America,* p. 115 n. 12. F. B. Johnston and T. T. Waterman, *The Early Architecture of North Carolina* (Chapel Hill: University of North Carolina Press, 1941), p. 5. Cited by Weslager, *The Log Cabin in America,* p. 146, n. 10.

30. Weslager, *The Log Cabin in America,* p. 210.

31. *Echoes of History* (The Pioneer American Society) 2:5 (Sept. 1972):61.

32. Candee, "Wooden Buildings," pp. 266ff.

33. Weslager, *The Log Cabin in America,* p. 135.

34. R. W. Brunskill, *Illustrated Handbook of Vernacular Architecture* (New York: Universe Books, 1971), pp. 62–63.

35. Henry Glassie stresses these resemblances in "Types of the Southern Mountain Cabin," passim. He not only shows that small log houses resemble small frame and masonry houses, but also emphasizes in many ways the resemblances between British-American and British small, traditional houses.

36. See note 1.

37. Fiske Kimball, *Domestic Architecture of the American Colonies* (New York: Scribner's, 1922), pp. 6–8.

38. Harold R. Shurtleff, *The Log Cabin Myth* (Cambridge: Harvard University Press, 1939).

39. See, for example, Weslager, *The Log Cabin in America,* chapt. 7, and Donald

and Jean Hutslar, "Log Architecture of Ohio," p. 177.

40. See note 4.

41. Kniffen and Glassie, "Building in Wood," pp. 58–59.

42. Jordan, *Texas Log Buildings,* p. 24.

43. Sarah Matthews, "German Settlement of Northern Chester County in the 18th Century," *Pennsylvania Folklife* 27:4 (Summer 1978):27.

44. Jordan, *Texas Log Buildings,* p. 24.

45. For Pennsylvania German log houses, see Mercer, *Origin of Log Houses,* figures 13–19. For German examples, see works such as Bedal, *Historiche Hausforschung,* pp. 67–72; Franke, *Ostgermanische Holzbaukultur ,* passim; and Hermann Phleps, *Holzbaukunst: Der Blockbau* (Karlsruhe: Dr. Albert Bruder, 1942), passim.

46. See my letter on Pennsylvania German log houses in *Pioneer America* 11 (1979):106.

47. Ibid.

48. See note 10.

49. Kniffen and Glassie, "Building in Wood," pp. 59–65.

50. Congden, *Early American Houses.*

51. Kniffen and Glassie, "Building in Wood," pp. 59–65.

52. David Thomas, *Travels Through the Western Country in the Summer of 1816* (Auburn, N.Y., 1819), p. 39. Cited by Weslager, *The Log Cabin in America,* p. 234.

53. Donald and Jean Hutslar, "Log Architecture of Ohio," p. 208.

54. Anonymous letter to the editor, *Michigan Agricultural Society Transactions* 8 (1851):398.

55. Thomas D. Clark, *Indiana University: Midwestern Pioneer I* (Bloomington: Indiana University Press, 1970), 13.

56. Manuscript Collection, Monroe County Public Library, Bloomington, Indiana.

57. Phillip Vickers Fithian, *Journal, 1975–76.* Ed. by R. G. Albion and L. Godson (Princeton: Princeton University Press, 1934), pp. 9–10. Cited by Weslager, *The Log Cabin in America,* p.147, n. 20.

58. John Schlebecker, *Living Historical Farms: A Walk into the Past* (Washington, D.C.: Smithsonian Institution, 1968), p. 19.

59. Weslager, *The Log Cabin in America,* pp. 289–91.

60. "Pioneer Farmstead, Great Smoky Mountains National Park, North CarolinaTennessee," published by the Great Smoky Mountains Natural History Association in Cooperation with the National Park Service, n.d.

61. For examples of photographs and drawings of hewn-and-chinked-log houses in Kentucky and Tennessee, see Clay Lancaster, *Ante-Bellum Houses of the Bluegrass* (Lexington: University of Kentucky Press, 1961); W. L. Montell and M. L. Morse, *Kentucky Folk Architecture* (Lexington: University Press of Kentucky, 1976); Edna Scofield, "The Evolution and Development of Tennessee Houses," *Journal of the Tennessee Academy of Sciences* 11 (1936):229–40; and Glassie, "Types of the Southern Mountain Cabin."

CHAPTER THREE

1. Thaddeus Mason Harris. *Journal of a Tour into the Territory Northwest of the Allegheny Mountains* . . . . (Boston, 1805), p. 15.

2. Robert Carlton (pseud.), *The New Purchase,* ed. by James A. Woodburn (Princeton: Princeton University Press, 1916), pp. 51–57.

3. In addition to Baynard Rush Hall, who wrote of his experiences in Indiana about twelve years after he had left the state and when he was living in Brooklyn, New York, others who have described early round-log structures in Indiana from personal knowledge of some kind include: S.W. Widney, *Pioneer Sketches: Containing Facts and Incidents of the Early History of Dekalb County* (Auburn, Ind., 1859), pp. 5–6; Howard Johnson, *A Home in the Woods* (Indianapolis, 1951), pp. 149–52; and [John M. Wasson], *Annals of Pioneer Settlers on the Whitewater and its Tributaries in the Vicinity of Richmond, Ind. from 1804 to 1830* (Richmond, Ind., 1875. Rpt. Indianapolis, 1962), pp. 14–15. While there are a certain number of disagreements in details, the main features of the round-log cabin are described by these writers with reasonable consistency, and these features agree with descriptions of similar structures from adjoining states such as that in John Woods, *Two Years' Residence in the Settlement on the English Prairie in the Illinois Country* (London, 1822), pp. 123–29.

CHAPTER FOUR

1. See, for example, Donald and Jean Hutslar, "Log Architecture of Ohio," p. 211.

2. Henry C. Mercer, *Ancient Carpenters' Tools* (3rd ed. Doylestown, Pa.: 1960), pp. 53–54.

3. Donald and Jean Hutslar, "Log Architecture of Ohio," p. 235.

4. George E. Evans, *The Pattern Under the Plough* (London: Faber and Faber, 1966), pp. 145–47.

5. Some seeming exceptions to this generalization are the "saddlebags" houses described in a later chapter. In each of the three examples found, a one-room house was first built with a fireplace in an exterior end wall. Later, a second log room was built in such a way that the fireplace and chimney were between the two rooms.

6. Mercer, *Ancient Carpenters' Tools,* p. 300.

7. See, for example, Janet Waring, *Early American Stencils on Walls and Furniture* (New York: Dover Publications, 1968). On pp. 63–65 painted designs are shown, although the rest of the book deals with the use of stencils.

CHAPTER FIVE

1. The one-room house with sleeping loft was common in England in the seventeenth century even though few have survived. In Wiltshire, a county in southern England, there are records dating from 1631–32 for 355 houses. Most of these had a single room on the ground floor. Over half had a full sleeping loft while

most of the rest had a half loft (R. B. Wood-Jones, *Traditional Domestic Architecture in the Banbury Region* [Manchester University Press, 1963], p. 72n). E. Estyn Evans gives data establishing the remarkable resemblances between traditional Ulster houses and the most common southern Indiana log houses: "That this variety of log-house [i.e., that in the southern mountains] can be associated with the Scotch-Irish is attested in other ways: not only is the ground plan almost identical with that of the traditional small Ulster farmhouse, but like the north Ulster house it was generally provided with two opposite doors . . . . The chimney was placed in one of the gables, ... The average internal dimensions of this type of log-house are 16 ft. by 22 ft., which compares closely with an average of 15 ft. by 21 ft. for the traditional Ulster kitchen: the external dimensions in fact are almost identical" ("The Scotch-Irish: Their Cultural Adaptation and Heritage in the American Old West," in *Essays in Scotch-Irish History*, ed. E. R. R. Green [London: Routledge and Kegan Paul, 1969], p. 79). Note that the external dimensions of the log house Evans describes are almost identical to log houses of southern Indiana. To the internal dimensions one must add one foot and a half to arrive at the external dimensions. Hence the external dimensions of the log houses he describes would average 171/2 ft. by 231/2 ft.

Evans maintains, following Glassie, that English one-room houses are square rather than rectangular (Henry Glassie, "Types of the Southern Mountain Cabin," pp. 404–7). Evans also states that the traditional rectangular one-room house of Ulster is derived from Scotland. Hence the rectangular southern Indiana log house could ultimately be from either Scottish or Scotch-Irish sources. It is clear, however, that by the time the settlers moved into southern Indiana they shared a common building tradition whether their ancestors came from Scotland, North Ireland, Ireland, England, or Wales.

2. Darwin Lambert, "Life Styles for Earthmanship," *Proceedings of the Pioneer America Society* 2 (1973):125.

3. Carlton, *The New Purchase*, pp. 69–70.

4. See, for example, Henry Glassie, *Pattern in the Material Folk Culture*, pp. 88–98.

5. For information on the I-house and its distribution, see Fred B. Kniffen, "Folk Housing: Key to Diffusion," *Annals of the Association of American Geographers* 55 (1965):553–56. Kniffen has said that he coined the term "I-house" when he first noticed examples in Indiana, Illinois, and Iowa. Later he realized that they are found in many other states as well, but the term has stuck.

6. See, for example, Glassie, *Pattern in the Material Folk Culture*, p. 78.

7. Dorothy Hartley, *Lost Country Life* (New York: Pantheon, 1979), p. 227.

8. See Elfrieda Lang, "German Immigration to Dubois County, Indiana, During the Nineteenth Century," *Indiana Magazine of History* 41 (June 1945):131–51.

9. The Hutslars give an illustration of an early house in Ohio using "plank walls" with the horizontal planks morticed into vertical posts. This is a construction method similar to that used in the Indiana house (Donald and Jean Hutsler, "Log Architecture of Ohio," p. 183). In this Ohio building, however, the horizontal timbers are relatively thin, having been sawed rather than hewed. They fit closely upon one another without the use of chinking. The Ohio building uses

exactly the same method as some of the buildings in Maine and New Hampshire described by Candee. In these early New England buildings the horizontal timbers fit into vertical posts. They are sawn, not hewn, and they fit atop one another without interstices (Candee, "Wooden Buildings," pp. 248, 277, 335).

10. See C. H. Dornbusch and J. K. Heyl, *Pennsylvania German Barns,* Pennsylvania German Folklore Society, vol. 21 (Allentown: Pennsylvania German Folklore Society, 1958), and Susanne S. Ridlen, "Bank Barns in Cass County, Indiana,"*Pioneer America* 4 (July 1972):25–43.

CHAPTER SIX

1. Logan Esarey, *The Indiana Home* (Crawfordsville, Ind.: R. E. Banta, 1943), p. 29.

2. Widney, *Pioneer Sketches,* p. 5.

3. C. A. Weslager, *Log Cabin in America* .

4. Donald and Jean Hutsler, "Log Architecture of Ohio," pp. 171–271.

5. Mercer, *Ancient Carpenters' Tools,* p. 300.

6. Peter C. Welsh, "Woodworking Tools, 1600–1900," *Contributions from the Museum of History and Technology,* Paper 51 of U.S. National Museum Bulletin 241 (Washington, D.C., 1966), pp. 178–228.

7. Carlton, *The New Purchase,* p. 278.

8. Henry J. Kauffman, *American Axes* (Brattleboro, Vt.: S. Green, 1972).

9. Belknap Hardware and Manufacturing Co., Catalog number 86 (1932), p. 15; Catalog number 88 (1937), p. 13. This firm was founded in 1840.

10. Carlton, *The New Purchase,* p. 278.

11. Ibid., p. 215.

12. See ibid., p. 247 n. 5.

13. Warren E. Roberts, "Wood Screws as an Aid to Dating Wooden Artifacts," The *Chronicle* of the Early American Industries Association 31:1 (March 1978):14–16.

14. See Esarey, *The Indiana Home,* p. 17 n. 1. In this popular book dealing with the settlement of and life in southern Indiana, the author estimates that about one-half of the settlers who came before 1816 came on foot or on horseback. Of these, he says, "The average household property was a quilt or coverlet, a change of clothing, a pot and 'spider' or three-legged skillet, an axe, hatchet, two or three steel knives, a hoe and a few other trinkets or trifles." One might well ask, "Of what use is an axe if one has no way of sharpening it?"

15. Tools by the makers named are owned by the author.

AFTERWORD

1. See my "Turpin Chairs and the Turpin Family: Chairmaking in Southern Indiana," *Midwestern Journal of Language and Folklore* 8:2 (Fall 1981).

BIBLIOGRAPHY

I. Works Cited

Anonymous. Letter to the editor. *Michigan Agricultural Society Transactions* 8 (1851):398.

Belknap Hardware and Manufacturing Company, Louisville, Kentucky. Catalog number 86 (1932) and Catalog number 88 (1937).

Bedal, Konrad. *Historische Hausforschung.* Münster: F. Coppenrath Verlag, 1978.

Brunskill, R. W. *Illustrated Handbook of Vernacular Architecture.* New York: Universe Books, 1971.

Candee, Richard M. "Wooden Buildings in Maine and New Hampshire: A Technological and Cultural History." Ph.D. Dissertation, University of Pennsylvania,1976.

Carlton, Robert. See Hall, Baynard Rush.

Clark, Thomas D. *Indiana University: Midwestern Pioneer.* Vol. 1. Bloomington: Indiana University Press, 1970.

Congden, Herbert Wheaton. *Early American Houses for Today.* Rutland, Vt.: Charles E. Tuttle Co., 1963.

Dornbusch, C. H. and Heyl, J. K. *Pennsylvania German Barns.* Pennsylvania German Folklore Society, vol. 21. Allentown: Pennsylvania German Folklore Society, 1958.

Editorial, *Echoes of History* (The Pioneer America Society). 2:5 (Sept. 1972):61.

Erixon, Sigurd. *Svensk Bygnads Kultur* Stockholm: Aktiebolaget Bokverk, 1947.

Esarey, Logan. *The Indiana Home.* Crawfordsville, Ind.: R. E. Banta, 1943.

Evans, George E. *The Pattern Under the Plough.* London: Faber and Faber, 1966.

Evans, E. Estyn. "The Scotch Irish: Their Cultural Adaptation and Heritage in the American Old West," in *Essays in Scotch-Irish History.* Edited by E. R. R. Green. London: Routledge and Kegan Paul, 1969. Pp. 69–86.

Fithian, Phillip Vickers. *Phillip Vickers Fithian. Journal, 1775–76.* Edited by R. G. Albion and L. Dodson. Princeton: Princeton University Press, 1934.

Franke, Heinrich. *Ostgermanische Holzbaukultur.* Breslau, 1936.

Glassie, Henry. *Folk Housing in Middle Virginia.* Knoxville: University of Tennessee Press, 1975.

————. *Pattern in the Material Folk Culture of the Eastern United States.* Philadelphia: University of Pennsylvania Press, 1968.

————. "The Types of the Southern Mountain Cabin." In *The Study of American Folklore: An Introduction.* Edited by Jan H. Brunvand. 2nd ed. New York: W. W. Norton, 1978. Pp. 338–70.

Greenaway, Cora. *South Shore: Seasoned Timbers.* Halifax, N.S.: Heritage Trust of Nova Scotia, 1974.

Hall, Baynard Rush (Robert Carlton, pseud.) *The New Purchase.* Edited by J. A. Woodburn. Princeton: Princeton University Press: 1916.

Harris Thaddeus Mason. *Journal of a Tour into the Territory Northwest of the Allegheny Mountains. . . .* Boston, 1805.

Hartley, Dorothy. *Lost Country Life.* New York: Pantheon, 1979.

Hill, R. N. and Carlisle, L. B., *The Story of the Shelburne Museum.* 2nd ed. Shelburne, Vt.: Shelburne Museum, 1960.

Hutslar, Donald and Jean. "The Log Architecture of Ohio." *Ohio History* 80 (1971):172–271.

Johnson, Howard. *A Home in the Woods.* Indianapolis, 1951.

Johnston, F. B. and Waterman, T. T. *The Early Architecture of North Carolina.* Chapel Hill: University of North Carolina Press, 1941.

Jordan, Terry. *Texas Log Buildings: A Folk Architecture.* Austin: University of Texas Press, 1978.

————. "Alpine, Alemannic, and American Log Architecture." *Annals of the Association of American Geographers* 70 (1980):154–80.

Kauffman, Henry J. *American Axes.* Brattleboro, Vt.: S. Greene, 1972.

Kimball, Fiske. *Domestic Architecture of the American Colonies.* New York: Scribners, 1922.

Kniffen, Fred B. "Folk Housing: Key to Diffusion." *Annals of the Association of American Geographers* 55 (1965):549–77.

————, and Henry Glassie. "Building in Wood in the Eastern United States: A Time-Place Perspective." *Geographical Review* 56 (1966):40–66.

Lambert, Darwin. "Life Styles for Earthmanship." *Proceedings of the Pioneer America Society* 2 (1973):125–35.

Lancaster, Clay. *Ante-Bellum Houses of the Bluegrass.* Lexington:University of Kentucky Press, 1961.

Lang, Elfrieda. "German Immigration to Dubois County, Indiana, During the Nineteenth Century."*Indiana Magazine of History* 41 (June 1945):131–51.

MacLaren, George E. G. *Antique Furniture by Nova Scotian Craftsmen.* Toronto, 1961.

Marshall, Howard W. "The 'Thousand Acres' Log House, Monroe County, Indiana." *Pioneer America* 3:1 (Jan. 1971):48–56.

Matthews, Sarah. "German Settlement of Northern Chester County in the 18th Century." *Pennsylvania Folklife* 27:4 (Summer 1978):25–32.

Mercer, Henry C. *Ancient Carpenters' Tools.* 3rd ed. Doylestown, Penn.: Bucks County Historical Society, 1960.

_____. *The Origin of Log Houses in the United States.* Doylestown, Pa.: Bucks County Historical Society, 1976. Reprinted from *Papers, Bucks County Historical Society* 5 (1926):568–83. The paper in essentially the same form was also published in *Old-Time New England* 18:1 (July 1927):2–20 and 18:2 (Oct. 1927):51–63.

Montell, William Lynwood and Morse, M. L. *Kentucky Folk Architecture.* Lexington: University Press of Kentucky, 1976.

Perrin, R. W. E. *Historic Wisconsin Buildings.* Milwaukee: Milwaukee Public Museum, 1962.

Phleps, Hermann. *Holzbaukunst: Der Blockbau.* Karlsruhe: Dr. Albert Cruder, 1942.

"Pioneer Farmstead, Great Smoky Mountains National Park, North Carolina-Tennessee." Published by the Great Smoky Mountains Natural History Association in Cooperation with the National Park Service, n. d.

Rempel, John I. *Building with Wood and Other Aspects of Nineteenth Century Building in Ontario.* Toronto: University of Toronto Press, 1967.

Ridlen, Susanne S. "Bank Barns in Cass County, Indiana." *Pioneer America* 4:2 (July 1972): 25–43.

Roberts, Warren E. "Letter to the Editor." *Pioneer America* 11 (1979):106.

_____. "Some Comments on Log Construction in Scandinavia and the United States." In *Folklore Today*, edited by L. Dégh, H. Glassie, and F. Oinas. Bloomington: Research Center for Language and Semiotic Studies, Indiana University, 1976. Pp. 437–50.

_____. "Turpin Chairs and the Turpin Family: Chairmaking in Southern Indiana." *Midwestern Journal of Language and Folklore* 8:2 (Fall 1981).

_____. "Wood Screws as an Aid to Dating Wooden Artifacts." The *Chronicle* of the Early American Industries Association 31:1 (March 1978):14–16.

Scheuttle, Frank A. "Log Architecture in Erie County, New York." M.A. Thesis, Cooperstown Graduate Program, 1978.

Schlebecker, John. *Living Historical Farms: A Walk Into the Past.* Washington, D. C.: Smithsonian Institution, 1968.

Scofield, Edna. "The Evolution and Development of Tennessee Houses." *Journal of the Tennessee Academy of Sciences* 11 (1936):229–40.

Shurtleff, Harold R. *The Log Cabin Myth.* Cambridge: Harvard University Press, 1939.

Stewart, John. "Letters from John Stewart to William Dunlap." *The South Carolina Historical and Genealogical Magazine* 32 (1931):1–33.

Thomas, David. *Travels Through the Western Country in the Summer of 1816.* Auburn, N.Y., 1819.

van Wagenen, Jr., Jared. *The Golden Age of Homespun.* New ed. New York: Hill and Wang, 1963.

Vlach, John. "The 'Canada Homestead': A Saddlebag Log House in Monroe County, Indiana." *Pioneer America* 4:2 (July 1972):8–17.

Wacker, Peter O., and Trindell, Roger T. "The Log House in New Jersey: Origins and Diffusion." *Keystone Folklore Quarterly* 13 (1968):248–68.

Waring, Janet. *Early American Stencils on Walls and Furniture.* New York: Dover Publications, 1968.

[Wasson, John M.] *Annals of Pioneer Settlers on the Whitewater and its Tributaries in the Vicinity of Richmond Indiana from 1804 to 1830.* Richmond, Ind.: 1875. Rpt. Indianapolis,Ind.: Indiana Historical Society, 1962.

Welsh, Peter C. "Woodworking Tools, 1600–1900." In U.S. National Museum Bulletin 241: *Contributions from the Museum of History and Technology.* Paper 51, pp. 178–228. Washington, D. C., 1966.

Weslager, C. A. *The Log Cabin in America.* New Brunswick: Rutgers University Press, 1969.

Widney, S. W. *Pioneer Sketches: Containing Facts and Incidents of the Early History of Dekalb County.* Auburn, Ind., 1859.

Wood-Jones, R. B. *Traditional Domestic Architecture in the Banbury Region.* Manchester: Manchester University Press, 1963.

Woods, John. *Two Years' Residence in the Settlement on the English Prairie in the Illinois Country.* London, 1822.

II. OTHER WORKS

Attebury, Jennifer Eastman. "Log Construction in the Sawtooth Valley of Idaho." *Pioneer America* 8:1 (Jan. 1976):34– 46.

Brandt, L. R. and Braatz, N. E. "Log Buildings in Portage County, Wisconsin: Some Cultural Implications." *Pioneer America* 4:1 (Jan. 1972):29–39.

Brunskill, R. W. *A Systematic Procedure for Recording English Vernacular Architecture.* Reprinted from the *Transactions* of the Ancient Monuments Society, vol. 13 (1965–66).

Davidson, William H. *Pine, Log, and Greek Revival: Houses and People of Three Counties in Georgia and Alabama.* Alexander, Ala.: Outlook, 1965.

Deetz, James. *In Small Things Forgotten: The Archaeology of Early American Life.* Garden City, N. Y.: Anchor Books, 1977.

Erixon, Sigurd. "Är den Nordamerikanska Timringstekniken Överförd fron Sverige?" *Folk-Liv* 19 (1955–56):56–68.

_____. "The North-European Technique of Corner-Timbering." *Folk-Liv* 1 (1937):13–60.

Glassie, Henry. "The Appalachian Log Cabin." *Mountain Life and Work* 39:4 (Winter 1963):5–14.

_____. "A Central Chimney Log House."*Pennsylvania Folklife* 18:2 (Winter 1968–69):32–39.

_____. "The Double-Crib Barn in South-Central Pennsylvania." *Pioneer America* 1:1 (Jan.1969):40– 45; 2:1 (Jan. 1970):47–52; 2:2 (July 1970):23–34.

_____. "The Old Barns of Appalachia." *Mountain Life and Work* 40:2 (Summer 1965):21–30.

_____. "The Smaller Outbuildings of the Southern Mountains."*Mountain Life and Work* 40:1 (Spring 1964):21–25.

Gregory, George C. "Log Houses at Jamestown, 1607." *Virginia Magazine of History & Biography* 44:4 (Oct. 1936):287–95.

Gritzner, Charles F. "Log Housing in New Mexico." *Pioneer America* 3:2 (July 1971):54–62.

Hale, Richard W., Jr. "The French Side of the 'Log Cabin Myth.'" *Proceedings of the Massachusetts Historical Society* 3rd ser., 72 (Oct. 1957–Dec. 1960):118–25.

Hulan, Richard H. "Middle Tennessee and the Dogtrot House." *Pioneer America* 7:2 (July 1975): 37–46.

Jordan, Terry G. "Log Construction in the East Cross Timbers of Texas." *Proceedings of the Pioneer America Society* 2 (1973):107–24.

_____. "Log Corner-Timbering in Texas." *Pioneer America* 8:1 (Jan. 1976):8–18.

Kelly, J. Frederick. *The Early Domestic Architecture of Connecticut.* New Haven: Yale UniversityPress, 1924.

_____. "A Seventeenth Century Connecticut Log House." *Old-Time New England* 31:2 (Oct. 1940):28–40.

Kniffen, Fred B. "On Corner Timbering." *Pioneer America* 1:1 (Jan. 1969):1–8.

Langdon, John U. "New Light on Charles Oliver Bruff, Tory Silversmith." *Antiques* 93:6 (June 1968):768–69.

Mercer, Henry C. *The Dating of Old Houses.* New Hope, Penn.: Bucks County Historical Society, 1973. Reprinted from *Bucks County Historical Society Papers* 5 (1923): 536–49.

Price, Beulah M. D. "The Dog-Trot Log Cabin: A Development in American Folk Architecture." *Mississippi Folklore Register* 4:3 (1970):84–89.

Roberts, Warren E. "Folk Architecture." In *Folklore and Folklife: An Introduction.* Edited by R. M. Dorson. Chicago: University of Chicago Press, 1972. Pp. 281–94.

_____. "Folk Architecture in Context: The Folk Museum." *Proceedings of the Pioneer America Society* 1 (1972):34–50.

_____. "Tools Used in Building Log Houses in Indiana." Illustrated by Ada L. K. Newton. *Pioneer America* 9 (1977):32–61.

_____. "The Whitaker-Waggoner Log House from Morgan County, Indiana." In *American Folklore.* Edited by Don Yoder. Austin: University of Texas Press, 1976. Pp. 185–207.

Visted, K., and Stigum, H. *Var Gamle Bondekultur.* Oslo: J. W. Cappelens Forlag, 1952.

Willis, Stanley. "Log Houses in Southwest Virginia: Tools Used in Their Construction." *Virginia Cavalcade* 21:4 (Spring 1972):36–47.

Wilson, Eugene M. "The Single Pen Log House in the South." *Pioneer America* 2:1 (Jan. 1970):21–28.

Wright, Martin. "The Antecedents of the Double-Pen House Type." *Annals, Association of American Geographers* 48 (1958):109–17.

Zelinsky, Wilbur. "The Log House in Georgia." *Geographical Review* 43 (1953): 173–93.